TEA-TIME

at the Inn

*For the bed & breakfast and
country innkeepers who offer travelers the experience
of tea-time in such variety and abundance.
This book is as much theirs as it is mine.*

GAIL GRECO

TEA-TIME

at the Inn

A Country Inn Cookbook

GAIL GRECO

RUTLEDGE HILL PRESS®
Nashville, Tennessee
A Thomas Nelson Company

Published by Rutledge Hill Press, a Thomas Nelson Company, P.O. Box 141000, Nashville, Tennessee 37214.

Photographs on pages 34, 55, 72, 128, 143, 176, and 182 by Tom Bagley.

Photograph on page 145 © 1990 by Celestial Seasonings.

Photographs on pages 153 and 154 by CHRIS.

Photograph on page 187 by Dennis Curran.

Photographs on pages 201 and 202 by Charley Freiburg.

Photographs on page 60, 74, 77, and 78 by Jeff Frey.

Photograph on page 149 courtesy of Fitz and Floyd, Inc.

Photographs on pages 44, 45 (both), 57, 59, 63, 66, 126, 174, 177, 179, 180, 191, 193, and 197 by George Gardner.

Photograph on page 140 by Havey Productions.

Photographs on pages 22 and 24 by Alegria Hayes.

Photograph on page 20 by Don Heiny.

Photograph on page 148 © 1988 by Grant Huntington and courtesy of Old Monterey Inn. Photograph on page 161 © 1988 by Grant Huntington. Photographs on pages 163 and 164 © 1990 by Grant Huntington.

Photograph on page 170 by Robert C. Jenks.

Photograph on page 105 by Paul Kopelow.

Photographs on pages 51, 52, 53, and 56 by Art Marasco.

Photographs on pages 15, 18, 19, 157, 159, and 160 (both) by Bruce Muncy.

Photograph on page 188 by Randy O'Rourke for *Insider*.

Photographs on pages 70 and 71 by Pal Parker Photography.

Photograph on page 100 by Linda Pearson.

Photographs on pages 38, 40, and 41 by Paul Russell.

Photographs on pages 82, 83, and 85 by George Salivonchik.

Photographs on pages 110, 111, and 112 by Bill Schwartz.

Photographs on pages 166 and 207 by Neil Sjoblom.

Photographs on pages 90, 115, 116, and 118 by Richard Smaltz.

Photograph on page 107 by Allen Smith.

Photographs on pages 122, 123, and 125 by Jack Weinhold.

Photographs on pages 33, 35, 36, and 37 by John Wilson.

Photographs on pages 93, 94, and 96 by P. Michael Whye.

Cover and text design by Bruce Gore, Gore Studios.

Typography by D&T/Bailey Typesetting, Inc., Nashville, Tennessee.

Library of Congress Cataloging-in-Publication Data

Greco, Gail.
    Tea-time at the Inn : a country inn cookbook / Gail Greco.
      p. cm.
    Includes index.
    ISBN 1-55853-848-8 (pbk)
    1. Afternoon teas. I. Title.
  TX736.G74 1991
  641.5'3—dc20   91–23461
                                    CIP

Printed in China
7 8 9—05 04 03

CONTENTS

CHAPTER FOUR
Specialty Teas
137

CHAPTER FIVE
Holiday and Seasonal Teas
167

Introduction

THE BEST LITTLE TEA HOUSES IN AMERICA

TEA CAN TAKE YOU ON A magical journey to places you've never been before. The best little tea houses in America are not on busy street corners or in shopping malls. The simple ceremony that surrounds this most poetic of all beverages is actually best found gracing the candlelit parlors, the Colonial keeping rooms, the sprawling Victorian front porches, the woodpaneled libraries, the Federal dining rooms, the fragrant gardens and the rustic brick courtyards of bed & breakfasts and country inns.

Brimming with architectural and decorative curiosities of yesteryear, small inns present the most inviting and appropriate stage for experiencing tea-time in the Old World spirit. As participants in these magnanimous occasions, we fall under their spell, ushering in a new-found passion.

Innkeepers are proliferating the art of afternoon tea. In fact, I believe they are largely responsible for the resurgence of tea-time in America because its spread coincides with the growing popularity of small inns. Innkeepers don't just write or talk about serving tea. They do it, making converts of us all. We partake of afternoon tea at an inn and never forget the refinement and grandeur of the occasion. As a result, we return home with a fervor to bring such symmetry into our own lives.

Hundreds of inns in America serve afternoon tea—30 percent of the inns surveyed in a recent study by the Professional Association of Innkeepers International. The survey revealed that afternoon tea is more available to inn guests as an amenity than such provisions as bicycles and whirlpools.

The innkeepers use tea-time as another means of cossetting their guests from the moment the traveler arrives on their doorstep. As Joan Wells of the Queen Victoria puts it, "Our reward is that guests will plan their day around tea-time."

Most inns offer tea-time only for overnight guests as a complimentary way of saying, "We care about you." They do this either formally at a tea table or informally from a sideboard where you help yourself. Many inns offer tea only on special occasions. Tea may also be served to outside guests or drop-ins in the style of a romantic country tea house.

The ways in which tea is served at America's small inns are as varied as the inns themselves. There will always be the traditional English tea to enjoy. However, tea-time is moving into the mainstream. As you will read, all types of theme teas are painting new portraits of an old ceremony. This is tea-time American style and what's important is not how the tea table is set or the tea served, but the experience of tea-time itself, however simple or decorous. Meanwhile, these novel ways of enjoying tea are refreshing. They open the tea-time door wide for everyone to come in and join in the pleasure the tea leaves brew.

This book presents myriad suggestions for tea flavors and finger foods. Since tea-time has replaced the cocktail hour in many circles, you'll find teas incorporating heavier foods such as hors d'oeuvres. I've included a variety of recipes so that you can pick and choose to suit your mood, time-frame, and occasion. Hold your own tea with the tea-time-at-home suggestions and let your guests know which inns provided the recipes. This adds to the experience and triggers great exchanges about inns and travel. By the way, inns vary their menus constantly, so you may not find these exact tea foods at a particular inn when you visit it.

Tea-Time at the Inn is certainly a book for armchair dreaming. But do try the recipes and enjoy tea the inn way. And then, pamper yourself by making your way to the inns for tea-time and a whole lot more.

Tea was once reserved for the upper classes who had time on their hands. Nowadays, it's the opposite. We're so busy that we take tea to escape from the pressure and the fast pace, especially when someone invites, "Oh, do come for tea. . . ." Now, you have an excuse to linger.

In some cultures, tea-time is a way of life. In America, it's a relatively new pastime. In any case, it's a luxury you certainly deserve to lavish upon yourself in sweet, heaping quantities.

Acknowledgments

*One person may hit the mark, another blunder. But heed
not these distinctions. Only from the alliance of one, working
with and through the other are great things born.*
—Antoine De Saint-Exupery, 1900-44

A GOOD BOOK IS A PRODuct of teamwork. I thank the other team players:

My brother-in-law, Robert Bagley, for first serving me tea the proper way. He also provided research, as did my sister, Dot, Aunt Margaret, and Billy Barnes. Artist Kathy Cox for preparing research materials.

The Montgomery County Public Library System in Rockville, Maryland, has a telephone reference hot line. It was invaluable for fact-finding and for editing the recipes. Thank you Fern Solomon, Linda Snidow, Chris Tuckerman and Sylvia Gear, whose faces I've never seen, but whose voices I'd recognize anywhere.

Elliot Engel, a literary scholar, for showing me the Dickens way of tea. Lillian Hatton, of the Tea Council of the United States, for research and encouragement. Nancy Smolak for fact-checking. Keith and Mary Millison, Susan Walsh, Cathy Gomez and The Gingerbread Angel Gift Shop in Cape May for photo props. My mother for her promotional effort. And her sewing group, for cheerleading.

It was a pleasure working for publisher Larry Stone. He cares about quality and has truly made writing this book a joy. And to the entire Rutledge Hill team, including Ron Pitkin for his vision and Teri Mitchell for her invaluable assistance in editing the recipes.

My husband, Tom Bagley, gets my biggest applause for his editorial expertise and advice, photography, and love.

*An excerpt
from a letter by guests of
The Mad River Inn,
Waitsfield, Vermont,
dated November 1990:*

In our hectic world . . . we so rarely took time
to find peace with each other. What we brought
back [from your inn] was tea-time, a special
time to stop and reflect.

As we left the inn, we set out on a task of finding
our special teacups, teapot, etc. The daintiness
and yet elegance of a china teacup focuses one
to be gentle, to think warmly and to feel close.

When we sit and have our tea, we are transport-
ed back to your wonderful inn, with its warmth
and caring. We find we leave our work behind
and talk of our future together, have wonderful
fantasies and make wonderful plans. All too
soon, our tea-time is over, yet the feelings linger,
allowing us to be in a more gentle and
acceptable place . . .

CAROL AND
MALCOLM COHEN,
Brooklyn, NY

TEA-TIME
at the Inn

One

STEEPED INN TRADITION

REGARDLESS OF WHETHER YOU BELIEVE TEA LEAVES CAN forecast the future, one thing is certain, they do have a story or two to tell. One of the most popular is the legend of the Chinese emperor Shen Nung, a man of divine healing. The emperor had observed that those who first boiled water before drinking, experienced better health. One day in 2737 B.C., the emperor's servant was cleansing the water for consumption when leaves from a nearby *camellia sinensis* bush blew into the bubbling liquid. The leaves enriched the taste and added an aroma that pleased the emperor so much that he continued to serve his drinking water flavored with *camellia sinensis* leaves.

Today, most of the tea leaves in the world come from this evergreen shrub found in mild climates. The plant's leaves may be harvested once a week before they are blended and processed into the many types and varieties of teas we enjoy today.

India and other tea-growing countries have their own versions of the beverage's beginnings. However, the Chinese story is the one most quoted as tea consumption spread very quickly from China to Japan and England. Eventually, tea became a beverage associated with taking time out to relax. Afternoon tea-time as we know it today was introduced around 1840 by Anna, seventh Duchess of Bedford (1783–1857). In those days in England, lunch was served early and dinner not until 8:00 or 9:00 P.M. The duchess conceived the idea of serving sandwiches and small cakes in the middle of the afternoon. The taking of afternoon tea was born and it quickly became a popular pastime with the prominent social classes.

American innkeepers serve afternoon tea between 3:00 and 5:00 P.M. As you will see, some are more formal than others. A few offer a high tea in the more traditional British way that harkens back to when the working class in

A distinctive marquetry sideboard paints another tea-time canvas at Morrison House.

England stopped for a light supper around 5:00 P.M. This meal centered around tea and included a sweet bread or scones and sweet cake, and at least one hot or cold main dish—which differentiates it from afternoon tea. This high tea refueled farmers and other laborers for returning to the fields while there were still a few hours of daylight.

Many in America use the term *high tea* to mean any tea that contains a non-sweet such as a finger sandwich, as well as sweets. But a sandwich is not a main course. Inns that hold high teas include at least one entrée or, in many cases, a variety of hearty finger foods. Some high teas are so bountiful that they may replace the evening meal or at least hold it off until much later.

Next time you rub tea leaves with your fingers, releasing the fragrant aroma, remember that this natural scent is the keeper of ancient legend, history, intrigue and romance. Locked up in those delicate dried leaves is a record of man's progress. Tea has transcended the ages, only to land at this point on the timeline at many bed & breakfast and country inns. Now, with their many interpretations of an old tradition, inns are making their own tea history.

*Imagine what the world would be like if everyone
had tea to look forward to each day!*
—Rita Maranda, The Mad River Inn,
Waitsfield, Vermont

FORMAL AFTERNOON TEAS

A Butler's Tea

**Smoked Chicken and Walnut Salad
Sandwiches**

Watercress and Cheddar Sandwiches

Stilton with Port Wine

Scones of Choice

Cream Puffs

IN THE MIDST OF ITS URBAN surroundings, the Morrison House appears like a palace on a cloud. Its crescent-moon stairway summons you to an enchanted castle. You are ushered inside, almost with a bowing gesture.

Regally set tables of silver and crystal sparkle in the midday sun as an English butler pours a magnificent combination of Darjeeling and Formosa Oolong. The golden-colored beverage, steeped to a peachy bouquet, filters through a strainer attached to the teapot's spout. The strainer is a most refined addition by innkeepers Rosemary and Bob Morrison who had a silversmith craft several of the strainers to match an antique one they discovered. As the teapot is tilted over the cup, the strainer (see photo below) levels and catches the tea leaves.

As the pouring continues, the "tea-totaler" absorbs the butler's description of the courses: *scones lapped with crème fraîche—fluffy, mountainous peaks of it; apple or pear butter or luscious wine grape preserves; perfectly packed piquant sandwiches and pert puff pastries.* Most tea-takers become so engrossed in conversation that they may forget to ask what they're eating. Tea keeps coming in an unhurried man-

ner. When the pot is empty, a butler reaches for more from a samovar on his sideboard.

During my visit, a mother was there with her daughter, dressed as though one of a queen's most courtly coquettes; a couple were engaged in joyful banter; two shoppers were relaxing after browsing boutiques and specialty shops; and old-time friends were exchanging palaver from the past over a piping pot.

"Tea-time is an inexpensive way to treat yourself to culture." This is how the Morrisons have viewed tea-time since 1985 when they first poured tea for their guests. Tea is so important that staff members must study *The Art and Civility of the Afternoon Tea.* The guide says, "Tea is a central element of the elegance and the mystique that is Morrison House. Our guests enter for an afternoon of quiet conviviality, where entertainment centers around the joy of conversation. No movies, no television, no games, no revelry and none of the distractions of the modern-day world. Only a hot cup of tea and warm conversation."

The guide was written by maître d'hôtel Declan David L. Jarry III, a delightful chap who is a connoisseur of fine wines and liqueurs and who matches spirits to tea-time treats. He chose a Lusteau Sherry, Delux Cream as my après-tea drink. It was a superb finish to an afternoon that found me focusing only on pleasantries.

Morrison House is the embodiment of European travel created by Bob and Rosemary, who built the inn in the Federal style to complement the architecture of Old Town Alexandria and blend the hospitality and cuisines of Europe with those of the New World.

As I left Morrison House, I exited the other side of the half-moon-shaped staircase. I knew I was on to a new way of looking at things.

Morrison House
116 South Alfred Street
Alexandria, VA 22314
Phone: **(703) 838-8000**
Rooms: **45**
Tea-Time: **3:00-5:00 P.M. daily for inn guests and drop-ins**

A BUTLER'S TEA AT HOME

- Act as butler by wearing black tails or a long dress, or anything you want to, allowing just a pair of white gloves to reflect the fact that you are at your guests' beck and call.
- Be sure you pour the tea for your guests.
- Decorate tables in traditional butler colors of black and white.
- Drape white gloves on tea tables.
- Offer only delicate foods and finish with a liqueur.

SMOKED CHICKEN AND WALNUT SALAD SANDWICHES

2 whole smoked chicken breasts

¼ cup chopped walnuts

¼ teaspoon fresh thyme

⅛ teaspoon fresh garlic

½ cup mayonnaise

Salt and pepper to taste

30 slices of bread, crusts removed

Purée all ingredients, except bread, in a food processor. • Spread mixture on half the bread. • Top with remaining slices. • Cut each sandwich in half. Yield: 30

WATERCRESS AND CHEDDAR SANDWICHES

1 bunch fresh watercress, finely chopped

½ cup mayonnaise

½ cup cream cheese, softened

16 slices bread, crusts removed

8 large slices cheddar cheese

Combine watercress with mayonnaise and cream cheese. • Spread layer of cream cheese mixture on half the bread. • Add a slice of cheddar cheese to each and another layer of spread. • Top with remaining bread. • Cut each sandwich in half. Yield: 16

STILTON WITH PORT WINE

| *1 ounce very good port* |
| *4 ounces Stilton cheese, softened* |
| *Cream* |

Work the port into the Stilton and thin with enough cream to make the mixture spreadable. • Serve with crackers. Yield: 1 cup

CREAM PUFFS

At Morrison House, they often form cream puffs into dainty swans. This recipe allows you to make them any shape you desire.

| *2 cups milk* |
| *2 sticks butter* |
| *1 teaspoon salt* |
| *1½ cups all-purpose flour* |
| *12 eggs* |

Preheat oven to 400°. • In a heavy saucepan, combine milk, butter and salt. • Bring to a rolling boil, stirring often. • Remove immediately from the heat and add the flour. • Return to medium heat and cook until the mixture is smooth and rolls free from sides of pan. • Add eggs, one at a time, stirring after each addition until paste is medium-stiff. • Carefully spoon mixture into a pastry tube and pipe into desired shape. • Bake for 8 minutes, then lower oven temperature to 350° and continue baking for 12 minutes. • When the cream puffs are done, they should feel very light and be golden brown. Yield: Depends on shape, but makes about 24 puffs.

Declan Jarry takes pleasure in pouring tea.

There's the teapot on the hob; there's the knuckle of ham; and there's the butter; and there's the crusty loaf and all. The fire was blazing brightly under the influence of the bellows, and the kettle was singing gaily under the influence of both. A small tray of tea things was arranged on the table, a plate of hot buttered toast was gently simmering before the fire, and the red-nosed man himself was busily engaged in converting a large slice of bread into the same agreeable edible, through the instrumentality of a long brass toasting fork.

—Charles Dickens

TEA SELECTING

Teas fall into three basic classifications:

Black Tea—This tea undergoes a special processing treatment (oxidation) that turns the leaves black and produces a brew with a rich, hearty flavor.

Oolong Tea—A semi-oxidized tea whose leaves are partly brown, partly green.

Green Tea—is not oxidized, so the leaves stay light in color when brewed.

Within these classifications, there are thousands of varieties of teas—which come principally from Sri Lanka, India, Indonesia, Kenya and other East African countries. The tea you buy in a food store is a blend of some 20 to 30 varieties—carefully selected by expert tea tasters to maintain the high quality and flavor of each brand.

John Harney is a master tea blender and owner of Harney & Sons, Ltd. in Salisbury, Connecticut. A former innkeeper, he now blends and supplies specialty teas to America's most prestigious hotels and inns.

***

Types and Blends of Popular Teas

Assam—India tea that produces a reddish brew with a brisk, strong flavor that is great to wake one up with in the morning.

Ceylon—Considered one of the world's best. Its golden color and full taste are suitable for drinking any time of the day with milk or lemon.

Darjeeling—A wonderfully large-leafed tea with a rich flavor and a bouquet reminiscent of muscat grapes. Darjeeling can be served anytime.

Earl Grey—A blend of Darjeeling and China teas flavored with oil of bergamot. This is a wonderful afternoon tea that should be served without milk or lemon, as it has such delicate flavor.

English Breakfast—A blend of Assam and Ceylon teas. Strong and full-bodied.

Lapsang Souchon—From the Fukian province of China, it has a distinctive smoky flavor that is best without milk. It is a great tea for blending.

Formosa Oolong—One of the best and most expensive teas in the world. It produces a pale yellow liquid with a light peach flavor. It is best served without milk, in the afternoon or evening.

Morrison House, Alexandria, Virginia

A Laura Ashley Tea

Chocolate Tea

———

Green Tea and Framboise Cocktail

———

Goat Cheese and Smoked Haddock Tarts

———

Fresh Crab and Zucchini Bread Sandwiches

———

Orange Currant Scones

———

Strawberry Pudding

———

Hand-Rolled Chocolate Truffles

IT WAS A CLEAR AUTUMN day when I visited the first inn of what someday may be twenty or more Laura Ashley inns nationwide. The Inn at Perry Cabin is the creation of Sir Bernard Ashley, who, with his late wife, Laura, founded the colorful, floral fashion and decorating empire that bears her name. The inn is situated on a grassy cove, tucked into the Miles River off the Chesapeake Bay. Sailboats shadowed the sun and bobbed slightly in the crisp wind as the falling leaves wrestled for position on the ground. It was a day to sip tea and watch the waves go by. Tea is served in the parlor, drawing room, library, morning room or on a brick patio, only a few feet from the water.

I stopped by the kitchen before tea-time. Chefs were crimping pastries, rolling dough, popping out trays of scones and squeezing custard into shells. The kitchen staff was also making preparations for the evening's dinner. One dish on the menu caught my eye—a lobster with whitefish quenelles, black truffles and vegetable caviar.

I sat in the parlor for tea. The wooden grilles on a pair of French doors offered a checkered view of migrating ducks and geese at the water's edge. I was surrounded by a mélange of geometric and floral wall and fabric designs, all working in perfect harmony—Laura Ashley of course. The artful array matched new patterns with antiques and English-garden paintings, creating an eclectic feeling, definitely patrician and decorous, but oh, so comfortable and unpretentious.

Four delicate strikes from an antique mantel clock announced the onset of tea-time. A hostess attended

A field of flowers for tea

guests by first unfolding a crisply starched linen napkin onto each lap. Tea was caddied in from the kitchen. I sampled randomly and sipped regularly until the pot was empty and the plate was a mere custodian of crumbs. My mind drifted with the small motorboats and schooners taking their runs during the final days of Indian summer and the impending winter. I thought about the purchases I had just made in the shops that line St. Michaels' main street.

Low voices and cheerful whispers filled the inn. The clock was tinging and the sun was giving clue to the changing time and tide. An hour had passed and The Inn at Perry Cabin was still catering to the murmur of hearty talk. Only one guest was alone, deep in the literary throes of a gothic whodunit.

The aura of tea-time is only the confection on the crumpet at Perry Cabin. At nighttime, for instance, the bed sheets are urbanely turned down—exactly one-and-one-half inches. One truly feels as though he or she is visiting English gentry in a stately country home. Tea-time reinforces that feeling with a lingering passion.

The Inn at Perry Cabin
308 Watkins Lane
St. Michaels, Maryland 21663
Phone: **(301) 745-2200**
Rooms: **39**
Tea-Time: **4:00–6:00 P.M. daily for inn guests only**

CHOCOLATE TEA

6 tablespoons loose Orange Pekoe tea
2 teaspoons cocoa powder
½ teaspoon grated orange peel
2 teaspoons brown sugar
1 cup sweetened whipped cream
1 tablespoon grated dark chocolate

Brew tea to desired strength. • Stir in cocoa, peel, and brown sugar. • Steep 30 minutes. • Pour into 6 cups. • Add a dollop of whipped cream to each and garnish with grated chocolate. Yield: 6 cups

GREEN TEA AND FRAMBOISE (RASPBERRY) COCKTAIL

6 ounces green tea
2 ounces framboise (raspberry) liqueur
Fresh mint to taste
6 ounces blush-colored champagne

Brew tea to desired strength. • Chill until ice cold. • Chill glasses. • Fill with crushed ice. • Add 1 ounce framboise liqueur to each glass; top with mint. • Pour tea over ice; top with champagne. • Serve immediately. Yield: 2 servings

For extra flavor, store tea bags in a jar with citrus peel, vanilla bean or cinnamon sticks.

Vermont Marble Inn

TEA MAKING

How to Prepare the Perfect Cup of Tea:

Loose Tea

Tea aficionados tell us that tea's best flavors are released by preparing the water and tea leaves most methodically. The secret of making a really good cup of tea revolves around ensuring that the water is as near boiling as possible when it hits the tea leaves, and that the infusion takes place as rapidly as possible. To achieve this, the Victorian Villa offers this method:

- Draw water for the teapot from a cold tap. Heat the water to boiling on the stove over high heat.
- Choose a tea of good quality.
- Warm the teapot by filling it with hot water before using.
- Fill the tea ball or infuser loosely, allowing 1 teaspoon for each cup of water and 1 teaspoon for the pot.
- Add the tea ball or infuser to the pot.
- Pour the boiling water into the teapot. Allow the tea to steep about 5 minutes. (Always take the teapot to the kettle, not the other way around, as you don't want the water to go off the boil.)

***

Tea Bags

Preheat your teapot by rinsing it out with hot water. This keeps the tea hot during brewing. Bring fresh, cold water to boil in your tea kettle. Use one tea bag per cup. Brew for 3 to 5 minutes.

Victorian Villa

GOAT CHEESE AND SMOKED HADDOCK TARTS

These are served open-face style.

1 stick goat cheese without ash
2 tablespoons freshly cracked black pepper
1 cup olive oil (extra virgin)
4 slices toasted oat grain bread
½ pound smoked haddock
Tomato slices
Chives

Roll stick of goat cheese in cracked pepper. • Marinate overnight in olive oil at room temperature. • Just before serving, remove crusts from toasted bread. • Place a generous slice of the marinated goat cheese on each piece of bread, followed by a piece of haddock. • Follow with a tomato slice and chives. • Cut each in half diagonally. Yield: 8

FRESH CRAB AND ZUCCHINI BREAD SANDWICHES

This is an interesting combination of sweet bread and meat.

6 ounces crab meat
2 ounces lightly seasoned crème fraîche
½ bunch fresh chives
4 slices fresh zucchini bread (see next recipe)
Fresh watercress

Toss crab meat with crème fraîche and chives. • Set aside. • Meanwhile, thinly slice zucchini bread and remove crusts. • Layer 2 slices of bread with the crab meat mixture. • Top with remaining slices. • Cut in half diagonally; garnish with fresh watercress. Yield: 4

The Inn at Perry Cabin is a monument to a quieter time.

ZUCCHINI BREAD

3 eggs
1 cup vegetable oil
2 cups sugar
2 cups grated zucchini
3 cups all-purpose flour
¼ teaspoon baking powder
1 tablespoon baking soda
1 teaspoon salt
1 teaspoon cinnamon
½ cup chopped nuts

Preheat oven to 350°. • In large bowl of electric mixer, beat eggs. • Add oil, sugar and zucchini. • Sift dry ingredients together; add to zucchini mixture. • Stir in nuts. • Pour into a greased 9x5-inch loaf pan. • Bake for 1 hour or until tester inserted in center comes out clean. Yield: 1 loaf

A LAURA ASHLEY TEA AT HOME

- If you have a chiming clock, place it where your guests can hear it easily and begin tea-time on the hour.
- Create an English garden atmosphere with lots of mini-print tablecloths and napkins.
- Serve tea from a pretty ceramic watering can.
- Add a fresh flower arrangement to every tea table.
- Leave coffee table books about England in view.
- Place scones into a pottery flower pot lined with small-print fabric.

ORANGE CURRANT SCONES

2 cups all-purpose flour
1 1/2 tablespoons baking powder
1/3 cup sugar
1/2 teaspoon salt
Grated peel of 1 orange
5 tablespoons butter
5 tablespoons shortening
1/2 cup buttermilk and more for brushing
1/3 cup currants

Preheat oven to 425°. • Place grease-proof (not waxed) paper on a baking sheet. • Combine first 4 ingredients by hand. • Add orange peel. • Flake in butter and shortening. • Add buttermilk. • Mix gently, just until ingredients are incorporated. • Fold in currants. • Roll dough out. • Cut out scones with 2-inch biscuit cutter; brush with a little buttermilk. • Bake for 15 minutes or until golden. Yield: 12

STRAWBERRY PUDDING

1 stick butter
1 cup sugar, divided
4 eggs
1 3/4 cups all-purpose flour
1/2 teaspoon salt
2 teaspoons baking powder
1 cup milk
1/2 teaspoon vanilla extract
2 pints strawberries, cleaned and hulled
1 pound bread scraps
Whipped cream
Cinnamon
Sugar

Preheat oven to 375°. • Cream together butter and half the sugar. • In separate bowl, beat eggs with remaining 1/2 cup sugar and add butter mixture. • Sift together flour, salt and baking powder. • Add to mixture, then stir in milk and vanilla. • Fold in strawberries and bread scraps. • Pour into a greased 9x5-inch loaf pan. • Bake for 30 minutes. • Serve warm with a dollop of whipped cream and a sprinkle of cinnamon and sugar over top of each serving. Yield: 6 to 8 servings

Stir a tablespoon of a favorite fruit preserve into a cup of hot brewed tea.

HAND-ROLLED CHOCOLATE TRUFFLES

2¾ pounds semi-sweet chocolate

2¾ pounds sweet butter, at room temperature

2 cups heavy cream

1 cup sweetened whipped cream

¼ pound unsweetened dark chocolate, melted

Melt semi-sweet chocolate in top of double boiler over simmering water. • Do not overheat. • Set aside to cool. • In small bowl of electric mixer, whip butter until soft. • Add slightly cooled chocolate to butter. • Whip until fully incorporated. • Scrape sides of bowl and whip again. • While the mixer is running, add heavy cream in a thin stream and mix until well blended. • Set mixture aside until firm. • Then, using a small scoop, form truffles by rolling into balls at least 1 inch in diameter. • Place each truffle onto a dollop of sweetened whipped cream and drizzle unsweetened chocolate over top. Yield: 40

Taking afternoon tea is one of the great British traditions. It is actually more akin to a ritual—experienced in the grandest and simplest of homes all over the world . . . To me there is nothing better than a good strong cup o' chá, sandwiches and scones to make me feel at home wherever I am in the world.

—Sir Bernard Ashley

Suites bloom botanical at this Laura Ashley inn.

An English Country Tea

Cucumber with Mint Butter Sandwich

Smoked Salmon with Caper Cream Cheese Spread

---

*Scones of Choice
with Blueberry Port and Rhubarb Ginger Jams*

Victorian Cream Cake

THEY ARRIVE IN PAIRS, IN threes, sometimes in fours and fives. They are dressed for a proper English afternoon in the country. Some don hats. Others have just come from the office and still have on their suits and ties. Some even dare to wear white gloves. They want to feel special. Pampered. Served. And they are. This could be a quaint tea house on a back road in the English countryside, but instead it's one of America's most authentic country inns, The Bee & Thistle. If I didn't already know that this inn is unique and individual, I'd say they're imitating a British tea house. But it's simply their style and their way of bringing English tea-time in the country to America. The cheerful at-mosphere, abundant English herb and floral gardens, and a chef from London are the natural props that help make you feel as though you're taking tea in bucolic England.

Some await tea-time sitting outside on benches under ageless trees that bow like lace parasols to shade them. The scalloped edges of the Lieutenant River offer a glistening reflection of the 1756 Bee & Thistle Inn as the waters run along the edge of the property.

This is no ordinary day for the guests who drop in at tea-time. They have set aside this time to get together with others. In the parlor, a

A pouf of nature joins afternoon tea at Bee & Thistle.

tea menu is set out on tables, trumpeting the day's comestibles and choice of aperitifs.

"Try the Earl Grey English Liqueur. I added it to our menu because it's perfect with tea," Penny Nelson suggested. I obliged. I was in heaven by the time the first delicate, fruity/tarty sip had reached my toes. Penny and I sat in plush armchairs. My tea equipage was served from a doilie-covered bench that usually seats the evening's pianist. Penny's was on a tea table. Everyone is brought their own individual antique Staffordshire teapot, part of Penny's personal collection which is on view in a china closet. I enjoyed pouring my own tea from the pot. As I glanced around the parlor, I realized that the inn had been transformed into a little tea room. Quaint and magical.

In the kitchen, tea-time delights were being prepared by the culinary staff, which includes the Nelsons' son, Jeff, who formerly served at the Ritz-Carlton in Boston and executive chef Francis Brooke-Smith, formerly of the Ritz in London. I asked Francis for a bottom-line recommendation on making better scones. He stated simply, "Don't overwork the dough!"

Following an aperitif and the serving of the teapots, out came the tea foods all at once—unlike most inns, which serve them in courses. At Bee & Thistle, tea guests are served an attractive dinner-plate-size arrangement filled with finger sandwiches, scones with such homemade jams as rhubarb and blueberry port, tea breads and a lavish dessert. "We decided to do it this way so that people would not be constantly interrupted and have their flow of good conversation stopped cold," explained Penny. She and her husband, Bob, have been serving afternoon tea since they opened the inn in 1983.

The back of the tea menu sums up the Nelsons' feelings about tea: "Good conversation is the heart of afternoon tea and talk seems to flow as cups are filled and refilled. The tone is usually light and animated, since it's considered poor form to bring up distasteful subjects at tea. The idea is to relax, socialize and recharge one's batteries for the evening." At the Bee & Thistle, one needs to recharge for the evening to sample a Bee & Thistle dinner. Like tea-time, dinner here is romantic and the food memorable. The inn constantly finishes first in state contests for the best food and atmosphere because the only thing they don't do very well at Bee & Thistle is rest on their laurels.

Bee & Thistle
100 Lyme Street
Old Lyme, CT 06371
Phone: **(203) 434-1667**
Rooms: **11**
Tea-Time: **Mon., Wed., Thurs., 3:30–5:00 P.M. for inn guests and drop-ins**

CUCUMBER WITH MINT BUTTER SANDWICH

2 tablespoons sour cream

1 ounce fresh mint leaves, chopped

4 sticks sweet butter

⅛ teaspoon salt

3 to 4 large cucumbers, peeled and sliced thin

60 slices thin white bread

In food processor, blend sour cream and mint. • Add butter, 1 tablespoon at a time. • Pulse. • Add salt. • Blend well. • Spread half the slices with a thin layer of the mint butter. • Add 5 to 6 cucumber slices to each half, overlapping slices slightly. • Add tops. • Remove crusts. • Cut sandwiches in half lengthwise. Yield: 60 sandwiches

SMOKED SALMON WITH CAPER CREAM CHEESE SPREAD

1½ pounds cream cheese, softened

1 heaping tablespoon capers

½ teaspoon salt

½ teaspoon pepper

120 slices thin wheat bread

3½ pounds smoked salmon, thinly sliced (1 ounce per full sandwich, before it's cut in half)

In food processor, blend cream cheese, capers, salt and pepper. • Spread mixture on half the bread. • Add a layer of salmon. • Do not overlap salmon. • Top with remaining bread. • Remove crusts. • Cut in half lengthwise. Yield: 120 sandwiches

The innkeeper's teapots muster for a march to the tea room.

AN ENGLISH COUNTRY TEA AT HOME

- Invite your guests to tea with an invitation written in calligraphy. Add some tea quotes and thoughts to the invitation, just to add flavor to your tea.
- Fill extra teacups with flowers as the centerpiece for each tea table.
- This is a good time to start collecting small teapots to serve individually to each guest.

BLUEBERRY PORT JAM

Serve this jam and the rhubarb ginger jam with your favorite scones.

6 pounds blueberries
2 cups port plus ½ cup port
9 cups sugar
½ cup lemon juice

Put all ingredients, except ½ cup port, in a pot and bring to a boil. • Simmer for about 20 minutes, gently stirring periodically to prevent sticking. Do not stir too much as it will break down the blueberries. • When set, about 25 minutes, remove from heat. • Allow to cool, then add ½ cup port. Mix well. • Place in sterile jars. Yield: 20 cups

RHUBARB GINGER JAM

4 pounds rhubarb, washed and cut into 1-inch pieces
1 cup water

1 tablespoon lemon juice
6 pieces fresh ginger (2-inches each), peeled, thinly sliced and chopped
6 cups sugar
8 tablespoons crystallized ginger

Place all ingredients, except crystallized ginger, into a large pot and bring to a boil. • Simmer for about 25 minutes. Just when it starts to set, stir in the ginger. • Cool. • Place in sterile jars. Yield: 15 cups

VICTORIAN CREAM CAKE

4 eggs
½ cup sugar
1 cup all-purpose flour
¼ stick butter, melted
Raspberry jam
1 pint heavy cream, whipped until very firm
Toasted almond slices

Preheat oven to 350°. • In a bowl over a pan of hot water, whisk eggs and sugar. • Continue until mixture is light, creamy and doubled in bulk. • Remove from heat and whisk until cold and thick (will resemble ribbons). • Gently fold in flour, then melted butter. • Place in a greased génoise mold. • Bake for 30 minutes or until tester inserted in center comes out clean. • Let cake cool. • Cut the cake into 3 layers. • Spread each layer with raspberry jam and whipped cream, about ¼-inch thick. • Assemble layers. • Frost the top and sides with remaining whipped cream. • Sprinkle tops and sides with toasted almond slices. Yield: 12 slices

A Cream Tea

English Tea Sandwich Loaf

———

Choux Puffs with Curried Chicken

———

Shrimp Puffs

———

Rose Manor Crumpets

———

Petite Chocolate Éclairs

———

Strawberry Puff Squares

———

Lemon Curd Mini-Tarts

———

Devonshire Cream American Style

"**N**OW LOVE, DON'T forget your daisies!" exclaimed innkeeper Don Bryant as we moved toward the foyer of the very British Rose Manor Bed & Breakfast.

Of course, Don, who was born and raised in England, wasn't talking about flowers. *Daisies*, he explained, is an English expression for shoes. Since my husband and I had removed our snow-caked boots upon entering the inn, Don was just reminding us about them.

The atmosphere at Rose Manor is all ease and please. Don and his wife, Carol Heeter, have fun as a couple. Their humor is contagious and sets the tone for a most cordial afternoon with tea. You would think tea would be a four o'clock ritual here, but Rose Manor provides such a bountiful table for tea-time that the innkeepers decided to hold their teas by request only, to ensure large numbers. Still, they serve several teas a month for up to 50 people a tea.

In summer, tea is served in a glass-enclosed conservatory overlooking a rose garden. Indoor teas are buffet-style in a dining room accented with rich chestnut wood, built-in sideboards, cupboards, and china closets.

Tea-time at Rose Manor is a cream tea because, as British tradition holds, clotted cream (American-style) or whipped cream is served. But it's also a cream tea because Carol is big on cream-filled pastries.

Carol and Don serve scones followed by sandwiches and as many as 13 different sweets. All that food takes a while to eat, but that's just what the guests come for, isn't it?

Rose Manor
124 Linden Street
Manheim, PA 17545
Phone: **(717) 664-4932**
Rooms: **5**
Tea-Time: **On special occasions and upon request**

ENGLISH TEA SANDWICH LOAF

1 large loaf of whole-wheat or white bread, un-sliced

Butter

4 ounces ham

2 tablespoons pickle relish

7 tablespoons mayonnaise, divided

4 ounces grated sharp cheddar cheese (yellow)

10 ounces red pimientos, drained (reserve 4 strips for garnish)

4 ounces cooked and cooled chicken, shredded

1 tablespoon curry powder

8 ounces cream cheese, softened

Pitted black and green olives, sliced

Cut crusts from bread, then cut loaf lengthwise into 4 slices. • Spread 3 slices with butter, leaving the top piece plain.

In food processor, blend ham with pickle relish and 2 tablespoons mayonnaise. • Spread on bottom layer. • Blend grated cheese, pimiento and 2 tablespoons mayonnaise; spread on second layer. • Blend chicken, curry powder and 2 tablespoons mayonnaise; spread on third layer. • Place remaining bread on top to complete the loaf.

In bowl of electric mixer, blend cream cheese and 1 tablespoon mayonnaise until smooth. • Ice entire loaf as you would a cake. • Fill a pastry bag, fitted with star tube, with remaining mixture and decorate the border on top and base of loaf. • Garnish with olives and pimiento strips. Yield: 12 one-inch slices

CHOUX PUFFS WITH CURRIED CHICKEN

Curried chicken may be substituted by minced ham or shrimp, tuna or crab salads. Puff shells can be made in advance and frozen for future use.

PUFF SHELLS

1 cup water

1 stick butter, cut into pieces

1/4 teaspoon salt

1 cup unsifted all-purpose flour

4 large eggs

Preheat oven to 425°. • Grease 2 large baking sheets. • In a 2-quart saucepan, heat water, butter and salt to boiling. • With wooden spoon or hand-held mixer, beat in flour until the mixture forms a ball and rolls free from sides of pan. Remove pan from heat. • Add eggs, one at a time, beating well after each addition until mixture is smooth.

Place dough into large pastry bag fitted with a round tip. • Pipe 1-inch-round by 1/2-inch-high circles onto baking sheets, leaving 1 inch between. • Bake for 10 minutes. • Reduce heat to 375°. • Bake 10 minutes longer. • Turn off oven and with fork, pierce shells once. • Leave in turned-off oven for 15 minutes. Cool on wire racks while preparing filling.

FILLING

2 boneless roasted chicken breasts

2 tablespoons curry powder

1/4 teaspoon salt

1/3 cup mayonnaise (or more if needed)

1/2 cup chopped walnuts

In food processor, blend all ingredients except nuts. • Don't overmix. • Fold in walnuts. • Cut top off each puff shell, about ⅓ of the way down. • Place 1 tablespoon of filling into the puff. • Replace the lid. • Refrigerate on a tray until serving time. Yield: 24

SHRIMP PUFFS

Puffs may be made ahead of time and frozen. You can make the basic pastry recipe that follows or substitute with a 9x15-inch sheet of puff pastry from the freezer section of the supermarket. Note: Pastry may also be filled with any savory or pie filling.

PUFF PASTRY

4 cups sifted all-purpose flour
1 teaspoon salt
4 sticks butter, chilled, separating out 6 tablespoons
1 tablespoon lemon juice
1¼ cups ice water

Sift together flour and salt into a medium bowl. • With a pastry blender or 2 knives, cut in 6 tablespoons butter. • Stir in lemon juice and water. • Knead in bowl for several strokes or until smooth.

On a lightly floured surface, roll out dough to form a 12-inch square. • Shape remaining butter into a 10x5-inch rectangle. • Place buttered rectangle on half the pastry square, leaving a 1-inch border. • Fold remaining pastry over butter, enclosing completely. Press edges to seal.

Roll pastry with a rolling pin several times, rolling out to a 24x8-inch rectangle. Fold into thirds. • Wrap in waxed paper or plastic wrap. Chill for 30 minutes. • Repeat rolling-

Shrimp Puffs in the sand

and-chilling process about 5 times. • Wrap and refrigerate pastry at least 1 hour longer before filling and using.

FILLING

5 ounces shrimp, peeled, cleaned and deveined (or use canned)
4 ounces cream cheese, softened
¼ teaspoon salt
1 tablespoon curry powder
2 teaspoons butter, melted

Steam shrimp about 3 to 4 minutes. • Place in food processor with next 3 ingredients. Blend well. • When ready to use, preheat oven to 350°. • Roll pastry out on a floured 9x15-inch board. • Brush all over with melted butter. • Cut into 3x3-inch squares and place a teaspoonful of shrimp filling in middle of each square. • Fold into triangles, sealing edges well. • Place on a lighly buttered baking sheet. • Bake for 20 minutes or until lightly browned. Yield: 15

A CREAM TEA AT HOME

- Decorate with baskets overflowing with fresh berries in season.
- Send guests home with a tea-party favor of a wire whisk to use in beating some of their own cream.
- Serve the Rose Manor Crumpets in an antique toast holder or a sorter, such as one used for the household's outgoing mail.

Rose Manor Crumpets

If you don't have crumpet rings, use a clean 6½-ounce tuna fish can with both lids removed.

½ ounce dry yeast (2 packages)
1 teaspoon sugar
3½ cups warm water
4 cups all-purpose flour
2 tablespoons baking powder
1½ teaspoons salt

Dissolve yeast and sugar in warm water. • Add flour, baking powder, and salt. • Whisk until frothy. • Heat griddle to 450°. • Grease insides of crumpet rings and place them on heated griddle. • Pour ¾ cup batter into each ring. • Cook until bubbles form and become dry on top. • Remove ring and turn crumpet to brown lightly. • Toast crumpet and serve with butter. Yield: 24

Petite Chocolate Éclairs

Éclairs

1 cup water
1 stick butter, cut into pieces
¼ teaspoon salt
1 cup unsifted all-purpose flour
4 large eggs

Preheat oven to 425°. • Grease 2 large baking sheets. • In a 2-quart saucepan, heat water, butter and salt to boiling. • With wooden spoon or hand-held mixer, beat in flour until the mixture forms a ball and rolls away from sides of pan. Remove pan from heat. • Add eggs, 1 at a time, beating well after each addition, until mixture is smooth.

Place dough into large pastry bag fitted with a large round pastry tip. • Pipe 24 oblongs (2½x1-inch) onto baking sheets, leaving 1 inch between. • Bake for 10 minutes. • Reduce heat to 375°. • Bake 10 minutes longer. • Turn off oven and with fork, pierce éclairs once. • Leave in turned-off oven 15 minutes longer. • Cool on wire racks. • Prepare vanilla custard filling.

Butter roses bloom among the crumpets and lace.

VANILLA CUSTARD FILLING

| ⅓ cup sugar |
| 1 tablespoon all-purpose flour |
| 1 tablespoon cornstarch |
| ¼ teaspoon salt |
| 1½ cups milk |
| 1 egg yolk, beaten |
| 1 teaspoon vanilla extract |

In a small saucepan, combine sugar, flour, cornstarch and salt. • Gradually stir in milk. Cook and stir over medium heat until mixture thickens and comes to a boil. • Cook 3 minutes longer. • Combine egg yolk with small amount of hot milk mixture. Add to pan. • Cook until mixture boils. • Stir in vanilla. • Remove from heat and cool completely. • Spoon filling into large pastry bag with a star tip. • Pipe filling into both small ends of éclairs, enough to fill to the center. • Decorate with icing.

ICING

| 8 ounces semi-sweet chocolate |
| 1 cup heavy cream |

Heat chocolate and cream in saucepan until chocolate is melted and mixture is smooth. • To thicken, cool in refrigerator. • Spread over éclairs. Yield: 24

DEVONSHIRE CREAM AMERICAN STYLE

- Rose Manor thinks it has come as close as can be to the real clotted cream made in Devon, England. Devonshire cream is made with unpasteurized cream from Jersey cows, and so because only pasteurized cream is available in the United States, it's hard to make the real thing here. Here's Carol and Don's recipe:
- Buy 2 cups of 40 percent butterfat cream from a real dairy or farm. Place cream in a bottle with straight sides (no neck) for ease of serving. Add 2 tablespoons lemon juice. Secure jar lid. Turn upside down, shaking. Leave at room temperature for 24 hours, away from drafts. Place bottle in refrigerator for another 24 hours and it's ready to serve.

Lemon, kiwi, and tea-time tarts

STRAWBERRY PUFF SQUARES

In addition to the ingredients for the vanilla custard filling and pastry, you will need ½ stick melted butter, strawberry jam or fresh fruit, and 1 cup of heavy cream, whipped. • First, prepare the Vanilla Custard Filling recipe from the Petite Chocolate Éclairs recipe on page 34. • Use the same pastry recipe (except for changes noted in the following puff pastry recipe) from the Shrimp Puffs on page 33.

PUFF PASTRY

Use the recipe from the Shrimp Puffs up to the point of rolling out the chilled dough.

Preheat oven to 350°. • Roll pastry out on a floured 9x12-inch sheet to an ⅛-inch thickness. • Brush all over with melted butter to cover. • Cut into 2x3-inch squares and pierce all over with fork. • Place squares on

lightly buttered baking sheet and bake for about 10 to 15 minutes, or until lightly browned and puffed. • Remove from oven and cool slightly. • When able to handle, insert point of sharp knife and pry apart to cool in sets of tops and bottoms.

Spoon vanilla custard filling onto bottom layers. • Next, spoon a layer of jam or fresh fruit over the filling. • Place pastry top on filling. • Add whipped cream in pastry bag fitted with star tube and decorate tops. • Refrigerate until serving time. Yield: 18

LEMON CURD MINI-TARTS

TART SHELLS

2¼ cups all-purpose flour
¾ teaspoon salt
½ cup shortening, well-chilled
2 tablespoons butter
5 to 6 tablespoons cold water

Preheat oven to 450°. • In large mixing bowl, sift together flour and salt. • Divide shorten-

Rose Manor's crumpets are a cinch compared to the time it must have taken in Charles Dickens' day:

Mix a gill of brewer's yeast with two quarts of luke-warm water and add sufficient flour to make a thinnish batter. Stand six hours in a warm place, stir with a wooden spoon and let stand further four hours. On a hot griddle lay a number of hoops, pouring a ladleful of batter into each. When the tops are bubbly turn them over, hoops as well, and in about five minutes they will be cooked.
—*Dining with Dickens*

ing and butter into 4 or 5 pieces and drop into bowl. • Set mixer to slow speed and continue cutting in shortening until particles are size of small peas, about 30 seconds.

Add water, 1 tablespoon at a time, until particles are moistened. • Use only enough water to make pastry form a ball. Do not overmix. • Cover with plastic wrap and chill for 15 minutes. • Roll pastry between waxed paper to ⅛-inch thickness. • Grease 48 1½-inch mini-muffin cups. • Cut pastry into circles with 3-inch cookie cutter. Press each circle into a muffin cup, forming a tart shell. • Prick with fork. • Bake for 8 to 10 minutes or until golden. • Fill with lemon curd.

Rose Manor's Strawberry Puffs

LEMON CURD

2 cups sugar
12 egg yolks, slightly beaten
1 cup lemon juice
2 sticks butter
2 tablespoons grated lemon peel
1 kiwi, cut into ¼-inch slices

In medium saucepan, blend sugar and egg yolks. • Add lemon juice gradually. • Cook over low heat, stirring constantly until mixture coats back of spoon. Do not boil. • Remove from heat. • Cool slightly. • Stir in butter and lemon peel. • Cool completely. When cooled, spoon lemon curd into tart shells, filling to rim. • Decorate each tart with one slice of kiwi. Yield: 48

INFORMAL TEAS

The Captain's House Inn

A FORMAL ATMOSPHERE does not have to exist in order to experience tea-time. "The point is that people make time to mingle and share conversation," says Dave Eakin of The Captain's House on Cape Cod. Dave and his wife, Cathy, say their guests break from the beach and shopping to go back to the inn for tea.

An English staff serves tea on white linen tablecloths, which contrast with the scene of lush greenery and colorful gardens visible through the glass-enclosed dining room.

The Captain's House Inn
369-377 Old Harbor Road
Chatham, Cape Cod, MA 02633
Phone: **(508) 945-0127**
Rooms: **11**
Tea-Time: **4:00–5:00 P.M. for inn guests only**

BUTTER CAKE WITH ORANGE ICING

CAKE

4 large eggs
1¾ cups sugar
2 cups cake flour
1 stick butter
1 cup milk
1 teaspoon vanilla extract
1 teaspoon baking powder

Preheat oven to 350°. • In large mixing bowl, beat eggs at medium speed for 3 minutes. • Add the sugar in 2 batches; beat just until combined. • Add the flour, 1 cup at a time. • In a saucepan, heat the butter and milk together until boiling; immediately beat into flour mixture. • Mix in vanilla and baking powder. • Pour into a greased bundt pan. • Bake for 45 minutes or until tester inserted in center comes out clean. • Remove from oven; cool in pan for 5 minutes and then invert onto a wire rack.

ICING

1 cup confectioners' sugar
2 tablespoons frozen orange juice concentrate, thawed
Heavy cream

Combine sugar and orange juice with enough cream to make a drizzling consistency. • Drizzle onto the cake. Yield: 12 slices

Ribbons of icing trickle down a butter cake while a lofty carrot confection poses atop a sideboard at the Captain's House.

NIG NOG COOKIES

1 stick butter
1 teaspoon golden syrup or honey
1 teaspoon baking soda, dissolved in 2 tablespoons hot water
1 teaspoon baking powder
1 cup old-fashioned oats
1 cup all-purpose flour
1 cup sugar
1 cup shredded coconut

Preheat oven to 350°. • Melt the butter and syrup. • Add baking soda mixture. • Add remaining ingredients and mix together. • Roll into balls (1 heaping tablespoon each) and place onto greased cookie sheet, at least 2 inches apart. • Press down, flattening slightly. • Bake 20 minutes or until golden brown. • Remove from cookie sheet. • Cool on rack. Yield: 24

FRUIT JEWELS

These add pretty bursts of rich, sparkling color to the tea-time table.

2 sticks unsalted butter
¹⁄₂ cup sugar
2 egg yolks
1 tablespoon lemon juice
2¹⁄₄ cups all-purpose flour
1¹⁄₂ teaspoons baking powder
¹⁄₄ teaspoon cinnamon
¹⁄₄ teaspoon salt
Assortment of jams

Preheat oven to 350°. • Cream together butter and sugar. • Add egg yolks and lemon juice. • Beat until smooth. • Add remaining

ingredients and blend into a dough ball. • Roll into smaller balls (1 tablespoon each) and place in mini-muffin tins lined with petits fours papers. • Make a small indentation in center of each and fill with an assortment of jams. • Bake for 30 minutes or until golden brown. Yield: 36

CARROT-WALNUT CAKE

CAKE

2 cups unsifted all-purpose flour
2 cups sugar
2 teaspoons baking soda
1 teaspoon salt
3 teaspoons cinnamon
4 eggs
1 cup vegetable oil
4 cups finely grated raw carrots

Fruit Jewels on a pedestal crown this Cape Cod table.

Preheat oven to 350°. • Grease and flour three 8-inch round cake pans. • Thoroughly stir together flour, sugar, baking soda, salt and cinnamon. • Set aside. • In a large bowl, beat eggs until frothy. • Slowly beat in oil. • Gradually add flour mixture to egg mixture, beating until smooth. • Add the carrots and blend well. • Pour into prepared cake pans. • Bake for 30 minutes or until tester inserted in center comes out clean. • Cool in pans for 10 minutes. Remove and cool completely on racks. • Make frosting.

FROSTING

8 ounces cream cheese, softened
4 tablespoons butter
2 cups confectioners' sugar
1 teaspoon lemon juice
1 teaspoon vanilla extract
1/2 cup finely chopped walnuts
Walnut halves for top of cake

Mix together the first 5 ingredients. • When well blended, spread some of the frosting over each layer, followed by the finely chopped nuts. • Assemble layers and add remaining frosting over tops and sides. • Decorate top of cake with walnut halves. Yield: 8 to 12 servings

SHORTBREAD WITH LEMON AND JAM

2 cups all-purpose flour
1/4 cup plus 1 tablespoon cornmeal
1/2 cup sugar
2 sticks butter
3/4 cup jam (any flavor)
1 teaspoon lemon juice

Sugar-dusted scones await a cloaking of rich cream and ruby preserves.

Preheat oven to 350°. • In large mixing bowl, combine flour, cornmeal and sugar. • Cut in butter until the consistency of very fine bread crumbs. • Grease two 7-inch square baking pans. • Sprinkle 1 1/2 cups flour mixture into bottom of each pan. Press down firmly. • In small saucepan, warm the jam and lemon juice to a spreading consistency. Spread onto bottom layer of each pan. • Sprinkle remaining shortbread mixture over top of each pan. • Press down gently with fingers. • Bake for 20 minutes or until golden brown and shortbread pulls away from sides of the pan. • Cool. • Cut into 2-inch squares. Yield: 14

The Vermont Marble Inn

TEA IS SERVED IN AN INTImate library at The Vermont Marble Inn and is the pride of innkeeper Bea Taub, who is also the pastry chef for the elegant desserts at her spacious Italianate mansion. Dinner, by the way, is so tasty and filling, that when I visited, I had to walk it off by traversing the town green across the street from the mansion. The view of The Vermont Marble Inn from the green includes an outline of tiny lights, reflecting against the exterior marble.

Fine china and porcelain teapots are set out for guests on top of heirloom tatting cloths for tea-time. "We like to set a dramatic table," says Bea, speaking for herself, her husband, Richie, and their innkeeping partner Shirley Stein. She does that by adding pedestal servers at varying heights and arranging the forks in a pattern. Spoons are held in an antique spoon holder.

Bea likes to serve sugar in cubes—"lumps" as she says—in keeping with tradition. "Tea-time helps newly arrived guests get acquainted immediately. Why wait for the next morning's breakfast?" Bea asks. Indeed.

The Vermont Marble Inn
12 West Park Place
Fair Haven, VT 05743
Phone: **(802) 265-8383**
Tea-Time: **3:00–5:00** P.M. **daily for inn guests**

CUCUMBER AND CHEESE SANDWICHES

| 1 cucumber, peeled and thinly sliced |
| 1/8 teaspoon salt |
| Freshly ground pepper |
| 1 tablespoon freshly squeezed lemon juice |
| 8 slices white bread, crusts removed |
| 1/4 cup butter, at room temperature |
| 8 ounces mild cheddar, grated |

Reserve 16 slices of cucumber for garnish. • Place remaining cucumber slices in a bowl and add salt, pepper and lemon juice. • Turn the cucumbers to coat each slice. • Spread bread slices with butter. • Sprinkle the cheese on half the bread. • Cover with slices of cucumber. • Top with remaining bread slices and cut into quarters on the diagonal. Garnish with reserved cucumber slices. Yield: 16

NUT TASSIES
This recipe freezes nicely.

CRUST

| 2 sticks butter |
| 8 ounces cream cheese |
| 2 cups all-purpose flour |

Mix all ingredients to form dough. • Press small amounts of dough into mini-muffin tins, just enough to cover each cup well.

FILLING

| 2 eggs |
| 1 1/2 cups firmly packed brown sugar |
| 2 tablespoons butter |
| 1/8 teaspoon salt |
| 1 1/2 teaspoons vanilla extract |
| 1 cup finely chopped walnuts or pecans |

Preheat oven to 350°. • In bowl with electric mixer, combine eggs, sugar and butter. • Add salt and vanilla. • Sprinkle nuts into bottom of each lined tart, reserving 1/2 cup. • Fill each tart with a tablespoon of filling. • Sprinkle remaining nuts on top. • Bake for 25 minutes or until crusts are lightly browned. Yield: 36

OATMEAL CHOCOLATE SANDWICHES

| 3 sticks butter, at room temperature |
| 1 cup sugar |
| 1 cup Grand Marnier liqueur |
| 3 cups quick or old-fashioned oats, uncooked |
| 2 cups all-purpose flour |
| 12 ounces semi-sweet chocolate, cut into small pieces |
| 2 tablespoons butter |

Preheat oven to 350°. • Beat butter and sugar until light and fluffy. • Blend in liqueur. • Add oats and flour, mixing well. • Chill mixture for 10 minutes. • Shape into 1-inch balls. • Place on ungreased cookie sheet 3 inches apart. • Press into 2-inch circles. • Bake for 10 to 12 minutes or until edges are a light golden brown. • Remove from cookie sheet and cool completely.

Melt chocolate and butter in top of double boiler, over simmering water. Stir until smooth. • Spread 2 teaspoons of melted chocolate on flat side of half the cookies. • Top with flat side of remaining cookies. • Drizzle with leftover chocolate. • Refrigerate 10 minutes. • Store, tightly covered, in a cool, dry place. Yield: 30

Inn Victoria

ONCE PATIENTS CAME TO see their doctor in the 12x20-foot little building. Now, they drop in for tea or ice cream. Inn Victoria's tea house looks as if it is from a Norman Rockwell painting or from England's country tea houses. It's filled with curious antique and modern tea equipage and a wonderful collection of teapots.

Inn guests may take tea here or in the 1850 bed & breakfast next door. At the heart of this cheerfully decorated inn and tea shop is KC Lanagan who runs Inn Victoria with her husband, Tom. KC has a distinct knack for innkeeping and a buoyant, giving personality. Selling antiques is another of KC's passions. The wonderful furniture of yesteryear and the innkeeper's creativity (she's an art major) have painted a delightful inn that shouldn't be missed—tea-time or otherwise.

Inn Victoria
On the Green
P.O. Box 788
Chester, VT 05143
Phone: **(802) 875-4288**
Rooms: **7**
Tea-Time: **4:00 P.M. daily at the inn; noon-8:00 P.M. daily in the tea shop in summer**

TEA-TIME ICE CREAM SODA

1½ cups boiling water
6 tea bags
¼ cup sugar
3 cups apple juice, chilled
3 cups ginger ale, chilled
Butter pecan, pistachio or ice cream of choice

Pour water over tea bags. • Steep for 5 minutes. • Remove tea bags. • Stir in sugar. • Cool. • In large pitcher, combine tea and juice. • Just before serving, add ginger ale and top with 1 scoop of ice cream. Yield: 8 servings

Popovers perch proudly on Inn Victoria's splendid table.

INN VICTORIA'S POPOVERS

$1^{1}/_{2}$ teaspoons vegetable oil
1 cup all-purpose flour
1 cup milk
2 eggs
$^{1}/_{4}$ teaspoon salt
1 tablespoon melted butter

Preheat oven to 450°. • Place $^{1}/_{4}$ teaspoon oil in each popover cup. • Place tin in heated oven. • Sift flour to measure 1 cup. • Combine milk, eggs, salt and melted butter. • Blend with flour until smooth. • Pour mixture into hot tins, filling each cup half full. • Bake for 30 minutes. Do not open oven door during baking. • Popovers are done when browned and puffy. Yield: 6

VANILLA RAISIN CAKE

2 sticks butter
8 ounces cream cheese, softened
$1^{1}/_{2}$ cups sugar
2 teaspoons vanilla extract
4 eggs
$2^{1}/_{4}$ cups sifted all-purpose flour
2 teaspoons baking powder
$^{1}/_{4}$ teaspoon salt
$1^{1}/_{2}$ cups raisins, cut in half

Preheat oven to 300°. • Cream butter with cream cheese until fluffy. • Gradually beat in sugar until dissolved. • Beat in vanilla and add eggs, one at a time, beating well after each addition. • Sift together flour, baking powder and salt. • Blend into the creamed mixture. • Fold in the raisins. • Transfer to a well-greased, 9-inch bundt pan. • Bake for 1 hour or until tester inserted in center comes out clean. • Leave cake in pan for 10 minutes. Shake loose and cool. Yield: 12 to 14 servings

The innkeeper's passion for collecting zany tea-ware is evident in this bird-watcher's pottery.

Maison du Pré

THE ANSONBOROUGH DIStrict of Charleston, South Carolina, surrounds you with history. And the place in the district for tea is Maison du Pré with its three historic homes and two carriage houses. Bob and Lucille Mulholland's inn is a reflection of the European influence on the city and the South's Colonial past. Impressionist paintings are everywhere, including one by Lucille, who is a serious artist. Tea-time is another way to taste the flavors of the region with recipes for the foods coming from regional cookbooks.

Maison du Pré
317 East Bay Street
Charleston, SC 29401
Phone: (803) 723-8691
Rooms: 15
Tea-Time: 4:00–6:00 P.M. daily for inn guests

SMOKED OYSTER CHEESE ROLL

8 ounces cream cheese, at room temperature

2 tablespoons mayonnaise

2 teaspoons Worcestershire sauce

Garlic juice and onion juice to taste

1 6½-ounce can smoked oysters

½ cup toasted, chopped almonds

Paprika

Mix together cream cheese, mayonnaise, Worcestershire and juices. • Spread onto waxed paper. • Place oysters on top of cream cheese mixture and turn up jellyroll style. • Roll in nuts and sprinkle with paprika for color. • Chill for 24 hours. • Serve with crackers. Yield: 2 cups

The innkeeper's art is everywhere, including on the tea table.

HUGUENOT TORTE

4 eggs
3 cups sugar
8 tablespoons all-purpose flour
5 teaspoons baking powder
½ teaspoon salt
2 cups chopped tart cooking apples
2 cups chopped pecans, divided
2 teaspoons vanilla extract
1 cup heavy cream, whipped

Preheat oven to 325°. • In bowl of electric mixer, beat eggs until frothy and lemon-colored. • Add next 7 ingredients in order listed, reserving ½ cup nuts. Mix until well blended. • Pour into two greased 8x12-inch baking pans. • Bake for 45 minutes or until crusty and brown. • To serve, scoop up with pancake turner (keeping crusty part on top). • Place each pancake on a serving plate. Cover with whipped cream. Sprinkle with remaining chopped nuts. Yield: 16 servings

If a recipe calls for using a pastry bag and you don't have one, you can make your own. Put your filling into a bottom corner of a clean, heavy plastic bag. Snip the corner with scissors. Squeeze the mixture out of the bag in the manner in which the recipe dictates.

The Mad River Inn, Waitsfield, Vermont

BENNE (SESAME) SEED WAFERS

Benne means sesame and was presumably brought to the South by West African slaves. It was a good luck plant to its growers. This recipe makes sweet, transparent biscuits.

1 stick butter, softened
2 cups loosely packed brown sugar
1 egg, beaten
1 cup all-purpose flour
½ teaspoon baking powder
¼ teaspoon salt
1 teaspoon vanilla extract
¾ cup sesame (benne) seeds, toasted

Preheat oven to 325°. • Cream together butter and sugar. • Add eaten egg. • Sift together flour, baking powder, and salt and add to butter mixture. • Add vanilla and sesame seeds. • Drop by teaspoonful on greased cookie sheet. • Bake for 12 to 15 minutes. • Allow to cool for 1 minute before removing from pan. Yield: 42

Sarah's Dream Bed & Breakfast

SARAH IS INNKEEPER JUDI Williams' mother, who had a dream to open a business some-day but never had the opportunity. A school teacher and farmer's wife, her mailbox would be overloaded with information she had requested about new business opportunities. But the material was filed away and never used. So, when Judi went into the bed & breakfast business, she named her and partner Ken Morusty's inn after her mother, in hopes that she could make her mother's dream come true.

Today it's also Judi's passion. Sarah's Dream is a vision of elegance during tea-time. Some six to eight tea treats are served at attractively decorated tables, spaced far enough apart for private conversations. Tea is so popular here that it's served three times a week, three times a day in an 1828 Greek Revival home that earned its place on the National Register of Historic Places.

Sarah's Dream Bed & Breakfast
49 West Main Street
Dryden, NY 13053
Phone: **(607) 844-4321**
Rooms: **7**
Tea-Time: **Tuesday, Wednesday, Thursday, 12:30, 2:00 and 3:30 P.M. for inn guests and drop-ins**

ZUCCHINI AND CHEESE MINI QUICHES

4 large eggs
½ cup half-and-half
½ cup milk
⅛ teaspoon garlic powder
¼ teaspoon white pepper
¼ teaspoon sage
½ cup shredded Swiss cheese
½ cup shredded sharp cheddar
1 cup shredded fresh zucchini
1 pastry for single crust pie

Preheat oven to 325°. • In a large metal bowl, beat eggs with wire whisk until foamy. • Add half-and-half, milk, garlic powder, pepper and sage; whisk together. • Add cheeses and zucchini and mix well. • Roll out pastry to an ⅛-inch thickness. • Cut into 2-inch circles and line 24 1¾-inch mini-sized muffin tins. • Pour egg mixture into each cup to fill. • Bake for 25 minutes or until set. • Set aside for 5 to 10 minutes before removing. • Serve hot or cold. Yield: 24

ENGLISH BANBURY TARTS

Use your favorite two-crust pie pastry recipe to make these traditional English cigar-shaped treats.

¼ cup sugar
1 teaspoon cornstarch
¼ teaspoon ground cloves
½ cup water

1 cup dried currants

1 tablespoon grated orange peel

½ cup finely chopped walnuts

Preheat oven to 350° • In a small saucepan, stir together all ingredients except nuts. • Cook over medium heat until mixture is thick and bubbly. Continue cooking for 5 minutes. • Remove from heat and stir in nuts. • Set aside to cool. • Roll out dough from 2-crust pie pastry recipe. Roll to an ⅛-inch thickness and cut into 2-inch circles. • Place 1 teaspoon filling in center of each pastry round. Bring 2 opposite sides together and pinch to secure, leaving other 2 sides open. • Bake on an ungreased cookie sheet for 15 minutes or until golden. Yield: 60

WATERMELON COOKIES
These delicate cookies add appropriate color to the tea table any time of year.

1½ sticks butter, softened

¾ cup sugar

1 extra large egg

1 teaspoon flavoring (lemon, almond or vanilla extract)

2¼ cups all-purpose flour

1 teaspoon baking powder

¼ teaspoon salt

6 drops red food coloring

4 drops green food coloring

Chocolate sprinkles

In a large bowl, beat together butter, sugar, egg, and flavoring. • Blend in flour, baking powder, and salt. • Form dough. Divide in half. • To first half add red food coloring. Blend color evenly. • Shape dough into a cyl-

A hardened and shameless tea drinker, who has for twenty years diluted his meals with only the infusion of this fascinating plant; whose kettle has scarcely time to cool; who with tea amuses the evening, with tea solaces the midnight, and with tea welcomes the morning.

—Samuel Johnson

inder about 2 inches in diameter. Wrap in waxed paper and chill until firm (about 1½ hours).

Meanwhile, divide the reserved half of dough again. Roll out 1 part between waxed paper to form a rectangle large enough in which to enclose the red-dough cylinder. • Chill, keeping the dough flat between 2 pieces of waxed paper.

Add the green food coloring to the remaining dough. Blend well and repeat rolling out as for the plain dough.

When reserved dough is chilled enough to handle, unwrap and place red dough cylinder along edge of plain dough. • Roll up to enclose red dough leaving ends exposed. • Repeat with the green dough, to cover the plain dough layer. • Wrap entire cylinder in waxed paper and return to refrigerator. • When dough is chilled, remove from refrigerator and unwrap. • Preheat oven to 350°.

To shape cookies, cut crosswise to make ¼-inch-thick whole watermelon slices. • Place 1 inch apart on ungreased baking sheet. • Reshape any lopsided pieces with your fingers. • Use chocolate sprinkles for watermelon seeds, decorating the red part of each cookie. • Bake for 7 to 12 minutes until set but not browned. • Remove. • Cut each cookie in half while still warm. • Cool and serve. Yield: 42

OLD-FASHIONED BREAD PUDDING

½ cup packed brown sugar

1 tablespoon vanilla extract

2 tablespoons melted butter

3 cups milk or half-and-half

3 large eggs, beaten until foamy

2 cups not-so-dry bread cubes (crust trimmings from tea sandwiches will do)

2 tablespoons sugar

½ teaspoon nutmeg

Whipped cream

Preheat oven to 325°. • Beat brown sugar, vanilla, melted butter and milk into beaten eggs. • Stir in bread cubes. • Pour mixture into a greased 13x9-inch glass pan. • Blend together sugar and nutmeg and sprinkle over top. • Bake for 1 hour or until tester inserted in center comes out clean. • Serve hot or chilled with whipped cream. Yield: 24 one-inch squares

Tiers of sugary creations sweeten dreams at Sarah's.

HIGH TEAS

A Chamber Music Tea

Finger Sandwiches of Choice

Village Inn Scones

Orange Blossom Muffins

Welsh Rarebit

Village Inn Trifle with Sherry

AS IF THE PLEASURE OF daily afternoon tea at The Village Inn isn't enough, add to it a concert of live chamber music, and you have an experience that is hard to put into words. The strains of such masters as Haydn and Beethoven gently purge the air with a pure and penetrating sweetness. Except for the modern-day fashions, everything seems as it must have been in the 1800s—not long after The Village Inn first opened (in 1771) to those traveling the picturesque Berkshire Mountain region of Western Massachusetts. High tea at The Village Inn, augmented by the au-

thenticity of its surrounding architecture and decor, is that seductive. And, of course, classical music is the heartbeat of this area. Tanglewood—summer home of the Boston Symphony—is just a few miles away from Lenox.

Following the concert, guests move into the dining room. Tables are set with dainty rose-print cloths and white linen. Creamy Wedgwood cups and plates are at each setting. Right away the staff begins pouring freshly brewed tea at each table.

Lightly browned scones with Village Inn-style clotted cream and finger sandwiches are served, followed by a hot savory—a Welsh Rarebit. This traditional dish is often

served at high teas in London. (See
recipe on page 55.) The rarebit is a
fine entreé to the last item served: an
incredible English trifle. Meanwhile,
the tea servers have made their
rounds several times, offering the
guests enough food for a meal.

However, if you eat later—say
around 8 or 9 P.M.—there will be
room for The Village Inn's dinners.
They are some of the best in all of
New England, with main courses such
as Veal Chanterelle, Shrimp and
Chorizo with Fettucini, and Orange
and Lingonberry Glazed Breast of
Duckling.

"Inns are places where people
come to share humanity," says Cliff
Rudisill. He and innkeeper Ray
Wilson were two of the first keepers
of country inns to serve a high tea in
America when they took over the inn
in 1981. "An inn is somewhere between a private residence and a public
domain," observes Cliff. In other
words, it's so wonderful that it's hard
to describe. And that's how one feels
after leaving The Village Inn.

The Village Inn
16 Church Street
Lenox, MA 01240
Phone: **(413) 637-0020**
Rooms: **29**
Tea-Time: **High tea with chamber music once a
month in winter and spring at 3:30 P.M. by
reservation only. Afternoon tea daily, 2:30–4:30
P.M. for inn guests and drop-ins.**

**Sandwiches and Welsh Rarebit make an inviting duo
for tea.**

A CHAMBER MUSIC TEA AT HOME

- Most colleges have music students eager
  to play for experience. Invite them or
  choose seasoned talent in your area.
- Prepare a hand-out for guests, listing the
  musical selections and the tea menu that
  will follow.
- Welcome everyone and quickly explain
  how the tea-time is going to be observed.
  Explain unusual dishes. Introduce the
  musician(s) and let the music begin.
- Since this is a high tea, seat guests at
  dining room-table height instead of tiny
  tea tables.

A tea-time composition includes Village Inn Trifle with Sherry (left).

VILLAGE INN SCONES

This recipe was adapted from the original of John Tovey, owner and chef at Miller Howe Country House Hotel at Windermere in the Lake District of England. He gave it to The Village Inn in 1982, when the innkeepers asked for the best scone recipe in all of England. It has never been released until now.

8 cups all-purpose flour
1 teaspoon salt
1 teaspoon baking soda
1 tablespoon baking powder
4 sticks butter, softened, cut into tiny cubes
7 tablespoons sugar
10 eggs, lightly beaten
1 cup milk
1 egg white, beaten (optional)

Preheat oven to 425°. • Sift together flour, salt, baking soda and baking powder. • Drop butter cubes over the flour mixture. • Blend gently with fingers until mixture resembles coarse cornmeal. Sprinkle with sugar and add beaten eggs. • Mix gently with hands until well combined. • Add enough milk to make pie-dough consistency. Do not over-work. • Pat out on floured table to form a large 1-inch-thick square. Cut into small triangles (bases about 2 inches). • Bake for 18 minutes or until golden. • For browner scones, coat top with beaten egg white. Yield: 75

Legend has it that orange marmalade was first introduced in the sixteenth century by Mary Queen of Scots. But the more practical belief has orange marmalade made in Dundee, Scotland, in the 1790s. Dundee is famous for its fruit growing.

Orange Blossom Muffins inspire thoughts for a budding missive.

ORANGE BLOSSOM MUFFINS
The marmalade adds a surprise and a marvelous taste.

4 eggs, slightly beaten
1 cup sugar
2 cups orange juice
½ cup vegetable oil
8 cups basic muffin mix (store-bought)
2 cups orange marmalade
2 cups chopped pecans

Preheat oven to 400°. • Whisk together eggs, sugar, orange juice and oil. • Add muffin mix and beat vigorously for about 30 seconds. • Stir in marmalade and pecans. • Fill greased muffin tins (2-ounce cups) about ⅔ full. • Bake for 20 to 25 minutes or until golden brown. Yield: 48

WELSH RAREBIT
The true name for this dish is Welsh Rabbit, which dates to a time when only the wealthy in Wales could afford game for dinner. Since rabbit was such a rarity, a dish of melted cheese over toast or biscuits must have been the "rabbit" of the lower classes, who jokingly referred to it as a rare and tasty bit or rarebit.

2 tablespoons butter
16 ounces dark beer
2 pounds cheddar cheese, grated
2 eggs, slightly beaten
2 tablespoons Worcestershire sauce
½ teaspoon salt
⅛ teaspoon red pepper
2 teaspoons lemon juice
Hot biscuits or toast

Melt the butter in a double boiler. • Stir in beer. • When well heated, stir in grated cheese with a fork. • When cheese is melted, stir in beaten eggs. • Add Worcestershire sauce, salt, and red pepper to taste, if desired. • Add lemon juice. • Serve immediately over hot biscuits or toast.
Yield: 16 servings

How to Eat a Scone
After opening the scone horizontally in half with a fork, put enough jam, then cream, on the scone for one bite. Return the half-eaten scone to the plate for another slathering of luscious jam and cream.

Hannah Marie Country Inn

Erica Pickaroff sets the tone at The Village Inn.

Village Inn Trifle with Sherry

Sherry is the secret ingredient in this most tasty trifle. You need two 9-inch cakes, so *make the cake recipe twice.*

Cake

6 egg yolks
1 cup sugar, sifted
¼ cup boiling water
1 teaspoon vanilla extract
1 cup cake flour, sifted
1½ tablespoons baking powder
¼ teaspoon salt
6 egg whites

Preheat oven to 350°. • In bowl of electric mixer, beat egg yolks until very light in color. • Beat in sifted sugar and gradually beat in boiling water. • Cool. • Beat in vanilla. • Add flour, baking powder and salt. • In separate bowl, whip egg whites until stiff. • Fold into batter. • Pour into a greased 9-inch cake pan. • Bake for 45 minutes or until tester inserted in center comes out clean. Yield: One 9-inch cake

Custard

¾ cup sugar
2 tablespoons cornstarch
⅛ teaspoon salt
1 cup milk plus 1 cup cream, mixed
4 egg yolks, well-beaten
2 tablespoons butter
1½ tablespoons vanilla extract
1 cup heavy cream, whipped

In top of double boiler, mix sugar, cornstarch and salt. • Stir in milk/cream mixture. Cook, covered, over medium heat for 8 minutes. • Uncover and cook 10 minutes longer. • Add beaten egg yolks, then beat in butter. • Continue to cook and stir for 2 more minutes. • Cool. • Stir in vanilla. • Fold in whipped cream. • Chill.

Trifle Assembly

1½ cups medium-dry sherry
Quality strawberry preserves
Whipped cream
Fresh strawberries

Cut the 2 cakes in half lengthwise. • Sprinkle all 4 layers with sherry. • Cover top of each cake with a layer of preserves. • Begin building the trifle by covering the bottom of the bowl with a layer of custard, followed by a layer of sherry soaked cake, and continue to alternate a layer of custard with a layer of cake, finishing with a layer of custard. • Top with whipped cream and garnish with a few fresh strawberries. Yield: 45 to 50 servings

High Tea Inn the 18th Century

Stuffed Turkey Roll

Choice of Cornbread and Pumpkin Bread

Kentucky Bourbon Cake

Fruit, Cheese and Smoked-Meats Platter

IT WAS THE VERMONT white birches that navigated my fog-filled course to the Inn at Weathersfield. Most poetically, it was also that type of tree that said goodbye to me as I left the inn. Although my suitcase was packed, innkeeper Mary Louise Thorburn and husband, Ron, insisted that I hear their poet laureate recite some Robert Frost. The laureate, who is often present at tea-time, was inspired by a picture Mary Louise had just hung, featuring white birches. This line from Frost's poem, "Birches," perked my ears: "He always kept his poise to the top branches, climbing carefully with the same pains you use to fill a teacup up

to the brim and even above the brim." (*Teacup* was substituted at the inn for *cup*—to fit the tea-time occasion.)

The birches were not my only memories of the 1795 inn. Hearty Vermont maples line the alley leading to the front of the inn, which features a pond, amphitheatre and a horse stable. It's not unusual to find guests arriving at the inn for dinner in their own horse-drawn sleighs.

Farm-raised partridge and pheasants are served here for some of the home-cooked, elegant meals prepared nightly and accompanied by Ron on

Vintage fashion, stenciled walls, wide-board floors and innkeeper Mary Louise Thorburn take tea-time back 200 years.

the piano. During the holidays, meat pies are cooked in a working 1795 hearth complete with cranes and iron utensils. Guests help churn butter. Special teas include a fiddler and a Colonial militia man who instructs guests in eighteenth-century dancing.

Tea is most appreciated. There's much to explore within twenty miles of the inn. During breakfast, Mary Louise and Ron talk about the people and places of the region. Whatever your interest, they will map out a day for you. High tea begins in the keeping room where fresh tea or hot cider is served from a cauldron. The tea is set out in the front parlor where Ron and Mary Louise dress in their favorite Colonial garb during holidays.

However, you don't need to see the costumes or hear the music to invite the 1700s into your heart. This is one of the most authentic country inns in America. Mary Louise has taken historic decorating classes and many of the rooms show off her interpretive talents. Mary Louise and Ron are caretakers of history and certainly of their guests.

The Inn at Weathersfield
Route 106, Box 165
Weathersfield, VT 05151
Phone: **(802) 263-9217**
Rooms: **14**
Tea-Time: **Daily from 3:30 P.M. to dinnertime for inn guests; eighteenth-century high teas on occasion for inn guests and drop-ins.**

AN EIGHTEENTH-CENTURY HIGH TEA AT HOME

- As hostess, dress in period garb—a long cotton dress. The gentleman of the house can wear knickers, a Jefferson shirt and round, wire-rimmed glasses.
- Hire a fiddler or play eighteenth-century tunes on the CD.
- Invite someone skilled in hearth cookery to give a short lecture on how the early Americans prepared foods.

STUFFED TURKEY ROLL

8 pounds turkey breasts
2 pounds mild sausage
1 large onion, finely chopped
½ pound mushrooms, finely chopped
3 large carrots, finely chopped
4 eggs
Bread crumbs (enough to solidify)
1½ teaspoons sage
1½ teaspoons rosemary
½ teaspoon garlic or more to taste
Butter
Salt
Pepper

Preheat oven to 375°. • Remove tenderloins from turkey breasts and trim any fat. • Grind trimmings and tenderloins in food processor and add next 9 ingredients. • Process well to form stuffing. • Pound turkey breasts to a 1-

inch thickness. • Spread stuffing on pounded turkey. • Roll up each breast, tucking the ends under. • Place in individual rectangular loaf pans. • Place into a larger pan filled half full with water. • Butter tops of breasts and sprinkle with salt and pepper. • Cover with double foil wrap. • Bake for 1½ hours. • Remove. • Cut into 1-inch-wide slices. • Cut each slice into quarters for tea-time. Yield: 48 tea-time pieces

KENTUCKY BOURBON CAKE

3 sticks butter, at room temperature

2 cups sugar

2¼ cups firmly packed light brown sugar

6 eggs

5½ cups sifted all-purpose flour

1 teaspoon salt

1 teaspoon mace

2 cups bourbon whiskey

3½ cups (1 pound) pecans, broken into pieces

Preheat oven to 300°. • In large bowl of electric mixer, cream butter until soft. • Combine sugars and gradually work half the mixture into the butter. • In separate bowl, beat eggs until light and fluffy. • Gradually beat in remaining sugar, until mixture is smooth and creamy. • Stir egg mixture into butter mixture. • In a separate bowl, sift together flour, salt and mace. • Add flour, then whiskey to the batter, alternating them, beginning and ending with flour. • Stir pecans into batter. • Pour batter into a well-greased 10-inch tube pan. • Bake for 1½ to 1¾ hours or until cake shrinks slightly from pan. • Cool cake in the pan for 15 minutes, then turn out onto rack. • Cool completely. Yield: 14 to 16 servings

The fact that in India my tea cost pennies and that in London I paid a tariff of nearly $25 was irrelevant: Cost has little to do with hospitality or the role of a guest. In both settings, I was served with attention and grace and was honored by the experience.

—L. Peat O'Neil, the *Washington Post*

Stuffed Turkey Roll, breads, fruits, cheeses, and Kentucky Bourbon Cake

ROMANTIC TEAS

TEA-TIME IS A PERFECT WAY TO SHARE CHERISHED MOments with that special someone, that person in your past, present, or hopeful future. Somehow, taking tea together, encourages an atmosphere of intimacy when you slip off the timepiece in your mind and cast your fate to a delight of tasty tea, tiny foods and thoughtful conversation.

Ralph Waldo Emerson once observed that there is a great deal of sentiment and poetry in a cup of tea. So it's not surprising that the very thought of tea is a romantic reflection—romantic in many ways besides affairs of the heart. Even just watching an outpouring of the golden beverage swirl into a china cup causes a rush of emotions—anything from a sense of calm to a feeling of excitement, adventure, intrigue, and mystery.

Tea invites passion even when it's sitting in a delicate cup next to a burning candle and a plate of sweets or alone with a linen napkin draped over the teacup's saucer. The visions of tea that dress country inns take many of these romantic forms.

Country inns, by their very nature, have a way of reinspiring the simple pleasures surrounding the taking of tea. Thorwood in Minnesota shows us that tea can underscore the romance of a picnic. A visit to The Pauline, a bed & breakfast that floats on the sea, demonstrates that tea-time can still be sentimental on board a boat along the Maine coast. Tea and tea foods are also a perfect combination for weddings and for enjoying privately in a room, served on a tray.

The inns prove that with a cup of tea in hand and love in your heart, romance can blossom no matter where you come together for tea-time.

Tea for two ties the knot at an Old Rittenhouse wedding.

Two for a Picnic Tea

Rose Petal Tea

Authentic English Welsh Cakes

Ribbon Tea Sandwiches

Thorwood Beef Crescents

Sweet Lemon Cream Scones

Sparkling Shortbread with Rosemary

Rosewood Fresh Raspberry Brownies

Chocolate-Covered Cherries

Fruit Pizza

ONCE UPON A TIME, NOT far from where the water falls like satin ribbons near the St. Croix River bluffs and the Vermillion River ravine, a young man desired to treat his lady friend to a special afternoon tea party. He sought the expertise of Thorwood Inn and this is what he got. In addition to a Victorian picnic hamper brimming with fine cuisine and tableware, he and his lady were escorted to the picnic site by limousine. As they pulled up to the park, the chauffeur requested that the couple remain seated until he ushered them out. Meanwhile, the chauffeur, now out of sight, sprinkled the walkway to the picnic table with a colorful train of velvety rose petals. A proposal of marriage was made and they lived happily ever after.

"It's a true story," innkeeper Pam Thorsen says of her Thorwood Inn where picnics, romance and fantasy are inseparable. The inn, which Pam hosts along with Rosewood, a sister inn in the same area, is known for its picnics in the guest rooms, inside the limousines, and, of course, at the area's many verdant parks.

Picnics and romance are the specialities of the house. The picnics are all designed so that the feeling of the inn's period (1880–1890) is transferred to the picnic site. Small books of posies and lines from magazines of the era are tucked into the picnic containers. A teddy bear accompanies the basket "to help with any details or instructions," says Pam. The rest of how the picnic unfolds, however, is left up to the participants!

Thorwood
4th & Pine
Hastings, MN 55033
Phone: (612) 437-3297
Rooms: 7
Tea-Time: Picnic teas for inn guests by reservation

Cascading water provides a breathtaking backdrop for a picnic.

ROSE PETAL TEA

2 cups black tea
1½ cups dried rose petals or buds (unsprayed)
¾ cup lemon verbena leaves
2 tablespoons dried lemon peel

Brew the tea. • In a large bowl, mix the tea with rosebuds, verbena leaves and lemon peel. Strain. • (Strong light will affect the delicate taste of the tea, so package in a dark, airtight container.) Yield: 2 cups

And quite a family it is to make tea for, and wot a happiness to do it! The privileges of the side-table included the small prerogatives of sitting next the toast, and taking two cups of tea to other people's one.
—Charles Dickens

AUTHENTIC ENGLISH WELSH CAKES

1 pound all-purpose flour
2 sticks butter
¾ cup sugar
2 teaspoons baking powder

6 ounces currants, plumped in water
1 egg
¼ cup milk (scant)
1 teaspoon lemon thyme
½ teaspoon freshly grated lemon peel
Sugar

Blend flour and butter with pastry blender. • Add sugar and baking powder. • Stir in drained currants. • In separate bowl, beat egg gently into milk and add to flour mixture. • Add lemon thyme and lemon peel. • Toss with hands until pastry is slightly soggy. • Spread out on flat surface to about ½-inch thickness; cut out with a heart-shaped cutter. • Fry on red-hot griddle. Flip and cook other side. • Put on rack to barely cool, then lightly coat with sugar and serve. Yield: 36

RIBBON TEA SANDWICHES

¼ cup basil leaves, loosely packed
¼ cup fresh parsley leaves, tightly packed
4 tablespoons butter, at room temperature
4 ounces cream cheese, at room temperature
2 tablespoons finely chopped chives
Salt and pepper to taste
8 thin slices white bread, crusts removed

In food processor, process basil and parsley until finely chopped. • Add butter, cream cheese, chives, salt and pepper. • Process until mixture turns green. • Spread mixture on half the bread slices. • Top with remaining slices. • Cut on the diagonal into 4 triangles. • Place on plate. Cover with slightly damp paper towel. • Refrigerate until packed in picnic hamper. Yield: 16

VICTORIAN PICNIC SANDWICHES

Sandwiches are the most appropriate form of food for picnics, especially the dainty, appetizing sandwiches made of home-made white or whole-wheat bread, filled with a mixture of chopped meat, daintily seasoned.

Many of the sandwiches are perfumed rather than seasoned. Clover or nasturtium sandwiches are made by packing the butter and bread in sweet clover or nasturtium blossoms in a tight box overnight. Next morning, with a sharp knife cut the end crust of the loaf, then spread the end of the loaf with butter that has been just a little warmed, that it may spread evenly. Then cut a slice, not more than one-eighth of an inch thick, and continue to butter and cut until you have the desired quantity. Two slices are then placed together, the crust trimmed off and the slices cut into squares or triangles or into long finger-shaped pieces. They are then placed in a pasteboard box that has been lined with waxed paper.

—***Ladies Home Journal,*** August 1887

Add elegance to iced tea by rubbing the rims of the glasses with lemon and then dipping them into white sugar.

THORWOOD BEEF CRESCENTS

½ pound lean ground beef
2 tablespoons chopped onion
2 tablespoons chopped green pepper
1 small tomato, seeded and diced
½ teaspoon salt
⅛ teaspoon pepper
1 tablespoon cornstarch
½ cup beef broth
1 tablespoon finely chopped almonds
2 tablespoons chopped raisins
Appetizer pastry dough (store-bought)

In a medium skillet, sauté beef until browned. • Drain. • Stir in onion, green pepper, tomato, salt, pepper, cornstarch and broth. • Cook, stirring for 4 minutes or until mixture is slightly thickened. Remove from heat. • Stir in almonds and raisins.

Preheat oven to 400°. • On a lightly floured surface, roll out pastry to form a 22x15-inch rectangle. Cut into 3-inch circles. • Spoon 1 to 2 tablespoons filling in center of each circle. • Fold dough over filling. • Press edges with tines of fork to seal. • Puncture top to let steam escape. • Repeat with remaining dough. • Arrange on 2 ungreased baking sheets. • Bake for 12 to 15 minutes or until golden brown. • Serve warm. Yield: 35

SWEET LEMON CREAM SCONES

2 cups all-purpose flour
1 teaspoon salt
¼ cup sugar
1 tablespoon baking powder
3 tablespoons butter
2 egg yolks, beaten well
1 tablespoon finely chopped lemon balm
½ teaspoon freshly grated lemon peel
⅓ cup heavy cream
Beaten egg white
Preserves
Mock Devonshire Cream (see next recipe)

Preheat oven to 450°. • Stir together flour, salt, sugar and baking powder. • Cut in butter with pastry blender. • Add beaten eggs, lemon balm and lemon peel to cream. • Stir together egg and flour mixtures to form a soft dough. • Turn out onto floured pastry board and knead about 20 times. • Roll out about ½-inch thick and cut with 2-inch round cutter. • Place on ungreased cookie sheet. • Brush tops with beaten egg white. • Bake for 10 minutes or until lightly browned. • Store in airtight container. • Serve with any flavor preserves and Mock Devonshire Cream. Yield: 24

MOCK DEVONSHIRE CREAM

½ cup heavy cream
2 tablespoons confectioners' sugar
½ cup sour cream

In a chilled bowl, beat cream until medium stiff peaks form, adding sugar during the last few minutes of beating. • Fold in sour cream and blend. Yield: 1½ cups

Thorwood's insulated tea cozy keeps tea hot on picnics.

SPARKLING SHORTBREAD WITH ROSEMARY

On an early summer evening picnic, add elegance with these cookies that will shimmer in the sun or candlelight.

1 stick butter
¹/₄ cup superfine sugar
1 ¹/₂ cups all-purpose flour
1 tablespoon finely chopped fresh rosemary
Sugar
Edible glitter

Preheat oven to 325°. • Cream together butter and sugar until smooth. • Add flour and blend. • Work in the rosemary to make a soft dough and then shape into a ball. • Roll out the dough on a floured board to a ¹/₄-inch thickness. Cut out with 1¹/₂-inch heart-shaped cutter. • Sprinkle lightly with sugar and add as much glitter as desired. • Bake on greased parchment-lined baking sheet for 15 minutes or until shortbread just begins to change color. • Cool on rack. Yield: 24

ROSEWOOD FRESH RASPBERRY BROWNIES

These brownies are so special and different and say "I care for you" in so many sweet ways.

Cocoa powder
3 ounces unsweetened chocolate
9¹/₂ ounces semi-sweet chocolate, divided
³/₄ cup plus 1 tablespoon unsalted butter, divided
1 tablespoon cognac
1 ¹/₂ teaspoons instant espresso powder
4 eggs
2 cups sugar
1 ¹/₄ cups all-purpose flour
¹/₂ cup sugar
6 tablespoons raspberry jam
3 ounces white chocolate
1 tablespoon water
1 cup fresh raspberries

Preheat oven to 325°. • Brush bottom of jellyroll pan with butter. Line with parchment. Butter paper and sprinkle with cocoa powder. • Combine unsweetened chocolate, 3¹/₂ ounces semi-sweet chocolate and ³/₄ cup

Iced tea was invented at the St. Louis World's Fair in 1904 during a heat wave when the English were introducing black tea from Ceylon to Midwesterners. Hot tea was not what fairgoers wanted, so ice was added to encourage people to try the tea. It became the thirst-quenching hit of the fair. Word spread quickly.

butter in top of double boiler. • Stir to blend over hot, not boiling, water until melted. • Cool for 2 to 3 minutes. • Stir in cognac and espresso powder.

Place eggs in bowl of electric mixer and beat for 1 minute or until slightly thickened. • Slowly add 2 cups sugar, about 2 tablespoons at a time, beating continuously for 8 to 10 minutes or until mixture remains in a pattern on surface when dropped from mixer's beater. • Fold in chocolate mixture just until blended.

Combine flour with remaining ½ cup sugar and sift over chocolate mixture while mixing in a folding motion. • Pour batter into jelly roll pan. • Bake 15 minutes. • Cover with foil and continue baking 10 minutes longer.

Scrape thin top crust from surface of brownie with knife, brushing crumbs away. • Turn out onto board and remove paper liner. • Cut the cake into 2 layers. • Cover and chill. • Spread the bottom layer with raspberry jam. • Cover with the top layer.

Melt remaining 6 ounces semi-sweet chocolate. • Spread on top. • Grate white chocolate and melt with remaining 1 tablespoon butter and 1 tablespoon of water in double boiler. • Drizzle over chocolate, and, using spoon or small spatula, make marble design. • Cut brownies into bars of desired size. • Garnish tops with raspberries. Yield: 30 to 50

Whenever you send a letter, enclose a tea bag for warm wishes. Enclose a box of loose tea whenever you return something you have borrowed.

A Thorwood picnic basket overflows with goodies including Fruit Pizza (to right of bear).

CHOCOLATE-COVERED CHERRIES

1 pound quality dark chocolate

2 to 3 tablespoons melted paraffin

1 pound confectioners' sugar

2 tablespoons evaporated milk

1 teaspoon vanilla extract

1 large jar maraschino cherries (about 60 cherries) with stems, drained

In top of double boiler, melt chocolate over medium heat. • Blend in paraffin. • In a bowl, mix together sugar, milk and vanilla. • Wrap a spoonful of the mixture around each cherry. • Dip into the chocolate to coat. • Place in petits fours paper cups. Yield: 60

FRUIT PIZZA

This looks pretty and adds a touch of whimsy to a picnic or any tea-time.

PIZZA CRUST

1½ cups all-purpose flour
¼ cup sugar
¼ cup butter
¼ cup vegetable oil
3 tablespoons cold water
Vegetable cooking spray

Preheat oven to 375°. • Mix together flour and sugar. • Cut in butter with pastry blender until mixture resembles coarse meal. • Stir in oil with a fork until all ingredients are moistened. • Stir in water, 1 tablespoon at a time, until dough rolls from sides of bowl and forms a ball. • Spray cookie sheet with vegetable spray. • With lightly floured rolling pin, roll pastry into an 11-inch circle. • Place on prepared cookie sheet. • Bake for about 12 to 14 minutes or until lightly browned. • Cool on baking sheet for 10 minutes. • Carefully remove to wire rack to cool.

Make good use of old teapots as planters or dispensers for balls of string or yarn.

PIZZA FILLING

6 ounces cream cheese, softened
¼ cup sugar
½ teaspoon vanilla extract
1½ cups thinly sliced strawberries
3 kiwis, peeled and sliced
1 banana, sliced (optional)
½ cup blueberries
½ cup red seedless grapes, halved

Beat together cream cheese, sugar and vanilla until smooth. • Slide crust onto serving platter. • Spread with cream cheese mixture. • Arrange fruit attractively over the crust, starting at outside edge. • Make glaze and spread evenly over fruit. • Chill for 2 hours (no longer) before serving. • Cut into pie-shaped wedges. Yield: 10 to 12 slices

GLAZE

1 teaspoon cornstarch
1 tablespoon water
¼ cup orange juice
3 tablespoons confectioners' sugar

In a small saucepan, combine all ingredients. • Over medium heat, stir constantly, bringing mixture to a boil. • Cook and stir 1 minute. • Cool. • Glaze fruit.

A Bridal Shower Tea

Maids-of-Honor Tarts

Seafood Mousse

Tomato Cheese Squares

Rum Custard Tarts

IF EVER THERE IS A PERFECT setting for the bridal party to get together before the wedding, it's for a tea. This quiet time provides the chance for close friends to share time together, reminiscing and looking to the future. Grandview Lodge is accustomed to such requests for teas for bridal showers, receptions and anniversaries.

Innkeepers Linda and Stan Arnold have a reputation for fine food, and so many nuptial events are scheduled here. Grandview Lodge has even done an afternoon reception as a way of introducing a new, out-of-town bride to friends of the groom's family.

The opening of gifts showered upon the bride for her new home, is the focus of this tea. Shower games may be played and because this is a

tea, a solo musician such as a harpist can provide some background entertainment.

A bridal shower tea suggests an afternoon affair and female guests find it the perfect occasion for wearing a favorite hat and gloves. The tea party is usually given by the maid-of-honor or bridesmaids. Grandview Lodge likes to do this tea buffet-style and in front of the fireplace.

Grandview Lodge
809 Valley View Circle Road
Waynesville, NC 28786
Phone: **(704) 456-5212**
Rooms: **11**
Tea-Time: **On special occasion**

TEA FOR THE BRIDAL PARTY AT HOME

• Consider the bride and groom's lifestyle and decorate with props that reflect their careers, hobbies or interests.
• For entertainment, have someone versed in how to give a proper tea share a quick lesson with the group.
• If the bride doesn't have a teapot to match her new fine china, this is a good occasion to give it to her.

MAIDS-OF-HONOR TARTS

These are classic English tea-time breads.

SHELLS

2 cups all-purpose flour
⅓ cup sugar
⅔ cup butter, chilled
1 yolk of a large egg
6 tablespoons ice water

In food processor, mix flour, sugar and butter until mixture resembles coarse meal. • Add egg yolk and water and process until dough forms. Don't overmix. • Flatten the dough into a disk. Store in plastic wrap in refrigerator for at least 1 hour. • Preheat oven to 400°. • On a lightly floured surface, roll out half the chilled dough at a time to fit heart-shaped muffin pans (cut heart shapes free-hand or with a cookie cutter, just slightly larger than each muffin pan size). Prick the shells with a fork and fill with pie weights. • Bake for 5 to 8 minutes. • Remove weights. • Return to oven for 5 to 8 minutes longer or until pastry is set but not browned. • Cool on wire rack.

FILLING

1 cup ricotta cheese
6 tablespoons butter, softened
⅓ cup sugar
2 large eggs
2 tablespoons almond extract
½ cup finely chopped almonds
¼ teaspoon ground nutmeg

Increase oven temperature to 425°. • Cream together ricotta, butter and sugar. • Add remaining ingredients and mix well. • Spoon 1 tablespoon of filling into each shell. • Bake for 8 to 12 minutes or until slightly browned. • Remove to wire rack and cool. Yield: 25

The tea bag was invented in 1904 when a New York City importer began sending samples to retailers in silk bags rather than in tins. Impressed by the convenience of the premeasured bags, retailers ordered the tea in bags, assuming that they were intended to steep in hot water.

SEAFOOD MOUSSE

| 2 envelopes unflavored gelatin |
| $\frac{1}{2}$ cup water |
| 1 pound mixture of cooked shrimp, crab meat and flounder, cooled |
| 2 hard-boiled eggs |
| 1 cup mayonnaise |
| 2 tablespoons vinegar |
| 2 tablespoons sweet pickle relish, drained |
| 2 tablespoons chopped parsley |
| 1 cup heavy cream, whipped |
| Lettuce |
| Lemon slices |

Maids-of-Honor Tarts (top) sweeten this bridal party.

In a small saucepan, combine gelatin and water. • Place over medium heat and stir constantly until gelatin is dissolved. • Remove from heat and set aside. • In food processor, chop seafood and eggs with quick pulses. • Do not purée. • In a mixing bowl, combine chopped mixture with gelatin, mayonnaise, vinegar, pickle relish and parsley. • Fold in whipped cream. • Pour mixture into an oiled 6-cup mold. Cover with plastic wrap and chill until firm. • Unmold and garnish with lettuce and lemon slices. • Serve with crackers. Yield: 6 cups

Herbal teas are not really teas, in that they don't contain any leaves from the tea plant. They are comprised of dried herbs, fruits, nuts and spices. Since herbal teas contain no real tea, they are naturally caffeine free.

TOMATO CHEESE SQUARES

DOUGH

2¼ cups all-purpose flour
1½ sticks butter, chilled
1 yolk of large egg
6 tablespoons ice water

In a food processor, mix flour and butter until mixture resembles coarse meal. • Add egg yolk and water and process until dough forms. • Do not overmix. • Flatten dough into a disk. Cover with plastic wrap; chill for at least 1 hour. • Preheat oven to 400°. • On a lightly floured surface, roll the chilled dough out to form a 20x12-inch rectangle. • Transfer into an 18x12-inch jellyroll pan, pressing the dough gently against the bottom and sides. • Line the dough with foil and fill with pie weights. • Bake for 5 to 8 minutes. • Remove foil and weights. • Return to oven for 5 to 8 minutes or until pastry is set but not browned. • Cool on wire rack.

FILLING

½ cup parsley
3 cloves garlic, peeled
1 cup vegetable oil
2 teaspoons dried basil
2 teaspoons salt
1 teaspoon dried oregano
1 teaspoon dried thyme
Freshly ground pepper
2 pounds Italian plum tomatoes, thinly sliced crosswise
¼ cup spicy mustard
1 pound shredded Swiss cheese

In food processor, chop parsley; drop in garlic until minced. • Add next 6 ingredients, pulsing to make a marinade. • Place marinade and tomatoes into a 1-gallon plastic bag or non-metallic, covered container. • Chill for at least 6 hours, turning the bag or container a couple of times. • Preheat oven to 350°. •

Tea-time after the bouquet's been caught

Spread the mustard evenly over the baked dough. • Sprinkle the shredded cheese over the mustard. • Arrange the marinated tomato slices down the length of the tart. • Bake the tart for 25 to 30 minutes. • Remove to wire rack and let stand for at least 10 minutes. • Cut into 2-inch squares. Yield: 54

RUM CUSTARD TARTS

Make the tart shells using the recipe for the Maids-of-Honor Tarts on page 70.

Preheat oven to 425°. • On a lightly floured surface, roll out half the chilled dough. • Press the dough into small tartlet pans. • Roll out remaining dough and continue pressing into additional tartlet pans. • Prick the shells with a fork and fill with pie weights. • Bake for 8 to 12 minutes or until lightly browned. • Cool on a wire rack. • Remove weights.

A decorative way to frost with confectioners' sugar is to use a flour sifter or sprinkle through a paper doilie.

FILLING

¼ *cup sugar*
3 tablespoons all-purpose flour
1 envelope unflavored gelatin
2 large eggs
1 yolk of large egg
1½ cups milk
3 tablespoons light rum or ½ teaspoon rum extract
½ cup heavy cream
Assortment of fresh berries, peaches and kiwis
1 cup apple jelly

In a large saucepan, combine sugar, flour and gelatin. • In a small bowl, beat eggs, egg yolk and milk. • Stir liquid into sugar mixture. • Cook over medium-low heat, stirring constantly until mixture thickens and boils. • Remove from heat. • Cover custard with waxed paper. • Chill for 1 hour or until mixture mounds slightly when dropped from a spoon. • Stir in rum. • Beat cream until soft peaks form. • Fold cream into custard. • Spoon into baked, cooled tartlet shells. • Chill. • Just before serving, garnish with fruit. • Heat apple jelly until melted. Brush melted jelly onto fresh fruit. Yield: 24

The Wedding Day Tea

Cranberry Fruit Consommé

Chocolate Mint Tea

*Smoked Turkey and Ham on Onion Dill
Bread with Watercress Butter*

*Wild-Fruit Drop Scones with
Blueberry Sauce*

*White Chocolate Muffins with
Crabapple Jelly*

*Lemon Cheesecake with Glazed
Raspberries*

Orange Blossom Wedding Torte

FROM WEEKEND GETAWAYS to dinner concerts and weddings, everything done at Old Rittenhouse Inn is cause for celebration. Whether you're in a singing or a sentimental mood, occasions are affairs of the heart here and a wedding tea is the ultimate portrait of love among the inns.

The Old Rittenhouse and its sister inns—Le Châteaú Boutin and Grey Oak—are veiled in romance any day but particularly for weddings. Innkeepers Mary and Jerry Philips decorate with the vintage linens, delicate lace, and bridal apparel they began collecting during their own courting days.

A wedding tea provides a calmer backdrop for this hectic day. The bridal reception is often less formal than a sit-down affair as the atmosphere for tea-time is quieter and more genteel. Guests receive the new Mr. and Mrs. over tea and finger foods following the ceremony.

It's only fitting that this inn be the backdrop for wedding and anniversary teas and dinners since Mary and Jerry discovered Old Rittenhouse while on their own honeymoon. It wasn't theirs until years later, however. Jerry, a choir teacher, and Mary, a professional pianist, helped couples write their own ceremonies and select their music before they added innkeeping to their repertoire.

Jerry, also a trained thespian, is a minister. (Although he suggests couples take a ferry ride to the nearby Apostle Islands, he recommends this park because it is a nature preserve and not for any apostolic reason!) With myriad talents, the staff at The Old Rittenhouse Inn provides those

A private moment before the wedding at Old Rittenhouse Inn

in love with everything it takes to become husband and wife: the Cinderella setting, the musical merriment, the wondrous food, and most of all, Mary and Jerry.

Most of Mary's recipes are original and for wedding teas they often include plenty of berries. Among the prepared foods are baskets of fruit, including Wisconsin's native cherries. Local farmers bring this bountiful produce to the inn where Mary buys it by the bucketful. As you toast the bride and groom with a cup of tea, you can't help but wish them indeed: "a life as it is at Old Rittenhouse—like a bowl full of cherries."

Old Rittenhouse Inn (Le Château Boutin, Grey Oak Guest House)
P.O. Box 584
Bayfield, WI 54814
Phone: **(715) 779-5111**
Rooms: **18**
Tea-Time: **On special occasions**

A WEDDING TEA AT HOME

- A nice wedding favor would be a sack of tea to take home. Tie small bundles of loose tea in pretty fabric with a bow that has the name of the bride and groom and wedding date printed on the ribbon.
- Many guests forget to bring rice to shower over the bride and groom. Pass out rice by the teacupful.

CRANBERRY FRUIT CONSOMMÉ

Serve the consommé warm as an appetizer to the tea and foods or as a cold beverage.

1 16-ounce package frozen, unsweetened rhubarb, sliced
¾ cup sugar
1 3-inch cinnamon stick
2 cups water
2 cups cranberry juice cocktail
½ cup Burgundy
½ cup club soda
Fresh mint
Strawberries

In a 4-quart saucepan, combine rhubarb, sugar, cinnamon stick and water. • Bring to a boil; reduce heat. • Simmer 5 minutes or until rhubarb is tender. • Remove cinnamon stick. • Remove rhubarb and press through a strainer, catching the juice in the saucepan. • Add cranberry juice, wine and club soda. • Mix gently. • Return to stove. • Serve warm. • Garnish with fresh mint and strawberries. Yield: 8 servings

CHOCOLATE MINT TEA

4 cups brewed mint tea (peppermint or spearmint)
4 cups hot chocolate made with milk
¼ teaspoon crème de menthe extract (or 1 teaspoon crème de menthe liqueur)
Whipped cream
Fresh mint sprigs

Blend mint tea and hot chocolate in a saucepan and heat. • Add crème de menthe. • Serve with a dollop of whipped cream and sprig of fresh mint. Yield: 8 cups

SMOKED TURKEY AND HAM ON ONION DILL BREAD WITH WATERCRESS BUTTER

ONION DILL BREAD

2½ teaspoons (¼-ounce package) active dry yeast

2 tablespoons sugar, divided

1¼ cups lukewarm milk, divided

½ cup minced onion

2 tablespoons dried dill

2 tablespoons unsalted butter, softened

1 teaspoon salt

1 large egg, slightly beaten

4 to 4½ cups unbleached flour

Romantic heart-shaped sandwiches (on pedestal) and Cranberry Fruit Consommé

In small bowl, proof (make sure it's active, i.e. it should bubble) the yeast with 1 teaspoon of the sugar in ¼ cup milk for 15 minutes or until foamy. • In a large bowl, combine remaining milk and sugar, onion, dill, butter and salt, stirring the mixture until butter is melted. • Stir in egg, yeast mixture and enough of the flour to make a soft but not sticky dough. • Knead the dough on a floured surface for 8 to 10 minutes or until smooth and elastic. Form into a ball. • Transfer to a lightly buttered bowl, turning once to coat with butter. • Cover with plastic wrap and allow dough to rise in a warm place for 1 hour or until doubled in size.

Punch the dough down and let it rest for 5 minutes. • Knead for 1 minute and place in a buttered 9x5-inch loaf pan. • Cover loosely with a towel and let rise in a warm place for 30 minutes or until doubled in size. • Preheat oven to 350°. • Bake for 45 minutes to 1 hour or until pan sounds hollow when bottom is tapped. • Remove bread from pan and cool on rack. Yield: 1 loaf

SANDWICH FILLING

1 bundle watercress, leaves only, rinsed

1 stick unsalted butter, softened

½ teaspoon sugar

½ teaspoon salt

20 slices Onion Dill bread

½ pound smoked turkey, thinly sliced

½ pound Virginia ham, thinly sliced

In small saucepan, blanch watercress leaves in boiling water. • Drain. Rinse under cold water. Squeeze out any excess water. • In food processor, purée the watercress with butter, sugar and salt. • Spread butter on bread slices. Remove crusts. • Add 1 slice each of the turkey and ham to 10 bread slices. • Top with remaining bread. • Cut sandwiches with large heart-shaped cookie cutter. Yield: 10

Wild Fruit Drop Scones with Blueberry Sauce

WILD FRUIT DROP SCONES WITH BLUEBERRY SAUCE

1 1/2 cups unbleached all-purpose flour
1/2 teaspoon baking soda
1 teaspoon cream of tartar
1/8 teaspoon salt
1 medium egg, beaten
1 1/4 cups milk
1 tablespoon sugar
1/2 cup blueberries
Butter
Blueberry sauce

Over large bowl, sift together flour, baking soda, cream of tartar and salt. • In separate bowl, beat egg, milk and sugar and stir into flour mixture slowly, until you have a thick batter. • Pour 1/3-cup each onto a hot, lightly greased griddle. • Drop blueberries onto

each scone. • When bubbles appear on top of cakes, flip to other side. • Slide onto a hot plate and keep scones covered with a cloth napkin until ready to serve. • Serve with butter and warm Blueberry Sauce. Yield: 8

BLUEBERRY SAUCE

1 cup fresh blueberries
1 tablespoon lemon juice
1 1/2 cups sugar

Blend blueberries and lemon juice. • Fold in sugar. • Heat to boiling, stirring constantly. • Serve with scones.

WHITE CHOCOLATE MUFFINS WITH CRABAPPLE JELLY

3 1/2 cups all-purpose flour
1/2 cup sugar
2 tablespoons baking powder
3/4 cup grated white chocolate
1/2 cup ground almonds
3 eggs
1/2 cup vegetable oil
1 cup frozen orange juice concentrate, thawed
1 cup milk
Crabapple jelly (see next recipe)

Preheat oven to 375°. • In a large bowl, blend together flour, sugar, baking powder, chocolate and almonds. • In another bowl, combine eggs, oil, juice and milk. • Make a well in the center of the dry ingredients and add wet ingredients all at once. • Stir to blend. Do not overmix. • Pour batter into greased muffin tins, filling each 2/3 full. • Bake for 15 to 20 minutes or until golden. Serve with Crabapple Jelly. Yield: 36

CRABAPPLE JELLY

3 pounds whole crabapples, stems removed
6 cups cold water
1 1³/₄-ounce package pectin
6 cups sugar

Place apples in an 8-quart (or larger) kettle. • Add water. • Bring to a rolling boil. • Reduce heat and simmer until apples split (about 15 minutes). • Strain the juice through a double layer of cheesecloth. This should yield about 4 cups of juice. • Add pectin to the juice. • Heat until juice boils. • Add sugar, stirring constantly for 1 minute. • Remove from heat. • Skim off foam with a spoon. • Pour into sterile canning jars and seal. Yield: 6 10-ounce jars.

LEMON CHEESECAKE WITH GLAZED RASPBERRIES

SHELL

2 cups all-purpose flour
¹/₂ cup sugar
2 teaspoons grated lemon peel
2 sticks unsalted butter, cut into bits
2 yolks of large eggs
¹/₂ teaspoon vanilla extract

Preheat oven to 400°. • Combine flour, sugar, and lemon peel; blend in butter until the mixture resembles coarse meal. • Add yolks and vanilla, combining the mixture until it forms a dough. • Remove the ring from a 10-inch springform pan. • Press ¹/₃ of the dough onto the bottom of the pan. • Bake for 8 minutes; let cool on rack. • Return the ring to the pan and pat the remaining dough at least 2 inches high onto the sides of the pan.

FILLING

2¹/₂ pounds cream cheese, softened
1³/₄ cups sugar
1 teaspoon grated lemon peel
¹/₄ teaspoon vanilla extract
3 tablespoons all-purpose flour
¹/₄ teaspoon salt
4 large eggs
2 yolks of large eggs
¹/₄ cup heavy cream

Preheat oven to 425°. • In bowl of electric mixer, beat cream cheese until smooth. • Beat in sugar, lemon peel and vanilla. • Beat in flour and salt; add eggs and egg yolks, 1 at a time. • Beat in cream. • Pour filling into baked shell. • Bake cheesecake for 12 minutes. • Reduce heat to 300° and bake for 1 hour longer. • Cool on rack.

TOPPING

³/₄ cup water
³/₄ cup sugar
3 tablespoons cornstarch
2 tablespoons light corn syrup
4 drops red food coloring
4 cups raspberries

In saucepan combine water, sugar and cornstarch. • Cook over moderately high heat, stirring until mixture is thick and clear. • Remove from heat and stir in corn syrup and food coloring. • Let topping cool to lukewarm. • Arrange berries on the cheesecake and pour the topping mixture over them. • Chill for at least 3 hours. Yield: 16 to 18 slices

ORANGE BLOSSOM WEDDING TORTE

CAKE

9 eggs, separated

1 cup sugar

1 tablespoon lemon juice

2 cups all-purpose flour

1 ounce grated white chocolate, melted

½ cup butter, melted and slightly cooled

½ cup Grand Marnier

Preheat oven to 325°. • Whip egg whites to a firm meringue, gradually adding sugar. • Beat egg yolks until golden and fluffy. • Carefully blend together egg whites and yolks. • Add lemon juice • Add flour and chocolate. • Stir in melted butter. • Turn mixture into 2 heart-shaped or 8-inch round baking pans. • Bake for 30 minutes or until tester inserted in center comes out clean. • Cool on wire racks. • Remove cakes from pans. • Split each layer in half horizontally. • Sprinkle each layer with ⅛ cup Grand Marnier. • Prepare filling.

FILLING

½ cup sour cream

8 ounces cream cheese, softened

2 sticks butter, softened

1 teaspoon finely grated orange peel

1 teaspoon orange extract

1 cup confectioners' sugar

In food processor, blend sour cream, cream cheese and butter until smooth. • Add orange peel, extract and sugar. • Blend just until mixed. • Spread about ¾ cup of filling on top of each layer.

CAKE ASSEMBLY

1½ cups heavy cream

1 tablespoon vanilla extract

1 tablespoon walnut extract

Orange slices for garnish

Whip cream with vanilla and walnut extracts until stiff peaks form. • Frost cake sides and top. • Garnish with orange slices or fresh flowers. Yield: 24 slices

Well before stoves and ovens were common, scones were made on a griddle over an open fire. Today drop-scones are made on a griddle on the stove. They look like plump pancakes but are eaten like biscuits with choice of toppings.

Tea Under a Canopy

William Overton's Plantation Tea

Miss Marcie's Plantation Cookies

Almond Crunch Cookies

Mammie Katie's Apricot Crescents

Russian Tea Cakes

MAYBE IT'S THE BOX-wood hedgerow with its scent compassing the way to the manor house.

Perhaps it's the inimitable style and dash of innkeeper Bill Sheehan, who greets you graciously at the front door. With a trademark mustachioed grin, he serves the tea. At dinner-time, he pours complimentary glasses of wine or cider for the guests as each arrives. Once everyone is seated, he delivers a blessing for the bounty about to be received. This is special.

Or perhaps it's the tasteful and al-luring decor of the guest rooms.

Whatever it is, from the moment you arrive at Prospect Hill everything and everyone flirts with your senses. Prospect Hill is alive with romance,

good cheer, and the potential for a visit of lasting impression.

The inn is purported to be the oldest continually occupied plantation in America. Since 1732, the main house has comforted aristocrats and land owners, and its outbuildings once housed the families of the slaves who tended the plantation. With tea-cup in hand, you can prance among the architectural curiosities of the main house, winding down a stair-case, lowering your head past a doorway, only to find tall ceilings round another corner. You can fanta-size in a cabin for two, such as the popular carriage house with its arched windows that bow to beehive bedposts.

No wonder couples of all ages flock here for anniversaries and wed-dings or a weekend getaway. There's even a dining room for couples only, and scattered about the grounds and in nooks and crannies are symbolic reminders of romance—statues of Cupid, which the inn uses as its logo. Is it any wonder why breakfast is served to you at bedside? Is it any wonder that this intimate tradition also carries over to tea-time?

Although tea is served in the par-lor or on the veranda, many take tea in their rooms at table side or under

A carriage to the canopy at Prospect Hill

a canopy. So you, dear reader, will have to fill in the blanks as to what tea-time at Prospect Hill is *really* like.

The fires of love are fed here. There's a reverence for life that makes everyone who enters a romantic. You can't help but be touched by the amorous magic that seems to sparkle like pixie dust over all of Prospect Hill.

Prospect Hill
Route 3, Box 430
Trevilians, VA 23093
Phone: (703) 967-0844
Rooms: 12
Tea-Time: 3:00–4:00 P.M. for inn guests

TEA UNDER A CANOPY

- Use a white wicker tray which conjures images of days gone by—very romantic. Cover the tray partially with a colored cloth and top with a lace doily. Add a bud vase with a flower. Set with your best china and silver and a two-for-tea teapot.
- Add a little Victorian calling card with a romantic saying or prophetic quote.
- Place a tea cozy over the teapot to keep it warm as you deliver the tray to your own guest room at home.

WILLIAM OVERTON'S PLANTATION TEA

This is a special blend of iced tea named after the original owner of the plantation.

8 Orange Pekoe tea bags (good quality)
12 sprigs fresh mint
1 cup sugar
1 quart boiling water
1 quart homemade lemonade*

Place tea bags, mint and sugar in a heat-resistant pitcher. • Pour in boiling water and stir. • Let stand for 30 minutes; then discard tea bags and mint, wringing them out over the pitcher. • Add lemonade. • Stir well. • Serve chilled. Yield: ½ gallon

*Homemade Lemonade: Juice of 4 lemons, 1 cup sugar, 1 quart cold water.

A bowl of leaf tea and a silver strainer await tea-timers at Prospect Hill.

MISS MARCIE'S PLANTATION COOKIES

1½ cups all-purpose flour
6 tablespoons butter, chilled and cut into ¼-inch pieces
1 tablespoon sugar
⅛ teaspoon salt
4 to 6 tablespoons ice water
Honey
Cinnamon
1 cup pecans, finely chopped

In a large bowl, combine the flour, butter, sugar and salt. • Using a pastry cutter or fingertips, cut the flour and butter together until mixture resembles coarse meal. • Pour ice water over mixture and knead until dough can be gathered into a ball. • Dust very lightly with flour and chill for at least 30 minutes. • On floured surface, roll chilled dough out to form a rectangle approximately 16x10 inches by ⅛-inch thick.

Preheat oven to 350°. • Spread dough with warmed honey until covered. • Sprinkle with a light covering of cinnamon, followed by chopped pecans. • Roll up dough jelly roll style. • Cut into ½-inch thick slices. • Place on very lightly oiled cookie sheet. • Bake for 10 minutes or until golden. Yield: 36

To make chocolate leaves for tea food garnishes, brush melted chocolate onto a real leaf. Let it harden and then gently remove the natural mold.

Peanut Cups

An easy-to-make add-on for tea-time: Use a basic sugar cookie dough found at your grocer's. Divide the dough into 9 thick slices, then cut each piece into fourths. Place each chunk into a greased mini-muffin tin cup. Bake at 350° for 10 minutes or until lightly browned. Remove from oven and immediately push a chocolate peanut butter candy into the middle of each. Yield: about 36.

Honeysuckle Hill, West Barnstable,
Massachusetts

ALMOND CRUNCH COOKIES

| 1 cup sugar |
| 1 cup confectioners' sugar |
| 2 sticks butter, softened |
| 1 cup vegetable oil |
| 1 teaspoon almond extract |
| 2 eggs |
| 4½ cups all-purpose flour |
| 1 teaspoon baking soda |
| 1 teaspoon salt |
| 1 teaspoon cream of tartar |
| 1 tablespoon honey crunch wheat germ |
| 2 cups coarsely chopped almonds |
| ½ cup sugar |

Preheat oven to 350°. • In large bowl of electric mixer, blend together 1 cup sugar, 1 cup confectioners' sugar, butter and oil until well mixed. • Add almond extract and eggs. • Mix well. • On low speed, gradually add flour, baking soda, salt, cream of tartar and wheat germ. • By hand, stir in almonds. •

Shape generous tablespoons of dough into balls. • Roll in sugar. • Place 5 inches apart on ungreased cookie sheets. • With fork dipped in remaining sugar, flatten in a crisscross pattern. • Bake for 12 to 18 minutes or until golden brown around the edges. • Cool cookies for 1 minute before removing from cookie sheets. Yield: 42

MAMMIE KATIE'S APRICOT CRESCENTS

DOUGH

| 1 3-ounce package cream cheese |
| 1 stick butter |
| 1 cup all-purpose flour |
| 2 tablespoons sugar |
| ¼ teaspoon salt |

FILLING

| ½ cup honey |
| ½ teaspoon ground cinnamon |
| ⅓ cup finely chopped pecans |
| Light cream |
| Apricot syrup* |

Cut the cream cheese and butter into the flour. • Add the sugar and salt and blend well. • Roll dough into a ball, cover with plastic wrap and chill for about 2 hours or overnight.

Preheat oven to 425°. • Separate chilled dough into 2 equal portions, leaving 1 portion in refrigerator. • On lightly floured

*To make apricot syrup, push 1½ cups apricot preserves through a sieve, leaving behind seed and extra pulp.

One of Prospect Hill's enchanting guest rooms

surface, roll out to an ⅛-inch thickness. •
Cut into 2-inch squares. • Mix together
honey, cinnamon and pecans. • Place ½ teaspoon filling in center of each square. • Roll
up crescent fashion, beginning at a corner. •
Place each crescent on ungreased cookie
sheet. • Repeat with remaining dough. •
Bake for 10 minutes or until lightly browned.
Do not overbake. • Remove from oven and
drizzle apricot syrup in criss-cross pattern
over each cookie. Yield: 24

RUSSIAN TEA CAKES

1 cup butter
½ cup confectioners' sugar
1 teaspoon vanilla extract
2¼ cups all-purpose flour
¼ teaspoon salt
¾ cup pecans, finely chopped
Confectioners' sugar

Cream together butter, sugar and vanilla. •
Stir together flour and salt. • Blend with
butter mixture. • Stir in pecans. • Chill
dough thoroughly. • Preheat oven to 400°. •
Roll chilled dough into 1-inch balls and place
on ungreased cookie sheet. • Bake for 10 to
12 minutes, until set but not brown. • Cool
only slightly. • Roll warm cookies in confectioners' sugar. • Allow to cool completely
and roll in sugar again. Yield: 48

"That's a Yacht o' Tea"

Geranium Iced Tea

**Lobster and Dill Butter Sandwiches on
Portuguese Sweet Bread**

**Maine Blueberry Scones with
Rose Hips Jam**

Rugelach

YOU PROBABLY CAN'T HAVE a more unusual tea-time than on board a 1948 cruising vessel. Yet every afternoon on the promenade deck of the 83-foot Pauline Inn Afloat, tea is served from a silver salver in a wood-paneled cabin as the boat floats romantically in Maine waters.

The inn-boat is the dream-come-true of Ken and Ellen Barnes. The couple had watched the former old sardine carrier go up and down the waters for many years. "We always admired her," says Ken. The ship was for sale for two years when they realized they could save the vessel by turning it into an "inn afloat."

Ellen and Ken totally refurbished the ship, replacing nearly everything except the hull, to accommodate twelve guests. Candlelight gourmet dinners that have earned high praise from critics in the three years the inn has been afloat, are served on bone china nightly by the ship's resident chef Wendell Holmes-Smith, a graduate of the Culinary Institute of America. Seafood, fresh-baked breads, and pies brimming with native fruit, are the specialties of the inn-boat. "Breakfast and lunch are often served *al fresco,* on the fantail, and we sometimes drop the hook while we dine," says an enticing line from the inn's brochure.

"It's a tradition to serve tea on board," says Ellen. "We rebuilt the ship in Victorian fashion and tea-time just goes with the atmosphere." It's true, drinking tea on board as the ship rocks gently, does add to the effervescence of tea-time. You make your way back to the ship for tea, after a day of self-planned activities or just relaxing on board. The ship is even more romantic in the evening—festively lit and wonderful for strolling. There's a wood-burning stove for chilly nights. Ellen, a knowledgeable open-hearth cook and cookbook author, sometimes prepares tea-time treats by the stove, especially the Rugelach.

The Pauline adds another dimension to cruising. On this ship, you get personal attention from a caring crew. Upon leaving the Pauline, you'll find yourself thinking, "Now, that's what I call the real love boat!"

Pauline Inn Afloat
Windjammer Wharf
P.O. Box 1050
Rockland, ME 04841
Phone: **(207) 236-3520**
Rooms: **6**
Tea-Time: **4:00 P.M. daily for inn guests May through October**

GERANIUM ICED TEA

3 scented rose leaves
3 lemon geranium leaves
½ cup sugar
2 quarts of herbed tea of choice
Ice cubes

In a small bowl, bury leaves in the sugar. • Cover and set aside for 3 days. • Brew tea as usual. • Add to a pitcher filled with ice. • Add geranium-flavored sugar, strain out the leaves. Yield: 2 quarts

LOBSTER AND DILL BUTTER SANDWICHES ON PORTUGUESE SWEET BREAD

Ellen Barnes has been making this dense sweet bread for 25 years. The bread is a nice contrast to the dill butter. Double the recipe for the butter if you're going to use all 4 loaves of the bread at once. These are open-faced sandwiches.

The Pauline

BREAD

4 tablespoons yeast
1 cup water
2 teaspoons sugar
1 cup warm milk
2 sticks butter, softened
2 cups sugar
6 eggs
2 tablespoons salt
8 to 10 cups all-purpose flour

Proof (make sure it's active, i.e. it will bubble) yeast in 1 cup warm water, adding 2 teaspoons sugar. • Mix milk, butter and sugar well; add to yeast mixture. • Beat eggs and salt together and add to mixture. • Add flour, 1 cup at a time, until dough is elastic enough to knead. • Knead for 10 minutes and let rise in a buttered bowl until doubled in size. • Punch down and divide into 4 greased 9x5-inch loaf pans. • Let rise. • Preheat oven to 350°. • Bake for 30 minutes or until browned. • (Note: This bread rises slowly. Don't panic. If the yeast is proofed, the bread will rise.) Yield: 4 loaves

DILL BUTTER

⅔ cup fresh dill weed
3 tablespoons fresh parsley leaves
2 sticks unsalted butter
1 tablespoon fresh lemon juice
¾ teaspoon salt
⅛ teaspoon cayenne

Finely chop dill weed and parsley leaves in a food processor. • Add butter and process until well combined. • With the motor running, add lemon juice through the feed tube. • Season with salt and cayenne. Yield: 1 cup butter

SANDWICH ASSEMBLY

Lobster meat
Watercress

Cut cooled bread into 2-inch wedges. • Remove crusts. • Spread with dill butter and add a piece of lobster meat. • Garnish with watercress.

MAINE BLUEBERRY SCONES WITH ROSE HIPS JAM

2 cups all-purpose flour
4 teaspoons baking powder
¼ teaspoon baking soda
½ teaspoon salt
2 tablespoons sugar
2 tablespoons grated orange peel
⅓ cup butter, cold
1 cup fresh blueberries
½ cup sour cream
⅓ cup milk

Tea-time on board

Preheat oven to 425°. • Combine flour, baking powder, baking soda, salt, sugar and orange peel. • Cut butter into flour mixture until it resembles coarse crumbs. • Fold in blueberries. • Combine sour cream and milk. • Blend into blueberry mixture and mix lightly until dough masses together. • Turn dough onto floured surface and roll out to a ½-inch thickness. • Cut dough with a 2-inch round cutter. • Place on ungreased cookie sheet. • Bake for 15 to 20 minutes or until golden brown. Yield: 24

ROSE HIPS JAM

The Pauline makes this jam with the wild *rosa rugosa* that grow on the islands of Maine. These hips are picked in late August and September in great quantity. You can use your own native rose hips and also serve this with the Portuguese Sweet Bread. (Do not use roses that have been in contact with pesticides.)

3 cups rose hips, rinsed and ends snipped
3 cups water
3 apples peeled, cored, coarsely chopped
4 cups sugar

Place rose hips in a non-metallic saucepan. • Add water. • Cook covered until rose hips are tender (about 20 minutes). • Transfer hips and water to processor and purée. • In another saucepan cook the apples in 2 tablespoons water until tender. • Add the rose hips purée and sugar to the apples. • Heat on low until sugar is dissolved. • Bring mixture to a boil and cook until it starts to jell. • Pour into sterile glass jars and seal. Yield: 12 ounces

RUGELACH

This was a favorite of Ellen Barnes' childhood in Brooklyn. "Every neighborhood had a bakery down the block or around the corner," remembers Ellen. When the bakeries disappeared, she searched for years before finding a Rugelach recipe that reminded her of those days.

1 stick butter
8 ounces cream cheese, softened
2 tablespoons sugar
½ teaspoon vanilla extract
2 cups all-purpose flour
½ cup sugar
2 tablespoons ground cinnamon
¾ cup plum jam or preserves
¾ cup chopped walnuts
¾ cup currants
Confectioners' sugar

Cream together butter and cream cheese. • Beat in 2 tablespoons sugar and the vanilla. •

Mix in flour, 1 cup at a time, until well blended. • Scrape dough onto well-floured surface. • With floured hands, knead for 30 seconds. • Divide dough into thirds; pat each into a 5-inch round circle. • Wrap tightly in plastic wrap and chill for 1 hour. • Mix together ½ cup sugar and cinnamon. • Remove 1 part of the chilled dough and roll in a 14-inch circle. • Spread dough with ⅓ of the plum jam, leaving a 1-inch border. • Sprinkle with ⅓ each of walnuts, currants and sugar/cinnamon mixture.

Cut filled dough into 4 quarters and each quarter into 4 wedges. Roll each wedge to form a crescent. • Repeat process with remaining dough. • Place on buttered cookie sheets. • Preheat oven to 350°. • Bake for 30 minutes or until lightly browned. • Cool on wire racks and sprinkle with confectioners' sugar. Yield: 48

A "THAT'S A YACHT O' TEA" AT HOME

- Place tea foods in children's small boats. The wooden, remote control boats will set a more elegant table.
- Place teapots in the center of life preservers which will help keep the tea warm.
- The tea server could sport a captain's cap.
- Charter a small boat for a tea-time party.

Three

THEME TEAS

There was a table set out under a tree in front of the house, and the March Hare and the Hatter were having tea at it . . .

"No Room! No Room!" they cried out when they saw Alice coming.

"There's *plenty* of room!" said Alice indignantly.

Alice sat herself down at the table anyway, and—as tea-time continued—she went through a lengthy discussion with the Hatter regarding his watch that seemed to stand still:

"It's always six o'clock now," said the Hatter . . .

"Is that the reason so many tea-things are put out here?" Alice asked.

"Yes, it's always tea-time, and we've no time to wash the things between whiles."

Lewis Carroll, *Alice's Adventure in Wonderland*

ALICE'S TEA-TIME ADVENTURE FROM LEWIS CARROLL'S THE Mad Tea-Party chapter reminds us that tea doesn't always have to be presented seriously. Ah, neither that it should replicate the one viewed "Through the Looking Glass" with its soiled napery and teacups, but it should have plenty of spirit and make people feel good.

A look at the tea-time habit in this classic story also suggests that tea-time had become a bit of a ho-hum-so-what affair in Wonderland. That's too bad. What the Hatter and his friends needed was a new twist to tea-time. Hatter, March Hare, and Dormouse should take a cue from the many fantasies in their fairy tale place, for Alice's adventure also suggests to us that you can make tea-time whatever you fancy it to be.

Choosing a theme for a tea is one way to bring fantasies to life and add to the tea-time experience. Now, you don't need to do anything more than hold a teacup in your hand and take time out to share with others to make tea-time special. However, themes bring added dimensions for more variety to tea-time.

Tea-time is not only on the table but also in the heart. Propping the tea-time stage only adds another facet to an already great experience.

Tara's Laura Ackley serves tea in antebellum fashion.

A Hats-Off-to-You Tea

**Minced Ham and Pineapple
Sandwiches with Honey Butter**

——————

Hannah Marie Country Scones

——————

Strawberry Bonnets

——————

Sugar Hats

——————

Brown Derby Drop Meringues

A YOUNG MILLINER, seated among colorful Paris hat fashions, is captured ever so winsomely in *The Millinery Shop,* a dreamy oil-on-canvas by French impressionist Edgar Degas. Hats were an essential part of everyday life in 1882 when Degas preserved this commonplace moment. Back then, gentlemen tipped their chapeaus to ladies and no one ventured outdoors without their crowning touch, worn ever-so proudly.

We may have dispensed with a dependency on headgear, but certainly not with its fascination as evidenced by A Hats-Off-to-You Tea at the Hannah Marie Country Inn. Once a year, the inn becomes a "grand millinery shop," not at all unlike the one in the nineteenth-century painting. Hats transform the Victorian dining room at the inn into a stylish boutique. Hand-held flirtation mirrors reflect the images of a playful tea-taking group, that giggles at the wonderful changes in their personalities and images as each person in the group dons a new brim. When the hat tea has ended, the Hannah Marie closes its "millinery shop" only to offer yet another unique tea experience later.

Innkeeper Mary Nichols is one of America's most popular theme-tea promoters. A former high school teacher and principal, Mary studied and worked for a year in England, where afternoon tea became a part of her lifestyle. Her inn, also owned and operated by her husband, Ray, sometimes serves tea twice a day for tea lunches and afternoon teas.

Theme teas include folk-art teas, Queen Victoria chocolate teas, storybook teas, teas with regional and historic crafts, doll-collector teas and ethnic teas. They all include instruction on how to serve a proper tea. "We talk about how one must be the 'keeper of the pot,' and serve the tea properly. It's important when doing a theme tea to make sure the traditional tea-time experience comes through," notes Mary, who offers similar instruction to tea-luncheon guests as well.

Tea is served in courses at Hannah Marie. Usually a black, leaf English tea is the beverage of choice, or a fragrant green tea such as Jasmine, followed by a savory, scones and a selection of confections.

Tea-time at Hannah Marie is enhanced by Mary's dedication to her role—first as innkeeper who openly shares her knowledge with warmth, personality and great individual flair, and secondly as purveyor of myriad afternoon-tea experiences. She is prophetic in her approach to life and tea-time—allowing everyone who listens a brighter way of looking at things. For all that, Mary Nichols, it's our hat that's off to you!

Hannah Marie Country Inn
Route 1, Highway 17 South
Spencer, Iowa 51301
Phone: **(712) 262-1286**
Rooms: **3**
Tea-Time: **Tea luncheon, Tuesday through Saturday, 12:30 p.m. for inn guests and by reservation from April through December; afternoon theme teas, 3:30 p.m. on dates according to the inn's schedule**

Tipping cups and hats

A HATS-OFF-TO-YOU TEA AT HOME

- Ask everyone to bring a favorite hat. Place them on a hat tree or on a table. Just before serving the tea, have everyone select a hat she thinks does not fit her personality. After the tea, ask everyone to explain her choice.
- Use decorated hatboxes to serve some of your tea-time treats. Scones would look inviting in a hat box. Pile hat boxes everywhere else for decoration.
- Ask everyone to bring a few yards of a favorite wallpaper. Buy the miniature, pre-made hatboxes from a crafts supply store and have everyone cover a box with the paper she or he brought.

A Strawberry Bonnet and a Brown Derby Drop Meringue top a Hats-Off-to-You plate.

MINCED HAM AND PINEAPPLE SANDWICHES WITH HONEY BUTTER

1 cup minced ham
½ cup chopped fresh (or canned) pineapple, drained
1 teaspoon Dijon-style mustard
Fresh pepper to taste
2 sticks butter, softened
2 tablespoons honey
20 thin slices whole-wheat bread

In bowl of electric mixer, blend ham, pineapple, mustard and pepper. • Blend together butter and honey. • Spread honey butter on all slices. • Top half the slices with ham mixture. • Top with remaining bread. • Remove crusts. • Cut each sandwich into 4 triangles. Yield: 40

HANNAH MARIE COUNTRY SCONES

3 cups all-purpose flour
2 tablespoons baking powder
½ teaspoon baking soda
1½ tablespoons sugar
2 sticks ice-cold butter, cut into 1-inch pieces
2 cups buttermilk
Buttermilk

Combine flour, baking powder, baking soda and sugar with a fork. • Using pastry cutter, cut butter into dry mixture. • Chill for 10 minutes. • Preheat oven to 400°. • Add buttermilk, mixing until all ingredients are moistened. • Gather into a ball and knead about 12 times. • Roll out pastry to 1-inch thickness. • Cut out scones with a 2-inch biscuit cutter. • Place on an ungreased baking sheet, close together, but not touching. • Brush tops with buttermilk. • Bake for 20 minutes or until golden brown. • Serve hot. Yield: 12

STRAWBERRY BONNETS

10 large strawberries
4 ounces cream cheese, softened
2 tablespoons strawberry liqueur (or vanilla extract)
3 tablespoons confectioners' sugar
1 cup heavy cream, whipped

Prepare strawberries; rinse, dry and hull. • Slice berries into quarters, but not straight through. Leave a ¼-inch base uncut. • When the berries are filled, they will resemble a tulip. • Set berries aside for filling. • Beat cream cheese until smooth. • Add liqueur and sugar, beating until smooth. • Fold in whipped cream. • Place mixture in pastry bag with star tip. • Pipe the mixture into each prepared strawberry. • Chill until serving time. Yield: 10

SUGAR HATS

The hats are made with a basic sugar cookie dough and decorated with icing. • You will make only 20 finished hats even though you're baking 80 cookies. • Each hat requires 3 two-inch cookies to form the crown and 1 three-inch cookie for the brim. • Make the 2-inch cookies first.

SUGAR COOKIE DOUGH

1¾ cups sifted all-purpose flour
½ teaspoon baking powder
½ teaspoon baking soda
½ cup sugar
1 stick butter
1 egg
2 tablespoons milk
1 tablespoon vanilla extract

Sift together flour, baking powder, baking soda and sugar into large bowl. • With pastry blender or 2 knives, cut butter into flour mixture until consistency of coarse cornmeal. • With fork, stir in egg, milk and vanilla. • Mix well with hands to form dough into a ball. • Wrap in waxed paper and chill for 2 hours. • Preheat oven to 350°. • Lightly grease cookie sheets. • Divide dough into 4 parts. • On lightly floured surface, roll out each part to an ⅛-inch thickness. • Cut dough with 2-inch round cookie cutters. • Bake for 7 minutes or until golden. • Cool completely. Yield: 60

To make the 3-inch cookies for the brims, repeat preceding recipe, cutting out 20 cookies with a 3-inch round cutter. • When both sets of cookies are made, you are ready for assembly and decorating. • Make the icing first.

ICING

1 cup shortening
2 pounds confectioners' sugar, sifted
2 teaspoons almond extract
½ cup water
Food coloring

In bowl of electric mixer, beat shortening until light and fluffy. • Add sifted sugar, beating until smooth. • Mix together almond extract and water. • Add to sugar mixture. • Beat until well blended. • Divide the icing evenly into bowls, as many as you wish according to your choice of decorating colors. • Mix in food colorings.

SUGAR HAT ASSEMBLY

For each cookie, place ¼ teaspoon icing on the 3-inch hat bottom (brim), just off center. • Place 1 small cookie on top, pressing gently. • (Icing is the glue.) • Add 2 more cookies, building crown with icing in the same manner. • Decorate hats with icing pumped through pastry bags: star tip for flowers; round tip for berries; flat tip for ribbons and bands. • Use your imagination!

Sugar Hats brim with sweet sentiments.

BROWN DERBY DROP MERINGUES

1 cup unsweetened cocoa powder
⅔ cup unsweetened grated coconut
3 cups superfine sugar
1 teaspoon vanilla extract
Whites of 10 large eggs, at room temperature

Preheat oven to 300°. • In small bowl, stir together cocoa and coconut; set aside. • In large heat-proof mixing bowl, combine sugar, vanilla and egg whites. • Transfer bowl of sugar/egg mixture to a large pan of simmering water. • Stir constantly with a whisk until meringue forms stiff and shiny peaks. • With a large rubber spatula, gently and quickly fold in the cocoa mixture just until evenly incorporated. • Using a pastry bag fitted with a number 6 (½-inch) tip, pipe the meringue into 1½-inch balls on prepared baking sheets, leaving 1 inch between. • Bake for 25 to 30 minutes. Yield: 80

Remember to pop a tea cozy onto the teapot to keep the tea hot and only after you've removed the tea leaves, or the tea will become bitter.

Hannah Marie Country Inn

A White Linen Tea

Russian Tea

Pear Nut Torte

Pecan Rum Meringues

*Golden Nuggets Candied
Grapefruit Peel*

Caramel Crunch Cake

Mint Chocolate Dipped Apricots

THE RED CASTLE INN IS often surrounded by snow, but the icicles you think you see in winter are part of the home's unique trim work. And the white that's even more striking than the snow comes from the delicate and lacy antique linens that innkeepers Mary Louise and Conley Weaver use so abundantly at tea-time. Everything is white except for the colorful foods. Mary Louise enjoys using white linens at tea-time. They are very special family heirlooms. Although the linens were monogrammed for her grandmother's trousseau, they look as crisp today as they were so many years ago. The linens have been in Mary Louise's family for quite some time and still bear the initial of her family name. Mary Louise also uses her grandmother's Limoges china teacups.

The white linen tea reflects the inn's glamorous past. Stories of gold

Write tea-time invitations on paper doilies and send in attractive envelopes.

miners and the ghost of the Lady in Grey are frequently the topics of conversation during tea-time when guests discuss the lore of surrounding Nevada City. In addition to daily afternoon tea for inn guests, Red Castle also has a tour of the inn once a month followed by a tea. A few times a month, in the evening, tea is served with a storyteller who weaves Gold Rush history with Victorian ghost tales by candlelight.

The Red Castle home was built in 1860 by a mine owner and is one of only two genuine Gothic Revival houses on the West Coast. It is set in the Sierra Nevadas in the heart of gold-rush country. One of Mary Louise's tea plates sums up tea-time at this inn: "Pleasant Dreams and Fond Recollections."

Red Castle Inn
109 Prospect Street
Nevada City, CA 95959
Phone: **(916) 265-5135**
Rooms: **8**
Tea-Time: **4:30–6:00 P.M. for inn guests. Once-a-month tea and inn tours 2–3:30 P.M. by reservation. Monthly tea and storytelling 6:00–9:00 P.M. by reservation.**

RUSSIAN TEA

12 cloves
2 to 3 cinnamon sticks, tied together
1 quart water
1½ cups sugar
3 tablespoons black tea
4 oranges
2 lemons
3 quarts boiling water

Tie cloves in a bit of cheesecloth or put in wire basket or tea ball. • Boil cinnamon sticks and cloves in 1 quart of water. • Dissolve sugar in the water and boil for 15 minutes. • Add the tea and allow to steep until strong. • Strain mixture into a 4-quart pitcher. (Cool mixture first if pitcher is heat-sensitive.) Add the strained juices of oranges and lemons plus 3 quarts of boiling water. • Let stand overnight or longer. • Reheat before serving. Yield: 32 cups

PEAR NUT TORTE

TORTE SHELL

1 16-ounce can pears
½ cup sour cream
½ teaspoon baking soda
1 package yellow cake mix
3 eggs
¾ cup chopped nuts
¾ cup sugar
1 tablespoon cinnamon

Pour varlet, pour the water,
The water steaming hot!
A spoonful for each man of us,
Another for the pot!

—Thomas Macaulay

Preheat oven to 350°. • Grease a large bundt pan. • Drain pears. • Reserve ⅔ cup syrup. • In blender, add pears, syrup, sour cream and baking soda. • Blend until smooth. • In a medium bowl, beat cake mix with pear purée until smooth. • Add eggs, one at a time, beating well after each addition. • In a separate bowl, mix nuts, sugar and cinnamon. • Shake half of the nut mixture into the bundt pan. • Pour in batter, adding second half of nut mix in two batches, layering the mix and batter. • Swirl through with a knife. • Bake for 45 to 50 minutes or until tester inserted in center comes out clean. • Cool for 30 minutes. • This can be frozen and filled later.

RUM FILLING

1 3¾-ounce package instant vanilla pudding
1½ cups milk
½ cup heavy cream, whipped
2 tablespoons dark rum

Beat pudding and milk until smooth. • Fold in whipped cream and rum. • Chill in airtight container until ready to use. • To serve, invert cake on dish or footed compote. • Mound filling in the center. Yield: 16 servings

PECAN RUM MERINGUES

Serve these in individual fluted paper cups.

2 egg whites, beaten foamy
¼ teaspoon salt
1 cup sugar
1 cup chopped nuts, chocolate chips, or ½ cup each
1 teaspoon vanilla extract or almond or rum flavoring

Preheat oven to 250°. • To beaten eggs, beat in salt. • Gradually add sugar while beating. • Continue until mixture holds its shape. • Carefully fold in nuts and flavoring. • Drop by teaspoonfuls onto a piece of foil. • Bake for 25 to 30 minutes or until firm, but not brown. • Remove at once from foil and cool on rack. Yield: 36

A WHITE LINEN TEA AT HOME

- Linens are relatively inexpensive antiques to buy. They are fun to collect and are best used rather than stored in a trunk where, ironically, they are more likely to become "tea-stained" by remaining idle than from actual use.
- Use the linens as backdrops for displaying your tea foods. (Keep hot teapots off the cloth.)
- Ask guests to bring examples of decorative white linen to your tea and have them explain what they know of the origins.

GOLDEN NUGGETS CANDIED GRAPEFRUIT PEEL

Hollowed out shells from 4 thick-skinned grapefruits

1 tablespoon salt

1 quart water

1 cup water

4 cups sugar

Remove membranes from grapefruit shells and cut each shell into 8 triangles. • (Be sure to wash outside of shells.) In a two-quart pot, combine peels, salt and 1 quart water, weighing peel down to keep submerged. • Soak for 24 hours. • Drain. • Cover well with fresh water. • Bring the pot to the stove, bringing the water to a boil. • Drain. • Repeat the fresh-water-and-boil process a total of 3 times to remove any bitterness. • Place peels, 1 cup water and sugar into a large pot and bring to a boil. Solution will be very thick. • Cook, stirring occasionally, until syrup begins to crystallize. • Then lay pieces out separately on aluminum foil to continue crystallization process. Let dry thoroughly. • May be kept indefinitely in plastic bags or jars. Yield: 32

CARAMEL CRUNCH CAKE

1¼ cups sifted cake flour

1½ cups sugar, divided

6 egg yolks

¼ cup water

1 tablespoon lemon juice

1 teaspoon vanilla extract

7 to 8 egg whites (1 cup)

1 teaspoon cream of tartar

1 teaspoon salt

Caramel Crunch Cake, Mint Chocolate Dipped Apricots, Pecan Rum Meringues, Golden Nuggets Candied Grapefruit Peel, and Pear Nut Torte

Preheat oven to 350°. • Mix together flour and ¾ cup sugar. • Add egg yolks, water, lemon juice and vanilla. • Beat until batter is smooth. • In a large bowl, beat egg whites, cream of tartar and salt, until foamy. • Gradually add remaining ¾ cup sugar and continue until meringue stands in firm peaks. • Fold batter gently into meringue with a spatula. Do not stir. • Gently spoon into an ungreased 9-inch tube pan. • Stir gently with a knife to level. • Bake for 50 to 55 minutes or until top springs back when touched. • Remove from pan by letting cake hang upside down over neck of a bottle until cool.

TOPPING

1½ cups sugar
¼ cup brewed coffee
¼ cup light corn syrup
3 teaspoons sifted baking soda

Combine sugar, coffee and corn syrup in a deep saucepan. • Cook to 310° (hard-crack stage). • Remove from heat and immediately stir in the baking soda, stirring vigorously until it thickens and rolls from the sides of the pan, but do not destroy the foam. • Quickly pour out onto an ungreased 9x9-inch shallow pan. • Do not spread or stir. • Cool, then knock out of the pan and crush into coarse crumbs.

FILLING

1 pint heavy cream
2 tablespoons sugar
2 teaspoons vanilla extract

Split cake into 4 layers. • Whip cream with sugar and vanilla, until stiff. • Spread half of the cream onto the layers. • Stack layers. • Frost top and sides with remaining filling. • Sprinkle crumbs over all and chill. Yield: 16 servings

MINT CHOCOLATE DIPPED APRICOTS

In top of double boiler, melt mint chocolate chips over medium heat. • Using tongs, dip dried apricots into chocolate to coat. • Place on waxed paper until ready to serve.

A Mystery Tea

Chilled Herbal Cooler

———

Pimiento Cheese Tea Sandwiches
with a Bite

———

Chicken Wings with Mark's Blueberry
BarbeClue Sauce

———

Double-Trouble Frosted Fudge Squares

———

Gingercake in a Blackened Skillet

———

Lemony Baked Apples with a Sting

———

Honeydew O'Shea's
Burgundy-Poached Pears

A MYSTERIOUS LETTER AR-rives at your door. It's your confirmation of a reservation for a mystery weekend at Dairy Hollow House. But what's this? Has the sleuthing begun? The letter asks, "Do you want to play a main, minor or silent character?" An answer is requested promptly so that the inn-keeper can decide who will play what role.

The excitement and sense of mystery has begun. Finally, mystery weekend arrives and so do you at the bright yellow door to Dairy Hollow House. You're on your guard from the moment you walk in—keeping your eyes open for anything that might later be referred to as a clue.

You are taken to your room where you discover your new role and have a few hours to get in character. The high tea starts at cocktail hour and all you know is that chicken will be served during Murder Most Fowl.

Whodunit? How? And why? All the classic questions are answered during any one of several original mysteries at Dairy Hollow House. As in many special events here, a high tea with heartier dishes is served on theme weekends.

"I love tea and have it whenever and wherever I can," quips Crescent Dragonwagon, who runs the inn with her husband, Ned Shank. She brings her knowledge of all the many teas she attended in England, New York, Chicago, and Atlanta to their inn. But she replaces a formal sit-down tea with a far more casual affair when it comes to mystery weekends.

Although Ned and Crescent hold events such as fireside weekends where guests partake in candlelight dinner, champagne, hot-tub baths and massages; and summer herb week-ends, "Nothing opened the 'tea-

Ned Shank notices that murder is afoot, but Crescent Dragonwagon is too engrossed in the pleasures of tea to be daunted by the ruckus.

opportunity field' quite so widely as the introduction of our mysteries," says Crescent. Tea and mysteries do go together. Even Agatha Christie's Miss Marple is constantly stopping for a cup of tea and sweet cake.

Tucked into a quiet mountain road, this award-winning inn provides a perfect setting for a mystery. The restored Ozark farmhouse, which serves regional cuisine Ned and Crescent call Nouveau 'Zarks, is off in a country setting overlooking the town.

Guests in disguise begin arriving—there's The Rev. Billy-Joe Bob Clayton as well as Mary-Jo Louise Umbecker, a spinster from Atlanta. Waiting in the wings is Mayor Ruth Ann Butter-

nut and the esteemed Wing Frysome and his family. Everyone finds out rather quickly that "Frysome's propensity for prosperity was perfected in poultry production." But as the food is served and the tea poured, someone queries, "But how long can Frysome remain cock of the walk?"

The answer comes rather quickly as Frysome's body is discovered in a hallway. "He's been fried," one guest remarks. Clues pointing to the killer are revealed to the guests through conversation and props as the tea continues. Guests soon begin making accusations as to who murdered the chicken à la king.

Crescent writes the whodunits for

> ### A MYSTERY TEA AT HOME
>
> - A high tea, because it is served in courses and includes heavier fare, is an ideal backdrop for a mystery at home. The mysteries take a while to solve and clues can be sprinkled throughout as the foods are served.
> - Tea should be the number one beverage so that everyone will be able to remain alert, calm and maintain a clear head.
> - When you invite guests and tell them what role they will play, ask them to dress in costume.

the inn, with the same pen she uses to write children's books. Another of her popular mysteries at the inn is The Fine Art of Murder. It's timed to coincide with the Eureka Springs May Fine Arts Festival. When local artist Jaybo Wolfe is named "Most Influential Artist of the Decade" by a popular magazine, jealousies trigger seething gossip. The mystery starts Saturday at the inn but the clues unwind at the galleries and studios of Eureka Springs. Part of the day involves a Saturday afternoon informal iced tea party with cookies that are baked in the shape of an artist's palette and then drizzled with colorful icings to resemble paint.

As a guest of Dairy Hollow House, you may return home hoping to hold your own mystery for friends. If you won't be writing the mystery, there may be a thespian group in your area that hosts mysteries with your guests participating. And there are boxed mysteries you can buy, including a series called, *How to Host a Murder,* where murders take place in a variety of settings including a yacht and a train. However, if it's a murder at an inn you're looking to solve, you need to make your way to Ned and Crescent's fast. You may even unravel the mystery behind Crescent Dragonwagon's quite colorful name.

Dairy Hollow House
515 Spring Street
Eureka Springs, AR 72632
Phone: **(501) 253-7444**
Rooms: **5**
Tea-Time: **On special occasions for overnight and outside guests**

CHILLED HERBAL COOLER

This is one of Dairy Hollow House's five most-requested recipes, perfect for sipping while hunting for mysterious clues.

8 (Celestial Seasonings) Red Zinger tea bags
1 quart boiling water
1 12-ounce can frozen apple juice concentrate
4½ cups cold water
1 orange, sliced
½ lemon, sliced
Sprigs of mint or honeysuckle

Stir a tablespoon of maple syrup into brewed tea and top with a scoop of butter pecan ice cream.

Steep tea in boiling water in glass container. • Cool to lukewarm. • Remove tea bags, squeezing to get out the last bit of flavor. • Add apple juice concentrate, cold water and fruits. • Chill thoroughly. • Serve in ice-filled glasses garnished with mint sprigs. Yield: 8 to 10 servings

PIMIENTO CHEESE TEA SANDWICHES WITH A BITE

Crescent says the colonel, a character who appears in many of the inn's mysteries, believes that the British are the greatest people on earth. But after being on campaign in India for so long, British cuisine became a trifle bland. That's why he enjoys this recipe with a kick when in the midst of a mystery.

3 ounces cream cheese, at room temperature
3 tablespoons mayonnaise
1 teaspoon Worcestershire or Pickapepper sauce
3 cloves fresh garlic
8 drops Tabasco
1 6-ounce jar pimientos, liquid drained and set aside
1 tablespoon chopped parsley
12 ounces grated cheddar cheese
½ cup coarsely chopped pecans
5 thin slices fresh tomato
Cress or clover sprouts
10 thin slices whole-wheat bread, crusts removed

In bowl of food processor, combine cream cheese, mayonnaise, Worcestershire, garlic, Tabasco and pimiento liquid. • Add parsley, pulsing a few more times. • Turn mixture into a large mixing bowl. • Stir in pimientos, cheddar cheese and pecans. • Chill for 6 hours. • To assemble, place tomato and a handful of sprouts on 5 slices of bread. • Spread pimiento mixture on remaining half. • Put tops and bottoms together. • Cut each sandwich into 4 triangles. Yield: 20

Honeydew O'Shea's Burgundy-Poached Pears, Lemony Baked Apples with a Sting, and Gingercake in the skillet may look innocent, but. . . .

CHICKEN WINGS WITH MARK'S BLUEBERRY BARBECLUE SAUCE

"These are wings to die for," says Dairy Hollow House.

CHICKEN

½ pound chicken wings
2 tablespoons vegetable oil

In glass dish, marinate chicken in oil and 1 cup sauce (recipe follows) overnight in refrigerator. • Next day, preheat oven to 350°. • Place chicken wings and ½ pint of the blueberry sauce into a well-greased, non-aluminum baking dish for about 30 minutes or till done. • Serve from a chafing dish.

SAUCE

4 pounds fresh blueberries
2 cups chopped onion
4 cups red wine
1 bulb garlic, skin removed, separated into cloves
1 medium lemon, peel on, seeded and quartered lengthwise
1 cup chopped fresh tomatoes
1 cup molasses
1 cup brown sugar
2 tablespoons Worcestershire or Pickapepper sauce
2 tablespoons prepared mustard
½ cup red wine vinegar
2 teaspoons salt
2 teaspoons coarsely ground black pepper
1 teaspoon cayenne

In a large stainless steel 6-quart pot, combine blueberries, onion, wine, garlic and lemon. •

Bring to a boil, then turn down to simmer. • Cook over medium heat, stirring often, for about 45 minutes. It will start to thicken. • Remove from heat. • Remove lemon and purée the mixture in batches. • Return to pot. • Add remaining ingredients. • Bring to a boil, then turn down to simmer. • Stir often. • Continue to simmer until quite thick, about 1 hour. • Store extra sauce in sterile glass canning jars. Yield: 5 to 6 pints

DOUBLE-TROUBLE FROSTED FUDGE SQUARES

There should be something dark and seductive in every mystery. These iced brownies are both. The clue to their powerful taste is in the selection of the chocolate.

8 ounces best-quality, unsweetened chocolate
2 sticks butter
5 eggs
3 cups sugar
2 teaspoons vanilla extract
½ teaspoon salt
1½ cups unbleached white all-purpose flour
¾ cup chopped walnuts

Preheat oven to 375°. • In small saucepan, melt chocolate and butter. • Set aside to cool. • Meanwhile, in bowl of electric mixer, beat together eggs, sugar, vanilla and salt. • Beat 8 minutes, until mixture is light and expanded in volume. • Beat in chocolate mixture, then hand-stir in flour and nuts. • Pour batter into a well-greased 9x13-inch pan. • Bake for 30 to 35 minutes or until tester inserted in center comes out clean. • Do not overbake. • Cool to room temperature.

FROSTING

12 ounces best-quality, semi-sweet chocolate morsels
1 cup sour cream or crème fraîche
1 teaspoon vanilla extract
Unbroken walnut halves

Melt chocolate morsels in separate pan over double boiler filled with very hot water. • As soon as chocolate is smooth and melted, remove from heat and stir in sour cream and vanilla. It will thicken as it cools. • Spread frosting on cooled brownies. • Cut into 1¼-inch squares and press half a walnut on top of each one. Yield: 40

The scene of the crime—Dairy Hollow House

GINGERCAKE IN A BLACKENED SKILLET

Caped in black iron, this comes out of the oven looking sinister. But the innkeepers claim, "This is the best gingerbread known to man or woman, lord or commoner."

½ cup port
½ cup raisins
1½ cups unbleached white all-purpose flour
1 cup sugar
2 teaspoons ginger
1 teaspoon cinnamon
½ cup shortening
½ cup chopped English walnuts
¾ cup buttermilk
1 teaspoon baking soda
½ teaspoon salt
1 egg, beaten
3 tablespoons dark molasses
Whipped cream (optional)

Preheat oven to 350°. • In small saucepan over medium-high heat, bring port to a boil. • Drop in raisins. • Let simmer 1 minute. • Remove from heat, allowing raisins to soak in port. • In a large bowl, combine flour, sugar, ginger and cinnamon. • Cut in shortening until mixture is crumbly. • Reserve ¼ cup of this mixture; adding walnuts to it. • Set aside.

Drain port into a 2-cup measure, reserving the raisins in another bowl. • Add the buttermilk to the port, to equal 1 cup of liquid, total. • Stir baking soda and salt into buttermilk-port mixture until dissolved. • Combine the larger portion of the flour/butter mixture (the part without the nuts) with the egg, molasses and port mixture. • Stir till well-combined. (It will be a bit lumpy). • Add raisins. • Pour batter into a well-greased 8- or 9-inch iron skillet. • Sprinkle the reserved flour/nut mixture over top. • Bake for 30 minutes. • Serve warm, plain or with whipped cream. • Cut like a pie. Yield: 12 to 16 tea-time-size slices

LEMONY BAKED APPLES WITH A STING

1 baking apple per person

1 teaspoon brown sugar

1 teaspoon cinnamon

1 butter pat

3 whole cloves

Lemon twist

Water or apple juice

1/2 teaspoon vanilla extract

Heavy cream

Preheat oven to 350°. • Core each apple. • Place in greased baking dish. • Sprinkle with sugar and cinnamon. • Dot with butter. • Place 3 cloves inside each apple and a twist of lemon in the center. • In base of baking dish, place ½-inch water or apple juice with ½ teaspoon vanilla. • Bake for 1 hour or until apples are soft but not mushy. • Serve with unwhipped, heavy cream. Yield: 1 apple

HONEYDEW O'SHEA'S BURGUNDY-POACHED PEARS

1½ cups Burgundy

1½ cups frozen apple juice concentrate, thawed

1 3-inch cinnamon stick

6 to 8 pears, peeled and halved lengthwise, seeds and core removed

Fresh mint leaves, for garnish

Combine wine, apple juice concentrate and cinnamon stick in a 10- or 12-inch skillet. • Bring to a boil, then turn down to simmer. • Place half of the pears, cut-side down, in the simmering syrup and cook for 5 to 7 minutes. • Gently turn each pear over, using a slotted spoon, and cook 5 to 7 minutes longer. • Remove from liquid and repeat with remainder of the pears. • Turn heat up under poaching liquid and reduce until just ½ cup or so of thick syrup remains. • To serve, spoon 1 tablespoon of syrup on the plate. Place 1 or 2 pear halves atop it. • For a more formal presentation, slice pear thinly and fan slices out in the syrup. • Garnish with mint. Yield: 12 to 16 servings

A Civil War Tea

Civil War Citrus Tea

Parsnip Chips

Green Pepper Dip

Civil War Peanut Brittle

General Doubleday's Toasted Pound Cake

Upside-Down Apple and Nut Cake

AS I CODDLED MY TEACUP and mused out The Doubleday Inn's parlor window beyond the stone tributes to battalions of unknown heroes, it wasn't hard to imagine how tea had rendered stalwart generals the common ground to let down their guard. Tea, with its power to heal the deepest wounds and bridge the widest rifts, proved a meaningful beverage during the Civil War. This most conciliatory of all drinks mediated a startling show of friendship and civility one warm day a year before this terrible war ended. I'm still entranced by the story of The Silver Tea Set:

"The American Civil War was the bloodiest war in our nation's history. Brother fought brother until 620,000 men were dead in just four years. However, as bloody as it was, Sir Winston Churchill said it was the last war fought by gentlemen." So begins the story of The Silver Tea Set as Gettysburg Battlefield guide Gary Kross launches into one of the many Civil War stories he recounts two times each week for captivated guests at the Doubleday Inn.

"In the summer of 1864, Confederate Major General George Pickett and his wife announced the birth of a baby girl," explains Kross. "Upon hearing the news, Union generals— all fellow graduates of West Point (as was Pickett)—did, under a flag of truce, cross into the Confederate lines, carrying a gift of a silver tea set for the general and his wife. After sharing a spot of tea, friendly congratulations and small talk, the Union generals departed, crossed back into their own lines and began an artillery bombardment of the Confederate fortifications."

The Doubleday Inn is along the route of a drive-by tour of the Gettysburg Battlefield and is one of America's few inns located on an historic battlefield. Only 75 yards from the inn, nearly 1,400 Confederate soldiers, under the command of Georgia General Alfred Iverson, were caught by surprise on July 1, 1863, killed, and buried in a mass grave. Union troops had concealed themselves behind a stone wall—that still remains in front of the inn—when they attacked. Gary Kross explains what happened afterward:

"The following year, the grave site was easily visible by green grass more lush than anywhere else and a climatic condition of 'blue fog,' hovering above. Farmhands refused to work the fields or go near the pits at dark. Many claimed, and some still do, that they've heard moanings from the pits—even though the bodies were re-interred to Raleigh, North Carolina in 1871."

While such stories are continually brought up at The Doubleday Inn, the bed & breakfast is as cheerful as can be. Innkeepers Joan and Sal Chandon and Joan's mother, Olga Krossick, see to that. The inn itself was built as a private home in the early 1900s and turned into an inn by the Chandons. Rooms are cheerfully decorated and filled with antiques and many homespun linens by Olga. Breakfasts often include regiments of blue-and-gray pancakes.

Innkeeper Joan Chandon dons period gloves to pour the tea.

The Doubleday displays Sal's collection of Civil War memorabilia. Scattered about the inn are a few daguerreotypes of General Abner Doubleday (purported originator of baseball and commander of Union troops here) for whom the inn was named. On special occasions, the innkeepers even wear period costumes.

The Doubleday Inn
104 Doubleday Avenue
Gettysburg Battlefield, PA 17325
Phone: **(717) 334-9119**
Rooms: **9**
Tea-Time: **4:00–6:00 P.M. daily for inn guests**

Tea-time overlooking the Gettysburg Battlefield

CIVIL WAR CITRUS TEA

6 tea bags
6 cups boiling water
2 tablespoons honey
2 cinnamon sticks
2 vanilla beans
1½ cups orange juice
1½ cups pineapple juice
¼ cup sugar
¼ cup brown sugar
1 tablespoon whole allspice
1 tablespoon whole cloves
Orange slices

Steep tea bags in boiling water for 5 minutes. • Remove. • Add remaining ingredients, except orange slices. • Warm in a crock pot for 2 to 3 hours. • Serve hot with orange slices as garnish. Yield: 10 cups

PARSNIP CHIPS
This is an invention of The Doubleday that happened when Joan wanted to make use of leftover parsnips. • Slice parsnips thin. • Deep fry. • Drain and sprinkle with garlic salt and oregano to taste.

A CIVIL WAR TEA AT HOME

- Use blue-and-gray colored linens and napkins.
- Get a copy of a Civil War battlefield map and enlarge it to the size of placemats for the table.

GREEN PEPPER DIP

Aside from the flavorful taste of this dip, the inn serves it in a large green pepper footed with dill and parsley.

1 cup sour cream, at room temperature
8 ounces cream cheese
¼ cup chopped dill
¼ cup chopped parsley
1 teaspoon garlic salt
½ teaspoon black pepper
1 small package chopped spinach, drained well
1 large green pepper
Dill and parsley

Blend sour cream, cream cheese, dill, parsley, garlic salt and black pepper. • Add spinach and mix well. • Chill 2 hours. • Transfer mixture into a large hollowed-out green pepper. • Arrange dill or parsley and lay fresh vegetables on top. • *Hint: When serving dips, be sure to cut vegetables in bite-sized pieces so there is no returning to the dip with a partially eaten vegetable. Otherwise, provide a spreading knife.* Yield: 2 cups

Tea was a favorite drink of Confederate officers, especially Robert E. Lee and his staff member Arthur J. L. Fremantle. Fremantle traveled with Lee and wouldn't go anywhere without his tea cozy. Lee's headquarters at Gettysburg was one-half mile south of The Doubleday Inn property. Tea was served there.
Gary M. Kross

Civil War memorabilia abounds at The Doubleday Inn.

CIVIL WAR PEANUT BRITTLE

The abundance of sugar and peanuts made this a famous sweet and tea-time treat during Civil War days.

1 cup sugar
2 tablespoons butter
¾ cup peanuts

In medium skillet, mix together sugar and butter until the mixture begins to thicken and turns dark tan. • Drop a teaspoon of the mixture into cold water. • When it hardens it is done. • Remove from heat. • Immediately mix in peanuts. • Let cool. • Break apart to serve. Yield: 1 large candy bar

GENERAL DOUBLEDAY'S TOASTED POUND CAKE

1 stick butter
1 stick margarine
1 cup shortening
2 cups sugar
6 eggs

2 cups all-purpose flour

1 tablespoon almond extract

Preheat oven to 325°. • Cream together butter, margarine and shortening with sugar until smooth. • Alternately add eggs and flour. Beat well while adding almond extract. • Pour into a greased and floured 16-inch-long loaf pan. • Bake for 1½ hours or until tester inserted in center comes out clean. • Let cake cool. • Before serving, slice into bread-sized pieces and toast. • Serve with preserves or apple butter. Yield: 14 to 18 slices

Most of the picking of tea is done by women and is an extremely labor-intensive process. A good gatherer can pinch about 70 pounds of green tea leaves per day. This makes about 18 pounds of tea.

UPSIDE-DOWN APPLE AND NUT CAKE

The Doubleday often makes this in a bundt pan.

6 large apples, cut into eighths

1 teaspoon cinnamon

2 eggs

½ cup chopped nuts

¾ cup sugar

1 cup all-purpose flour

½ cup melted shortening

½ teaspoon lemon juice

1 teaspoon vanilla extract

Cinnamon

Preheat oven to 375°. • Place apples in a greased pie plate and cover with cinnamon. • In a bowl, mix together eggs, nuts, sugar, flour, shortening, lemon juice and vanilla. • Pour mixture over the apples. • Sprinkle with additional cinnamon. • Bake for 45 minutes or until browned. Yield: 12 to 14 servings

A Gone With The Wind Tea

Rhett's Chocolate Pecan Bars

———

Miss Melanie's Chocolate Strawberries

———

Ashley's Almond-Filled Cookie Cake

———

Red Petticoat Swiss Jellyroll

———

Katie's Kahlúa Fudge

———

*Belle Watling's Midnight
Chocolate Cake*

———

Twelve Oaks Almond Tuiles

A HOSTESS IN AN ANTE-bellum gown pours you a cup of tea. As you wander around the inn and into Miss Pittypat's Parlor, a scene from another parlor in another time, comes to mind. There's Scarlett O'Hara, learning of Ashley's intent to marry Melanie. She smashes a china bowl, barely missing the head of Rhett Butler, sleeping out of sight on the other side of a sofa. He slowly rises and calmly tells Scarlett she's not a lady. Scarlett counters with stinging retorts and scurries up a staircase, "her heart hammering so hard from anger, insult and exertion that it seemed about to burst through her basque. . . . Mammy's lacings were too tight, and she thought she would faint . . . She had wished she carried smelling salts, like the other girls, but she . . . always felt so proud of not feeling giddy. She simply could not let herself faint now."

Only the energy from the tea in your cup keeps you from using the inn's own Victorian fainting couch to cushion the fluster brought on by the beauty and intrigue of Tara: A Country Inn.

Built in 1854, the same era as its fictional counterpart, Tara: A Country Inn was once the private home of Charles Koonce, a senator who made his fortune in coal and real estate. Innkeepers Donna and Jim Winner, passionate *Gone With The Wind* historians, scoured the South for their own Tara, but found it in the North. In 1986, after two years of restoration, they created Tara and opened the inn with the Winners' personal collection of fine antiques. A prized acquisition that's on display is the robe that actress Vivien Leigh wore during the honeymoon scene in the movie version.

Each room at Tara bears a name from the romantic epic. Ashley's dining room is for gourmet eating. It reminds one of how Scarlett satisfied her hunger in style with Rhett in New Orleans, after living on goobers and dried peas when her Tara was ravaged. Margaret Mitchell wrote, "Scarlett felt that she could never eat enough of these rich dishes. . . . Her appetite never dulled . . . and [she] ordered another pastry, thick with chocolate and stuffed with meringue."

Casual fare is served at the inn's Stonewall's Tavern, once used to hide slaves escaping to free states. A boarded-up, hidden staircase leads from Miss Pittypat's Parlor to the tavern. Another dining room is set up as Mammy's Quarters with an authentic rope bed. Family-style meals are served in the Old South dining room, which is furnished with rare rosewood tables. The inn also has an exercise room, pool, wine cellar and conference rooms. Guest rooms have names such as Fiddle Dee Dee, Chickamauga, and Carpetbaggers.

As you put down your empty teacup, you reflect on the Tara that Donna and Jim have "written"—find-

ing it hard to separate the fictional from the real. The Winners—true to their name—have won you over by making you feel fanciful. The memory of your visit and the time you took for tea there, lingers on as does the classic story itself. When you need to escape the stress of your modern world, you'll find the answer—and the place—in the words of Scarlett O'Hara: "I'll think of it all tomorrow, at Tara. I can stand it then."

Tea! Thou soft, thou sober, sage and venerable liquid . . . to whose glorious insipidity, I owe the happiest moments of my life, let me fall prostrate.

—Colley Cibber, *The Lady's Last Stake*, 1708

Tara: A Country Inn
3665 Valley View Road
Clark, PA 16113
Phone: **(412) 962-3535**
Rooms: **27**
Tea-Time: **4:00 P.M. daily for inn guests and drop-ins**

Red Petticoat Swiss Jellyroll, plain and stuffed tuiles, midnight and almond cookie cakes

RHETT'S CHOCOLATE PECAN BARS

1 cup firmly packed light brown sugar
2 sticks butter, softened
1 egg yolk
1 teaspoon vanilla extract
2 cups all-purpose flour
¼ teaspoon salt
1¾ cups semi-sweet chocolate chunks
½ cup coarsely chopped pecans

Preheat oven to 350°. • Mix together sugar, butter, egg yolk, vanilla, flour and salt. • Spread into a greased 13x9-inch pan. • Bake for 30 minutes. • Remove from oven. • Sprinkle chocolate over top, allowing it to melt (about 10 minutes). Spread the melted chocolate evenly with a spatula. • Sprinkle nuts over top. • Cut bars into 1½-inch squares, then cut on the diagonal to form triangles. Yield: 48

A GONE WITH THE WIND TEA AT HOME

- Greet guests in an antebellum dress.
- Offer ladies a colorful paper fan and the gentlemen, a cigar upon arrival.
- Make up trivia cards with questions from Margaret Mitchell's novel and have a game after the tea is served.
- End tea-time with a sing-along of Southern melodies such as "Old Folks at Home" (Swanee River) or "Summertime" (from *Porgy and Bess*).

MISS MELANIE'S CHOCOLATE STRAWBERRIES

8 ounces semi-sweet chocolate chips
Vegetable shortening
24 plump strawberries

Melt chocolate and add a small amount of shortening to make the mixture smooth. • Dip the strawberries into the chocolate. • Set on parchment or waxed paper to cool. Yield: 24

ASHLEY'S ALMOND-FILLED COOKIE CAKE

CRUST

2⅔ cups all-purpose flour
1⅓ cups sugar
1⅓ cups unsalted butter
1 teaspoon salt
1 egg

Preheat oven to 350°. • Grease a 10-inch springform pan. • In large bowl of electric mixer, blend all ingredients at low speed until dough forms. • Divide dough in half, rolling out one piece to fit a 10-inch pie pan. • Place rolled crust in bottom of pan.

FILLING

1 cup finely chopped almonds
½ cup sugar
1 teaspoon grated lemon peel
1 egg, slightly beaten
Whole almonds
Confectioners' sugar

In small bowl, combine all ingredients, except whole almonds and confectioners' sugar. • Spread over crust to within ½ inch of the sides of the pan. • Press remaining dough between waxed paper to form a 10-inch circle. • Remove paper. • Press dough into place over the filling. • Garnish with whole almonds. • Bake for 55 minutes or until light golden brown. • Cool for 15 minutes, remove from pan and sprinkle with confectioners' sugar. Yield: 14 slices

RED PETTICOAT SWISS JELLYROLL

The raspberry filling gives this cake its naughty name.

¾ cup all-purpose flour
½ teaspoon baking powder
3 eggs
1 cup superfine sugar, divided
1 tablespoon water
¼ cup raspberry jam

Preheat oven to 400°. • Grease a 13x9-inch pan. • In a small bowl, sift together flour and baking powder. • In a large bowl, using wire whisk, beat together eggs and ½ cup sugar until thick and creamy. • Fold in dry ingredients, then stir in water. • Pour batter into pan. • Bake for 10 minutes or until top springs back when lightly touched. • Lay out a sheet of waxed paper and sprinkle it with remaining sugar. • As soon as cake is done, turn it onto paper. • Trim off crusty edges with sharp knife. • Spread cake with jam. • Roll up firmly from short end. • Cool on wire rack. Yield: 8 to 10 slices

A tea-time fantasy at Tara

KATIE'S KAHLÚA FUDGE

1⅓ cups sugar

1 7-ounce jar marshmallow creme

⅔ cup evaporated milk

½ stick butter

¼ cup Kahlúa liqueur

¼ teaspoon salt

2 cups semi-sweet chocolate pieces

1 cup milk chocolate pieces

⅔ cup chopped pecans

1 teaspoon vanilla extract

Line an 8-inch square baking pan with foil. • In a 2-quart saucepan, combine the sugar, marshmallow cream, milk, butter, Kahlúa and salt. • Bring to a rapid boil, stirring constantly. • Remove from heat. • Add all chocolate. • Stir until melted. • Add nuts and vanilla. • Pour into pan. • Chill until firm. • Cut into 1-inch squares. Yield: 64 pieces

BELLE WATLING'S MIDNIGHT CHOCOLATE CAKE

CAKE

2 cups cake flour

1¾ cups sugar

¾ cup unsweetened cocoa

1¼ teaspoons baking soda

½ teaspoon baking powder

1 teaspoon salt

1¼ cups milk

¾ cup shortening

3 large eggs

1 teaspoon vanilla extract

Preheat oven to 350°. • In large bowl of electric mixer, combine (with fork) flour, sugar, cocoa, baking soda, baking powder and salt. Add milk, shortening, eggs and vanilla. • Turn mixer on at high speed and blend all ingredients until smooth. • Pour into 2 greased 9-inch round cake pans. • Bake for 30 minutes or until tester inserted in center comes out clean. • Allow cake to cool, then slice each cake into 2 layers, making a total of 4 layers. • Spread the filling between the layers. • Assemble the cake.

FILLING

2 large eggs, separated, at room temperature

1½ cups confectioners' sugar, divided

⅓ cup water

2 sticks butter, softened

2 squares unsweetened chocolate, melted

1 teaspoon vanilla extract

In small bowl of electric mixer, beat egg whites at high speed until peaks form. • Gradually sprinkle in ¼ cup confectioners' sugar, beating until sugar is dissolved and whites stand in stiff peaks. Do not scrape bowl during beating. • In separate large bowl at medium speed, mix remaining sugar with egg yolks, water, butter, melted chocolate and vanilla. • Fold in egg white mixture, using rubber spatula.

FROSTING

12 ounces (2 cups) semi-sweet chocolate chips
¼ cup shortening
3 cups confectioners' sugar
½ cup milk

In double boiler over hot, not boiling, water melt chocolate pieces with shortening. • Stir in sugar and milk. • Remove from heat. • Beat with spoon until smooth. • Frost sides and top of cake. • Decorate cake with extra frosting and chocolate shavings, if desired. Yield: 14 slices

TWELVE OAKS ALMOND TUILES

These wafer-like, crusty cookies can also be shells for mousse or fruit. The trick is to mold the wafer while still warm.

½ cup confectioners' sugar
¾ cup sifted all-purpose flour
⅛ teaspoon salt
2 eggs
1 teaspoon vanilla extract
2 tablespoons butter, melted
¾ cup slivered almonds

Preheat oven to 475°. • Whisk together sugar, flour, salt, eggs and vanilla. • Blend in butter and almonds. • Using a teaspoon, place small quantities of the mixture about 3 inches apart on a greased baking sheet. • Spread dough out slightly with the back of a fork which has been dipped in cold water. • Bake for 4 minutes or until tuiles are golden brown on the outside and white on the inside (watch closely). • Remove from oven and leave sitting on baking sheet, on the opened oven door so that tuiles remain warm. • Work quickly. • Mold each tuile around a rolling pin while still warm, or mold into other desired shape. Yield: 8 to 12

A Scottish Tea

Kipper Pâté Sandwiches

Mocha Shortbread Sticks

*Millionaire's Caramel and
Chocolate Shortbread*

Rock Cakes

Dundee Cake

Stuffed Brandy Snaps

FLOWERS EMBRACE YOUR stroll along the cobble footpath to the Corner House gardens where tea is served in summertime. Patches of lavender and scapes of roses eclipse the scent of raspberry tea in your china cup. In winter, Lapsang Souchon or a Darjeeling specially blended in London to complement Corner House water, is served in the inn's sitting rooms.

When Corner House serves a Scottish tea, you feel as though you are a Cameron or a Dunne, or certainly a Knox-Johnson. Innkeepers Sandy and John Knox-Johnson frequently offer a potpourri of tastes from Scotland. It's their way of sharing John's heritage. John was born in England and raised in Scotland. His mother was Scottish and his father was a British high commissioner in East Africa. John usually talks about his homeland during tea-time.

When on Nantucket, one feels as though he or she is walking through a photo album. Lighthouses and craggy cliffs appear as one strolls the bluffs. The skyline meets sandy roads and Nantucket's own moors. I love the picket fences, the window boxes bursting with flowers, and the architecture of the old sea captains' houses.

Surrounded by Colonial American antiques in this 1790 home, you almost forget about Scottish tea-time until you bite into Sandy's shortbread. It's then that you begin to see baronial houses and castles, marshy moors kissed by crystal beads after a warm soft rain, seas of bright purple heather, misty lochs with anchored rowboats bobbing by wind-blown dunes, and you hear the tunes of "Annie Laurie" and "The Braes of Yarrow." Yes, tea-time can take you places you've never been before.

Corner House Inn
49 Centre Street
Nantucket, MA 02554
Phone: **(508) 228-1530**
Rooms: **12**
Tea-Time: **4:00–6:00 P.M. daily for inn guests**

A SCOTTISH TEA AT HOME

- Sew napkin rings from tartan fabric and make cotton plaid doilies as the stage for hills of shortbread.
- Play Scottish bagpipe tunes on a stereo.
- Set out dominoes, the favorite game in Scottish pubs.

KIPPER PÂTÉ SANDWICHES

This is a traditional Scottish high tea dish from the Midlands. Kippers and other foods (often potted or preserved) arrived on the tea table in the 1800s. You can buy kippers in supermarkets or substitute with the less tasty haddock or mackerel.

2 boned kippers (about 1½ pounds)
1 tablespoon heavy cream
1 stick butter, softened
1 tablespoon fresh lemon juice
⅛ teaspoon cayenne pepper
¼ teaspoon ground mace
30 slices thin whole-wheat bread

Place kippers head down in a jug. • Pour boiling water to cover all but the tails. • Set aside for 5 minutes. • Pour off the water and remove skin. Set aside to cool. • Pound kippers till smooth or pulse in food processor. • Blend in cream, butter and lemon juice; add pepper and mace. • Store in a jar in refrigerator until ready to use. • Spread pâté on all bread slices. • Assemble sandwiches. • Remove crusts. • Cut as for finger sandwiches—three rectangles per sandwich. Yield: 45

Tartan plaids nobly flatter Kipper Pâté Sandwiches, Dundee Cake, Millionaire's Shortbread, Rock Cakes with strawberries, and Mocha Shortbread in an antique biscuit box.

MOCHA SHORTBREAD STICKS

Sandy brought this back from a Scottish friend in Edinburgh.

2 sticks butter, at room temperature
⅓ cup confectioners' sugar
2 teaspoons instant coffee powder
2 teaspoons hot water
1 tablespoon cocoa powder
1 cup all-purpose flour
1 cup corn flour
Confectioners' sugar

Preheat oven to 375°. • Cream together butter and confectioners' sugar. • Divide mixture into 2 bowls. • Dissolve coffee powder in hot water. Cool. Add to 1 of the bowls. • Add sifted cocoa to the other bowl and mix well. • Sift the flours together, adding half to each mixture. • Mix well.

Using pastry bag fitted with large star tube, spoon coffee mixture to one side of the bag. Spoon chocolate mixture into same bag, keeping mixture to other side of the bag, giving the shortbread a two-toned appearance. • Pipe onto 2 greased cookie sheets in 2-inch lengths. • Bake 15 minutes or until firm to the touch. • Cool slightly on cookie sheets—then place on wire rack to cool completely. • Dust with confectioners' sugar. Yield: 60

Scones originated in Scotland, where the word is pronounced "scaun." The name originally came from a parish in Perthshire which was the site of the historic abbey and palace where the kings of Scotland were crowned on the Stone of Scone (Destiny.) Tradition has it that this stone was Jacob's pillow. The name is the only thing that is like a stone, however, for scones are light as a feather and don't stay around long enough to gather any moss.

Alice Upham Smith
Woman's Day Encyclopedia of Cookery

MILLIONAIRE'S CARAMEL AND CHOCOLATE SHORTBREAD

The Scots prefer this rich recipe be made with ground rice, resulting in a coarser biscuit. However, rice flour is often substituted because it offers a finer texture. Another hint: Corner House has been known to use a good quality caramel sauce and chocolate topping in a pinch, instead of making their own.

4 sticks butter, at room temperature
4 tablespoons ground rice or rice flour
1/2 cup confectioners' sugar
4 cups all-purpose flour

Preheat oven to 325°. • Mix butter into ground rice, sugar and flour. • Press ingredients together firmly. • Turn onto lightly floured surface. • Knead until smooth. • Press mixture into an 11x18-inch jellyroll pan. • Make very deep cut marks for 48, 2-inch squares. • Prick dough all over top with a fork. • Bake for 35 minutes. • Cut again but not fully through. • Set aside for 10 minutes; turn onto wire rack and cool. • Turn back into jellyroll pan to spread on a layer of caramel and then chocolate.

CARAMEL FILLING

2 cups sugar
2/3 cup water

Add sugar to a small saucepan. • Add enough water (about 2/3 cup) just to cover. • Place a tight-fitting lid on top. • Bring sugar and water to a simmer. • Swirl pan by handle to be sure sugar is completely dissolved and liquid is perfectly clear. • Cover pan tightly again and boil syrup over fairly high heat until bubbles are thick (keep checking but do not stir) and it reaches a soft-ball stage (240°). • Remove from stove. • Set base of pan into cold water for a few seconds or until thick enough to spread on top of cooled shortbread.

CHOCOLATE TOPPING

8 semi-sweet chocolate squares
1 cup heavy cream
1 tablespoon rum

Melt chocolate slowly in cream. Bring to a boil, then cool, stirring occasionally. • When it begins to thicken, beat until fluffy and thick. • Spread on top of caramel layer before it sets. • Cut out squares as marked. Yield: 48

Damask napkins surround Rock Cakes, a sandwich, and shortbread sticks. A whalebone diorama tops the mantel.

*If a recipe calls for superfine sugar and you don't
have any handy, pulse granulated sugar
in a food processor.*

Hannah Marie Country Inn

ROCK CAKES

These are Scottish biscuit-like cakes you may
serve with butter or cream and jam or
preserves.

2 cups all-purpose flour
1/8 teaspoon salt
2 teaspoons baking powder
1/2 stick butter
1/4 cup shortening
1/4 cup golden raisins
1/4 cup currants
2/3 cup firmly packed light brown sugar
Grated peel of 1 lemon
1 large egg
1 to 2 tablespoons milk

Preheat oven to 400°. • Over a large bowl,
sift together flour, salt and baking powder. •
Cut in butter and shortening until mixture
resembles coarse crumbs. • Stir in raisins and
currants, sugar and lemon peel. • Beat egg
with 1 tablespoon milk. • Using fork, stir egg
mixture into dry ingredients, adding a bit
more milk if necessary to give a stiff
dough. • Mixture should just hold together. • Use 2 forks to place mixture into 12
small heaps on 2 greased cookie sheets. •
Bake for 15 minutes or until light golden
brown. • Cool on wire rack. Yield: 12

DUNDEE CAKE

This is a traditional Scottish fruit cake. The
city of Dundee in Scotland is known for its
fruit gardens. Make this 1 week before
serving time or earlier to release its fullest
flavor.

2 cups all-purpose flour
1 1/2 teaspoons baking powder
1 1/2 sticks butter, at room temperature
3/4 cup sugar
3 large eggs
2 1/2 cups mixed dried fruit (such as light and dark raisins, apricots, currants)
1/2 cup chopped mixed candied peel
1/3 cup small glacé cherries
Grated peel of 1 lemon
1 tablespoon brandy
1/2 cup whole almonds

Preheat oven to 325°. • Sift together flour
and baking powder. • In large bowl, cream
butter and sugar until light and fluffy. • Beat
eggs into mixture, one at a time. • Fold in
flour mixture until evenly combined. • Fold
in dried fruit, candied peel, cherries and
lemon peel. • Stir in brandy and mix well. •
Batter should be soft, not too stiff. • Blanch
almonds. Remove skins. • Chop 1 tablespoon
of almonds and add to mixture. • Spoon into
a greased 8-inch round cake pan. • Split remaining almonds in half and arrange on top
of cake in a pinwheel pattern. • Bake for 1 1/2
hours. • (If cake begins to show browning
before cooking time has elapsed, put a circle
of damp, greaseproof paper on cake. • Reduce oven heat to 300°. • Bake for 30 to 45
minutes longer or until tester inserted in center comes out clean. • Cool cake on wire
rack. • Wrap cooled cake in foil for at least 1
week before serving. Yield: 14 slices

An antique child's bed is a luggage rack and flower stand.

Don't twist the biscuit cutter when stamping out scones. This causes uneven baking and the scones may appear lopsided.

STUFFED BRANDY SNAPS

This recipe harkens back to John's childhood days in Scotland. It remains one of his favorites today.

½ stick butter, plus 2 tablespoons
½ cup firmly packed light brown sugar
¼ cup light corn syrup
1 teaspoon ground ginger
¾ cup all-purpose flour, sifted
1 teaspoon brandy
1 cup stiffly whipped cream

Preheat oven to 350°. • In a medium saucepan, mix together butter, sugar, syrup and ginger. • Heat until butter is melted. • Add flour and brandy and stir just to incorporate. • Place well-rounded teaspoons of the mixture onto a greased heavy baking sheet, about 2 inches apart. • Bake for 10 minutes. • Remove, leaving on open oven door as you mold snaps into cones while still warm. • Lift snaps off baking sheet with spatula and while still pliable, wrap each around the handle of a large wooden spoon handle. • Just before serving, fill pastry bag with fresh whipped cream and pipe into the large end of each cone. Yield: 10 to 12

An Amish Tea

Grape Pie

———

Cracker Pudding

———

Shoo-Fly Pie

———

Blueberry Supreme

———

Chocolate Chiffon Cake

———

Strawberry Whip

WHETHER YOU'RE JUST waking under morning sunlight or having tea in the parlor, the tranquility of the moment is heightened by what at first may seem an unfamiliar sound: the tapping of the shoe-clad hooves of horses on blacktop. This is the music of Amish buggies, bouncing and wheeling their way every day past The Churchtown Inn.

Throughout Pennsylvania Dutch country, buggies orchestrate the errands of the Plain People, mixing with modern-day traffic for a trip to the wheelwright for repairs or to market to sell fresh produce. Many times, a driver yanks the reins and the trotting halts in front of the inn. Local farmers and bakers drop off homegrown and homemade goods so innkeepers Stuart and Hermine Smith and Jim Kent can serve their guests the traditional foods.

The same authenticity is found whenever the evening tea is poured at the 1725 stone inn which is so characteristic of Lancaster County. At the Churchtown Inn, tea is held in the evening rather than the afternoon. There are usually Pennsylvania Dutch treats among the sweets—such as Grape Pie or Cracker Pudding.

The Churchtown Inn is known for its unusual special events: road rallies and treasure hunts, costume balls and jazz festivals. But it also escorts its guests to dinner at a Mennonite farmhouse. Then, not only do you hear

those ubiquitous clip-clops, but the lyrical sounds of Pennsylvania Dutch conversation, music and prayers as well. If you don't make the dinners, enjoying the Amish inspired tea-time dishes will give you some of the flavor of these humble people—literally. One bite and you know you must have come close to heaven on earth.

The Churchtown Inn
Route 23
Churchtown, PA 17555
Phone: **(215) 445-7794**
Rooms: **8**
Tea-Time: **Daily for overnight guests**

AN AMISH TEA AT HOME

- Set the table with an old quilt or a solid fabric in dark green, purple or black—Amish colors.
- The centerpiece can be a straw hat and a lady's bonnet.
- Let the tea cart be an antique wheelbarrow.
- Open the Bible to a page that contains one of your favorite verses.
- In addition to the Amish-inspired tea foods, add a bowl filled with large Pennsylvania soft or hard pretzels.
- Hold an Amish tea just for friends who enjoy sewing, and include a project to make before serving the tea.

GRAPE PIE

3 cups Concord grapes, seeded
1 cup sugar
3 tablespoons all-purpose flour
⅛ teaspoon salt
½ stick of butter, cut into 1-inch pieces
Prepared 9-inch pie shell and top crust
Butter

Hull the grapes. Set hulls and grapes aside. • In small saucepan, cook the grapes to a pulp and put through a sieve. • Add the hulls to the pulp and bring to a boil. • Stir in sugar, flour and salt and cook until thick. • Preheat oven to 450°. • Place mixture into unbaked pie shell. • Place butter pats on top. • Cover with top crust. • Bake for 10 minutes. • Reduce heat to 350° and bake for 30 minutes. Yield: 8 servings

CRACKER PUDDING

4 cups milk
1 cup sugar
1¼ cups salt-topped crackers, crumbled
2 eggs, beaten
1 teaspoon vanilla extract
Whipped cream

In small saucepan over medium heat, blend milk and sugar. • Slowly add cracker crumbs, stirring constantly. • Remove half of the hot mixture and stir it into the beaten eggs. • Return egg mixture to remaining hot mixture and boil for 1 minute, stirring constantly. • Remove from heat. • Stir in the vanilla. • Chill and serve with a topping of whipped cream. • Yield: 8 servings (4 ounces each)

SHOO-FLY PIE

2 cups all-purpose flour
4 tablespoons butter, softened
1½ cups firmly packed brown sugar
2 cups molasses
2 beaten eggs
1½ cups hot water
2 teaspoons baking soda

Preheat oven to 325°. • Mix together flour, butter and sugar. • Reserve 1½ cups for crumbs. • In another bowl, mix together the molasses, eggs, water and baking soda. • Add to crumb mixture. • Pour into 2 ungreased 9-inch pie plates. • Top with reserved crumbs. • Bake for 1 hour. Yield: 2 pies, 8 servings each

BLUEBERRY SUPREME

2 cups graham cracker crumbs
½ stick margarine, melted
4 cups marshmallows
⅓ cup milk
8 ounces cream cheese, softened
1 teaspoon vanilla extract
1 cup heavy cream, whipped
1 16-ounce can blueberry pie filling

Combine crumbs and margarine. • Press into a 10-inch-round baking dish. • Melt marshmallows in milk on top of double boiler. • Remove from heat. • Chill until thickened. • In mixing bowl, combine cream cheese and vanilla. Beat until well-blended. • Whip in marshmallow mixture. • Fold in whipped cream. • Pour into cracker crust. • Chill. • Top with blueberries. Yield: 10 to 12 servings

CHOCOLATE CHIFFON CAKE

8 eggs, separated
½ teaspoon cream of tartar
¾ cup boiling water
½ cup cocoa
1¾ cups all-purpose flour
1¾ cups sugar
1½ teaspoons baking powder
1 teaspoon salt
2 teaspoons vanilla extract
½ cup vegetable oil

Preheat oven to 325°. • Beat egg whites with cream of tartar until very stiff. • Combine boiling water with cocoa. • Let cool. • In a large bowl, sift together the flour, sugar, baking powder and salt. • Beat together egg yolks, vanilla and oil. • Add to dry ingredients. • Add cooled cocoa mixture. • Mix well. • Fold beaten egg whites into the batter. • Bake in a tube pan for 55 minutes or until cake springs back to the touch. • Increase temperature to 350° and bake 10 minutes longer. Yield: 12 to 14 servings

STRAWBERRY WHIP

1 20-ounce can crushed pineapple with juice

2½ cups water

½ cup sugar

1 6-ounce box strawberry-flavor JELL-O

2 envelopes Dream Whip

8 ounces cream cheese, softened

Heat in medium saucepan, pineapple with juice, water and sugar, stirring to combine. • Remove from heat. • Add JELL-O. • Mix well; set aside to cool. • In another bowl, whip Dream Whip according to package directions. • Add cream cheese. • Beat well. • Lightly combine with JELL-O mixture. • Pour into 9-inch mold. • Chill in refrigerator. Yield: 10 servings

Tea-time in Pennsylvania Dutch country

The serving of afternoon tea became a fashionable English social event in the 1840s, nearly 200 years after the first tea was brought to the royal family from China. During this time, tea was considered a precious commodity and was kept in decorative chests under lock and key. The lady of the house had the only key and carefully guarded access to the treasure. Servants suspected of stealing tea were immediately dismissed. When it was time to prepare for afternoon tea, the housekeeper would summon her mistress to open the chest and together they would oversee the careful measuring of the tea leaves.

The Governor's Inn, Ludlow, Vermont

An Italian Tea

Zuppa Stracciatella

Ricotta and Roasted Red Pepper Spread

Pesto, Pumante and Sweet Sausage Roll

Dolci con Frutta alla Ferentino

Chocolate Almond Pizzelles

WINTERS IN WESTERN North Carolina have quite a nip, and so tea-time, which frequently takes on an ethnic flavor, becomes a hearty afternoon respite at Applewood Manor. Red, green and white linens (colors of the Italian flag) accent an antique sideboard where guests can help themselves to an interesting assortment of Italian treats cooked up by Jim LoPresti.

The menu for this tea is complete from soup to nuts and each dish is most complementary. "Being a bed & breakfast, we don't serve dinner so we like to offer our guests something a little heartier during our tea-times," says Jim's wife, Linda. Even in sum-

mer, there's always a soup such as cold spice peach or strawberry soup, plus a finger food and a sweet. Tea-time here is informal and in warmer months may include an activity such as croquet.

Applewood Manor is a tastefully decorated Colonial-style home, accented with American antiques. It was built around the turn of the century in the shadow of George Vanderbilt's famous Biltmore estate where guests can spend several hours touring the manor house and gardens. Tea-time conversation often centers around comments about the Biltmore's incredible conservatory and the interesting summer kitchen.

The LoPrestis thoroughly enjoy entertaining and offer their guests the right blend of hospitality and privacy. They will also pack you a picnic should you want to further explore the Great Smoky Mountains National Park. Oh, and they will even give you a thermos of tea in case you don't get back for tea-time at the inn.

Applewood Manor
62 Cumberland Circle
Asheville, NC 28801
Phone: **(704) 254-2244**
Rooms: **5**
Tea-Time: **4:00–5:00 P.M. daily for inn guests**

Zuppa Stracciatella

The LoPrestis like to serve a soup with their teas. This one is healthy and delicious. Serve with croutons or slices of crusty garlic bread.

2 cups homemade chicken broth
8 ounces frozen chopped spinach
⅓ cup acine di pepe pasta
1 egg
2 tablespoons grated Parmesan cheese
½ teaspoon dried basil
¼ teaspoon salt
⅛ teaspoon fresh black pepper

Keep chicken broth warm. • Boil spinach separately. • Drain. • Cook pasta until al dente. • Drain. • In a small bowl, lightly beat egg, cheese, basil, salt and pepper. • Add egg mixture, spinach and pasta to warm broth. Yield: 2 cups

Ricotta and Roasted Red Pepper Spread

1 pound ricotta
3 tablespoons grated Parmesan cheese
2 tablespoons extra virgin olive oil
¼ cup finely chopped roasted red peppers
¼ teaspoon garlic powder
⅛ teaspoon salt
Freshly ground pepper to taste
2 tablespoons finely chopped parsley
¼ teaspoon nutmeg

Mix all ingredients thoroughly. • Serve with garlic toasts, celery, carrot and fennel spears or any crusty bread. Yield: 2 cups

Cupid oversees an Italian buffet.

Pesto, Pumante and Sweet Sausage Roll

¾ cup sweet Italian sausage, cases removed
¼ cup finely chopped onion
2 tablespoons olive oil
1 9-inch pie crust or frozen puff pastry sheet
¼ tablespoons pesto sauce
3 tablespoons finely chopped, dried tomatoes
4 ounces mozzarella, shredded
1 egg white

Preheat oven to 350°. • Cook sausage and onion in olive oil. • Set aside in a large bowl. • Roll pie crust out on waxed paper. • Spread a thin coating of pesto sauce over top. • Add tomatoes and mozzarella to the sausage mixture. • Spread mixture over entire pie crust, except for 1 inch on all sides of the crust. • Roll the crust up jellyroll style, wetting the clean edge with water to seal. • Brush top of rolled crust with egg white. • Bake for 45 to 50 minutes or until lightly golden brown. • Slice into ½-inch slices. Yield: 10 servings

> ### AN ITALIAN TEA AT HOME
>
> - Place a votive candle under a cheese grater for an Italian tin "candleholder."
> - Sprinkle elbow pasta around the tea table as Italian confetti.

DOLCI CON FRUTTA ALLA FERENTINO (APPLE AND PEAR TRIFLE)

3 ounces raisins
¼ cup sweet vermouth
3 tart baking apples
3 ripe pears (preferably Comice)
6 tablespoons light brown sugar, divided
½ cup water
2 ounces hazelnuts, lightly toasted
2 ounces almond slivers, lightly toasted
1½ ounces pine nuts, lightly toasted
8 amaretti (Italian macaroons)
5 eggs, separated
Grated peel of 1 lemon
2 tablespoons fresh lemon juice
1 tablespoon all-purpose flour

Soak raisins in vermouth for 30 minutes. • Wash, peel, core and slice apples and pears into very thin slices. • Put slices in pot with 2 tablespoons of brown sugar and ½ cup water. Cover and cook over medium heat for 30 minutes or until fruit is mushy. • Purée fruit in food processor. • Remove. Set aside. • Chop nuts and amaretti finely in food processor. • Preheat oven to 375°. • Add the remaining 4 tablespoons of sugar to egg yolks and beat until pale yellow ribbons form. • Add puréed fruit slowly to yolks. • Add the grated lemon peel and trickle in the lemon juice while stirring constantly. • Mix in chopped nuts and amaretti.

Drain the raisins in a strainer, dusting them with flour and shaking to eliminate excess flour. • Mix them into egg batter. • Beat egg whites until stiff and fold into batter.

Grease bottom of a 10-inch springform pan. • Cut out a waxed-paper disk the size of the pan bottom, grease it and place in pan. • Pour batter into pan and place in the uppermost level of the oven. • Bake for 50 minutes or until tester inserted in center comes out clean. • Cool to lukewarm. • Serve plain or topped with whipped cream or ice cream. Yield: 10 small servings

CHOCOLATE ALMOND PIZZELLES

These are flavorful Italian chocolate almond cookies. They are made with a pizzelle iron and resemble very fancy waffles or crocheted, starched doilies.

3 eggs
¾ cup sugar
3 tablespoons cocoa
1 stick butter, melted and cooled
2 teaspoons almond extract
1 teaspoon vanilla extract
1¾ cups all-purpose flour
2 teaspoons baking powder

Beat eggs, sugar and cocoa. • Add cooled, melted butter, then the almond and vanilla extracts. • Stir in flour and baking powder. • Blend. • Spoon batter onto pizzelle iron. • Cook until iron indicates readiness. Yield: 30

A Mexican Tea

Mexican Sombrero Dip

Spinach and Feta Triangles

Hot Mexican Cornbread

Spicy Toast Hearts

Chocolate Pound Cake

WALKING INTO THE ELEgant White Swan Inn with its parlor and library done in warm woods, hunting prints and designer fabrics influenced by England, you wouldn't expect to be served tea with Mexican foods and a few Mediterranean props on the table. "But we like to offer many theme teas here as a means of entertaining especially our repeat visitors," says Kim Post-Watson. "The Mexican idea came about because we enjoy making tea-time a little bit different, so why not a Mexican tea?"

Kim is vice president of Four Sisters Inns, owned by her parents, who wanted to honor their daughters. Four Sisters is comprised of the White Swan and five other California inns.

The Mexican Tea is informal, served around the time most guests arrive at the inn. The theme is all in the foods served for this tea. I like the use of the straw sombrero as the caddy for tortilla chips. All theme teas at the inn include a combination of sweets, vegetables or fruit with complementary dips and a savory hors d'oeuvre or finger sandwich.

Classical music and candlelight provide the atmosphere during all the teas at The White Swan. Guests find many spots around the inn where tea foods and a cup and saucer fit nicely for two. Another idea for the White Swan is a Chinese tea. After all, the inn is located only a few blocks from Chinatown!

The White Swan Inn
845 Bush Street
San Francisco, CA 94108
Phone: **(415) 775-1755**
Rooms: **26**
Tea-Time: **4:00–6:00 P.M. for inn guests**

. . . it took her a long time to prepare her tea; but when ready, it was set forth with as much grace as if she had been a veritable guest to her own self.

A New England Nun
Mary Wilkins Freeman

A fiesta tea at The White Swan Inn

MEXICAN SOMBRERO DIP

1 8-ounce can spicy refried beans (or 8 ounces black beans)
½ cup grated cheddar cheese
½ cup grated Monterey Jack cheese
½ cup chopped tomatoes
½ cup shredded lettuce
¼ cup minced green onion
½ cup sour cream

Spread the beans in the bottom of a small baking dish no larger than 5 inches square. • Spread ingredients in order listed. • Bake for 15 minutes. Serve with tortilla or other favorite chips. Yield: 2 cups

SPINACH AND FETA TRIANGLES

3 onions, finely chopped
¼ cup olive oil
24 ounces frozen spinach, thawed and drained
2 tablespoons chopped dill
8 ounces feta cheese, crumbled
2 eggs, beaten
6 tablespoons sour cream
¼ teaspoon salt
⅛ teaspoon pepper
⅛ teaspoon nutmeg
Puff pastry, cut into 35 four-inch squares

Preheat oven to 400°. • Sauté onions in oil until tender (not browned). • Stir in spinach. • Cook 5 minutes longer. • Stir in dill and cheese. • Cool. • Mix in eggs, sour cream, salt, pepper and nutmeg. • Chill until cold. • Place 1 tablespoon filling in center of each pastry square. • Fold opposite corners over to form triangle. • Press edges together. • Seal with tines of fork. • Place on lightly greased baking pan. • Bake for 15 to 20 minutes or until golden brown. Yield: 35 to 40

Hot Mexican Cornbread

¼ cup vegetable oil
1 cup cornmeal
1 cup milk
½ teaspoon baking soda
1 teaspoon salt
2 jalapeño peppers, diced
1 16-ounce can cream-style corn
2 eggs, beaten
1 cup chopped green onion
½ pound cheddar cheese, grated

Preheat oven to 350°. • Heat oil in a medium skillet. • In a 10- or 12-inch baking dish, mix remaining ingredients, except half the cheese. • Pour hot oil over mixture. • Top with remaining cheese. • Bake for 40 minutes. • Cool. • Cut into 2-inch squares. Yield: 20 to 25

Spicy Toast Hearts

1 loaf thin-sliced bread (more if needed)
12 ounces cream cheese, at room temperature
1½ cups finely chopped radishes
2 tablespoons chopped chives
1 tablespoon horseradish
½ teaspoon salt
¼ teaspoon pepper
Parsley, for garnish
Red caviar, for garnish

Preheat oven to 325°. • With a 1-inch heart cookie cutter, cut bread. • Place a single layer on a cookie sheet and bake until lightly toasted. • Turn and toast again. • In bowl of electric mixer, beat cream cheese, radishes, chives, horseradish, salt and pepper until blended. • Refrigerate until firm. • Spread on toast. • Garnish with parsley and caviar. Yield: 1½ cups

Chocolate Pound Cake

2 cups boiling water
4 ounces unsweetened chocolate
4 cups all-purpose flour
2 teaspoons baking soda
2 sticks butter, at room temperature
3½ cups firmly packed brown sugar
4 eggs
2 teaspoons vanilla extract
1 cup sour cream
Confectioners' sugar

Preheat oven to 325°. • Pour water over chocolate. • Set aside for 20 minutes. • Stir flour with baking soda. • Cream together butter, sugar, eggs and vanilla until light and fluffy. • Add dry ingredients alternately with sour cream, mixing well. • Stir in cooled chocolate mixture until combined. • Pour into 2 well-greased bundt pans. • Bake for 60 to 75 minutes or until tester inserted in center comes out clean. • Cool for 15 minutes. • Remove from pan and cool completely on racks. • Sprinkle with confectioners' sugar. Yield: 2 bundt cakes

Four

SPECIALTY TEAS

SOMETIMES THERE ARE UNIQUE REASONS FOR HOLDING TEA-time. Certainly a tea-tasting, where you want to introduce friends to the pleasures of various teas, is one such special excuse. Or tea-time can be a relaxing and friendly way to conduct a business meeting.

Inns have a wonderful habit of responding to their guests' every need. The specialty tea is the answer to any occasion when a guest should be fêted or an unusual set of circumstances calls for a custom menu. Such is the case with a tea for people who are watching their weight. Another specialty tea might be one where children, from tots to young teens, can enjoy the new experience of sitting at a pretty table and eating pastries and cakes while being waited on in a manner they never imagined.

A specialty tea is not usually theme-oriented nor connected to a holiday or time of year. It's any tea-time that suits a more rudimentary purpose—perhaps an everyday gathering such as breakfast or a Sunday brunch. No one is the guest of honor. There's little romance to these teas, but plenty of good feelings go along with sharing tea in the company of others whether they are business associates, strangers, or close friends.

In most cases, the specialty tea is a bit unusual and may take your guests by delightful surprise. Foods can be abundant, but serve with respect for the occasion. Especially for a business tea, you want to be quick and quiet and let the meeting go on if the participants aren't going to break for the afternoon respite.

The teas in this chapter are de rigueur at many inns. I think you will also find them in good taste for celebrating important occasions for your own special guests.

Pinafores and frocks and childhood fancies make a special tea at Honeysuckle Hill.

A Tea-Tasting

A Wide Assortment of Teas

———

Baked Cinnamon Sticks

———

Stuffed Strawberries

———

Fruit Sandwiches Cornucopia

———

Mini-Cheesecakes

———

Chocolate Crème de Menthe Dreams

PEOPLE WHO MAKE A LIV-ing tasting tea to ensure the quality of the beverage may try several hundred teas in a day. They sample tea by spraying a teaspoonful of it at the back of their mouth. This atomizes the tea, allowing the taster the full range of taste and smell. The taster then expectorates the tea, rather than swallowing it.

This kind of professional tea-tasting starts wherever the tea is grown. Tasters make sure the tea has a consistency of quality. Next, samples are sent to the packager, who also tastes it. If he or she approves, the tea is sent to the company's buying department.

A tea-tasting party at the Queen Anne Inn or in your own home is quite different from professional tea-tasting. The purpose of the party is your enjoyment of the characteristics of the teas. And you don't have to sample tea through a spray bottle!

A tea-tasting is similar to a wine-tasting, only much less formal. Inn-keeper Chuck Hillestad, who owns the Queen Anne with his wife, Ann, explains: "The range in taste for teas is at least equal to and possibly greater than wines. Even someone who doesn't know the difference be-tween a Claret and a Pinot Noir can differentiate between a Rose Hips and an Orange Pekoe."

Chuck recommends contacting the

A TEA-TASTING AT HOME

- Prepare a chart to hand out to your guests for comparison purposes. Leave space so that your guests can write their own taste comments and take the list with them when they leave.
- Demitasse cups are ideal for a tea-tasting as you don't offer each guest a full cup of tea—just a sampling. If you use your regular china, fill each cup only halfway.
- Tea-tastings are also a great time for tea-pot collectors to serve each tea flavor from a different pot.
- Place a large, attractive bowl on the table so that each guest can discard his or her tea. Empty the bowl often.
- It's your choice whether you're going to hold a tea-tasting with loose tea or with tea bags. The latter is certainly easier and the many varieties of herb and regular teas are found in abundance in tea bags. Also, you can make full pots of tea already brewed or have each guest dip a tea bag into his or her own cup. Have a small bowl at each guest's place-setting for discarded tea bags.
- Begin the tea-tasting by pouring one flavor for everyone to taste. Encourage your guests to taste the tea without any sugar, honey or milk, so that the pure flavor comes through. Show your guests how to observe the tea by noting its color, clarity and bouquet (scent).
- You'll want to enhance the tasting with sweets and snacks. There are no rules concerning what food to serve with what tea, as there are with wine.

makers of the teas you're going to serve for promotional material on the growing, varieties and ingredients of their teas. The Queen Anne works with the Celestial Seasonings tea company—which is situated near the inn in Boulder, Colorado.

The award-winning Queen Anne Inn is a romantic place to visit. It was voted by *Bridal Guide* magazine as one of the top ten places to spend a wedding night. This is no surprise. Chuck and Ann never stop coming up with ways to enchant all of their guests and their tea-tasting is just one of many thoughtful creations.

Queen Anne Inn
2147 Tremont Place
Denver, CO 80205
Phone: **(303) 296-6666**
Rooms: **10**
Tea-Time: **Christmas holidays and special occasions**

BAKED CINNAMON STICKS

These are the kind of cinnamon sticks you can eat. They're full of fun and flavor.

1 cup sugar
¼ cup ground cinnamon
1 loaf white bread, unsliced
2 sticks butter, melted

Preheat oven to 400°. • Combine sugar and cinnamon. • Remove crusts from bread. • Cut bread into 1-inch thick slices. Cut each slice into 1x4-inch sticks (about 4 per slice). • Dip in melted butter and roll in cinnamon mixture. • Place on foil-lined cookie sheet. • Bake for 15 minutes or until crisp and slightly browned. Yield: 64

Thermal pots keep water hot for a tea-tasting.

STUFFED STRAWBERRIES

These add color, interest and a gourmet touch to your tea-time spread. Try to find the biggest strawberries with the richest red color.

18 extra large fresh strawberries
³/₄ cup freshly whipped cream cheese
2 tablespoons finely chopped walnuts
1½ teaspoons confectioners' sugar
½ teaspoon milk

Cut a thin slice from the stem end of each strawberry. • This allows the berries to stand upright. • Cut ¼ inch off tip-end of berries, reserving tips. • Scoop out half of the pulp from each berry, leaving strawberry shells intact. • Combine pulp with cream cheese, walnuts, sugar and milk, mixing well. Add extra milk if needed to make a creamy consistency. • Spoon mixture into a decorating bag, fitted with a large tip. • Pipe mixture into strawberries and top with reserved strawberry tips. Yield: 18

FRUIT SANDWICHES CORNUCOPIA

There are lots of surprises in these sandwiches, which have a sweet and savory taste.

2 8-ounce packages cream cheese, softened
8 ounces crushed pineapple, drained
¹/₃ cup orange marmalade
3 tablespoons ginger preserves
1 cup chopped pecans
¼ cup finely chopped green pepper
1 tablespoon minced onion
½ teaspoon celery salt
½ teaspoon onion salt
8 fresh or maraschino cherries, pitted and chopped
Sliced raisin bread, crusts removed

Combine all ingredients, except bread. • Mix well. • Spread on half the bread slices. • Top with remaining slices. • Cut sandwiches in quarters on the diagonal. Yield: 4 cups

MINI-CHEESECAKES

This is a nice way to serve cheesecake as a finger food in keeping with tea-time.

18 vanilla wafers
2 8-ounce packages cream cheese, softened
³/₄ cup sugar
2 eggs
1 tablespoon lemon juice
1 teaspoon vanilla extract
1½ teaspoons Grand Marnier
¼ cup semi-sweet chocolate mini-morsels

Preheat oven to 375°. • Line mini-muffin tins with paper cups. • Place a vanilla wafer in each cup. • In bowl of electric mixer, beat cream cheese until light and fluffy. • Gradually add sugar, beating well. • Add eggs, one at a time, beating well after each addition. • Stir in lemon juice and vanilla. • Divide mixture into 3 portions. • Add Grand Marnier to first portion, mixing well. • Add ¼ cup chocolate morsels to second portion. Combine with plain portion and pour mixture into each cup, filling cups ¾ full. • Bake for 20 minutes.

TOPPING

1 pint sour cream
3 tablespoons sugar
½ teaspoon vanilla extract
Mandarin oranges, for garnish

Combine sour cream, sugar and vanilla; mix well. • Place a heaping teaspoon of sour cream mixture over cheesecakes as soon as they are removed from the oven. • Spread mixture to the edges. • Bake an additional 5 minutes or until topping is set. • Leave in muffin pans and chill overnight. • Garnish with orange slices before serving. Yield: 18

CHOCOLATE CRÈME DE MENTHE DREAMS

This recipe gets a bit of a double frosting. The mint flavor is a palate cleanser for all that tea-tasting.

COOKIES

4 1-ounce squares unsweetened chocolate
2 sticks butter
4 eggs

2 cups sugar
1 cup all-purpose flour
1 teaspoon vanilla extract

Preheat oven to 350°. • In a small saucepan, combine chocolate and butter. • Over low heat, stir until chocolate is melted. • Remove from heat. • Set aside for 10 minutes. • In bowl of electric mixer, beat eggs until thick. • Gradually add sugar, flour, and vanilla. • Beat on low speed for 1 minute longer. • Blend in chocolate mixture. • Pour into a lightly greased and floured 13x9-inch baking pan. • Bake for 25 to 30 minutes or until tester inserted in center comes out clean. • Cool 10 minutes before frosting.

FROSTING

4 cups sifted confectioners' sugar
1 stick butter, softened
¼ cup light cream
¼ cup crème de menthe
1 cup chopped walnuts
½ cup semi-sweet chocolate morsels

In medium bowl of electric mixer, combine all ingredients, except walnuts and chocolate morsels. • Beat at high speed until smooth. • Stir in nuts. • Frost cake. • Chill for 4 hours. • Remove cake from cooler. • Place chocolate morsels in a small saucepan. Cook over low heat, stirring constantly, until melted. • Drizzle over frosting. • Cut into bars. • Chill at least 1 hour. • Store in airtight container in refrigerator. Yield: 48

A Low-Fat Herb Tea

Iced Citrus Tea

Hot Geranium Tea

Herbed Cheese Spread on Pita

Yogurt Cheese

Cheese Pepper Melt

Applesauce Mint Nut Bread

Mandarin Mint Muffins

EACH BED & BREAKFAST and country inn offers its own unique experience. At Shash and Bill Georgi's place, Back of the Beyond, guests are surrounded by the Georgis' affinity for and desire to save the environment. Shash and Bill want you to take advantage of their good nature in more ways than one.

At breakfast and snack times, Shash and Bill provide healthful fare with many of the ingredients grown or raised in their organic gardens.

Even the honey in the tea is raised organically on the premises.

"Ours is an 'herby' B&B," laughs Shash, whose roots in organic gardening stem from growing up in her mother's Swedish kitchen "where food was in abundance and prepared attractively."

You can't help but get caught up in the Georgis' enthusiasm for nature. Guest rooms and common areas are filled with aromas from drying herbs. In warmer weather, you can stroll the rows of vegetable and herb gardens and clusters of growing flowers.

When you're served tea at Back of the Beyond, it's usually a blend of fresh Georgi-grown herbs with fruits, nuts and herb breads. Imagine what the royal classes would have said to this! A low-fat tea is not, I'm sure, what the English had in mind when they brought about this afternoon respite. But for today, it's nice to have another option. Dietary constraints are no longer an excuse for not taking time out for tea.

Back of the Beyond
7233 Lower East Hill Road
Colden, NY 14033
Phone: **(716) 652-0427**
Rooms: **3**
Tea-Time: **3:00–5:00 P.M. for inn guests**

Herbed Cheese Spread and pita bread

ICED CITRUS TEA

This keeps for a week or more when refrigerated and even mellows—if it lasts that long!

3 tablespoons lemon balm leaves	
3 tablespoons apple mint leaves	
3 tablespoons orange mint leaves	
3 tablespoons peppermint leaves	
2 tablespoons chamomile flowers	
1 tablespoon calendula petals (optional)	
4 cups water	
4 teaspoons honey	

Gather listed fresh herbs in the morning, if possible. • Wash and pat dry. • In a stainless or ceramic pan, add water and wring whole herbs into water with your hands. • Add honey. • Cover and bring just to a boil. • Stir to mix herbs. • Let steep for 10 to 20 minutes. • (You will be adding ice to the tea and will need double strength.) • Remove herbs by straining the liquid into an attractive jar or decanter. • To serve, pour over ice, adding a fresh sprig of mint or lavender as a stirrer. Yield: 1 quart

A LOW-FAT HERB TEA AT HOME

- Tuck a sprig of colorful herbs between the napkin and the napkin ring at each place setting.
- Be sure to have sugar substitutes available for those who prefer their tea sweetened. Honey is a nice alternative.
- If you don't have a honey stick, you can prevent drips of honey by quickly turning (twirling) your teaspoon upside down, once it's filled with honey.
- Make the tea with spring water.

HOT GERANIUM TEA

1 heaping teaspoon dried herbs, consisting of equal parts apple mint, orange mint and peppermint, lemon balm and chamomile.

1 cup water

1 teaspoon honey

1 fresh mint leaf

1 scented geranium

Place herbs in bottom of teapot. • Add boiling water and honey. • Let steep 5 to 15 minutes depending on desired strength. • Strain. • Float a fresh mint leaf or scented geranium in cup. Yield: 1 cup

HERBED CHEESE SPREAD ON PITA

1 cup low-fat cottage cheese or yogurt cheese (see recipe below)

3 tablespoons bleu cheese

2 teaspoons ground sage

¼ cup Parmesan cheese

1 teaspoon lemon juice

Herb salt to taste

Pita bread

Watercress

Mix first 6 ingredients. • Chill for several hours. • Fill small pita breads and add watercress. • Cut into fourths. • Or, cut up the pita bread and let guests apply their own spread. Yield: 24 bite-size sandwiches

YOGURT CHEESE

This is a substitute for cottage cheese. Spread on crackers, vegetables or muffins. Overnight in the refrigerator, drain plain yogurt (any amount) through a cheesecloth. In the morning, remove the solids left in the cheesecloth and turn into a bowl. Add your choice of herbs and seasonings and or minced vegetables to taste. The texture will be smooth and calories and cholesterol low.

CHEESE PEPPER MELT

½ cup grated Jarlsberg cheese

¼ cup grated sharp cheddar cheese

¼ cup grated Parmesan cheese

¼ cup low-cal mayonnaise or homemade mayonnaise

¼ cup plain yogurt or more

1 teaspoon chopped scallions

1 teaspoon chopped shallots

2 tablespoons finely chopped green, red and yellow peppers

¼ teaspoon chopped dillweed

¼ teaspoon chopped marjoram

¼ teaspoon chopped lemon thyme

1 teaspoon Worcestershire sauce

4 whole-wheat English muffin halves, lightly toasted

Calendula, nasturtium or fresh dill blossoms for garnish

In medium-size bowl, mix together cheeses, mayonnaise and enough yogurt to hold mixture together. • Mix in scallions, shallots and peppers. • Incorporate the herbs with a whisk. • Season with Worcestershire. • Spread mixture on English muffin halves. • Place under broiler for 2 to 5 minutes or until bubbly and lightly browned. • Cut halves into 4 quarters each and serve with garnish. Yield: 16 pieces

APPLESAUCE MINT NUT BREAD

A quick bread to make ahead as it slices better and has more flavor after 2 to 3 days.

2 cups unbleached all-purpose flour
¾ cup firmly packed brown sugar
1 tablespoon baking powder
½ teaspoon baking soda
½ teaspoon cinnamon
½ teaspoon nutmeg
1 cup chopped nuts
1 egg, beaten
1 cup natural applesauce
1 teaspoon chopped fresh mint or ¼ teaspoon dried mint
¼ cup sunflower oil

Preheat oven to 350°. • Mix dry ingredients and nuts together. • In another bowl, combine the egg, applesauce, mint and oil. • Add to dry ingredients and stir just until evenly blended. • Pour batter into 2 greased mini-loaf pans and bake for 50 minutes or until golden brown. • Cool on rack. Yield: 2 loaves

MANDARIN MINT MUFFINS

1 cup unbleached all-purpose flour
½ cup whole-wheat germ
½ cup oat bran
½ teaspoon baking powder
1 teaspoon baking soda
¼ teaspoon salt (optional)
¾ cup flaked coconut
1 generous tablespoon dry mint
½ cup lightly packed brown sugar

Dried herbs in an antique printer's tray

1 large egg
½ cup vegetable oil
½ cup orange juice
1 11-ounce can mandarin oranges, drained

Preheat oven to 400°. • Prepare muffin tins with vegetable oil spray. • Combine dry ingredients in one bowl. • In another bowl, mix wet ingredients and mandarin oranges. • Mix wet ingredients with dry, turning just until moist. • Spoon into prepared muffin tins. • Bake for 15 to 20 minutes or until tester inserted in center comes out clean. Yield: 12

My dear if you could give me a cup of tea to clear my muddle of a head I should better understand your affairs.
—Charles Dickens

Tea-Time for Tots

Mini-Lobster Rolls

Irish Scones

Cherry Pecan Bread

Sand Tarts

Oreo Cookie Cheesecakes

Whoopie Pies

PARENTS FIND SMALL INNS to be the perfect getaways for renewing romance. Bed & breakfast and country inns are the fantasyland of adults. The antiques are their toys; the social climate has the same electricity that was generated whenever a new kid arrived on the block; and the gourmet breakfasts and dinners delight the now grown-up palate as shakes, burgers, and fries did in teenage days. That's why many inns are not really for young children.

But Honeysuckle Hill has found tea-time a way to enliven the inn's lifestyle with the laughter of youth. While innkeepers Barbara and Bob Rosenthal offer tea to their adult guests every day, they also hold several teas each year for children's clubs in their area. "It's our way of honoring them for their efforts," says Barbara.

There's always a Nutcracker Tea for the youngest dancers of a local production company, an Easter Tea with the inn's collection of animal tea-pots, and a Bring Your Teddy to Tea for a sewing group called The Cape Cod Scallop Smockers.

"It's very important for us to use our best china, silver and linens," says Barbara. "The children feel so grown-up—giggly and thrilled at being served so finely." Chamomile is often the tea served to the youngsters.

When the children first approach the tea table, they are a little shy and unsure, even though the table and chairs are their size and height. Once seated, there's no stopping this group from digging in. What's so much fun about children at tea is watching how their imagination takes over. They try conversing as though a group of adults at tea, especially if they have been dressed in grownups' clothing. At Honeysuckle Hill, Barbara has also observed their imagination turning them into bakers. Barbara's cookie dips allow for new creations. "They've made all kinds of things with the dips

TEA-TIME FOR TOTS AT HOME

- At Honeysuckle Hill, the Rosenthals also make three sweet sauces for cookie dipping. Make a batch of sweetened whipped cream and separate into three bowls. Add chocolate chips and some cocoa to one, pink food coloring and crushed peppermint canes to another and crushed Heath bars to the third. Surround each dip with a different type of cookie: sand tarts (recipe follows), chocolate wafers and gingersnaps.
- Serve tea with a child-size tea set or demitasse cups.
- Use linen napkins but have some warmed, dampened face towels ready for sticky fingers and possible spills.

and other sweets on the table, such as a layer cake with the dips and cookies."

They love to pour the tea and pass the sugar and for a while, this is more fascinating to them than eating the sweets. "I've had many children's teas and nothing gets broken," says Barbara. "In fact, it's the parents that are watching, worrying that my good china will be broken. I don't worry at all. It never happens," says the innkeeper.

Actually, Honeysuckle Hill is quite a capricious inn. Although the finery of English rose chintz and Victorian handmade quilts decorate the rooms, storybook characters and featherbeds are its real hallmarks. As you drive up to the 1800s farmhouse, there's an antique wicker baby carriage holding summer's greenery and a fish pond with a small waterfall out back. Croquet and a hammock offer an invitation to play. The Peter Rabbit bedroom has a china cabinet filled with memorabilia. Tea-time for adults is often served with whimsical teapots and fairy tale cups and saucers. Even the breakfast table, although set elegantly, includes a ceramic menagerie.

Bringing your favorite teddy bear to Honeysuckle Hill is not a requirement. However, packing along the child in you is a must!

Honeysuckle Hill
591 Main Street
West Barnstable, MA 02668
Phone: **(508) 362-8418**
Rooms: **3**
Tea-Time: **5:00 P.M. daily for inn guests.**
Children's teas on special occasions.

"I can just imagine myself sitting down at the head of the table and pouring out the tea," said Anne, shutting her eyes ecstatically. "And asking Diana if she takes sugar! I know she doesn't but of course I'll ask her just as if I didn't know."

Anne of Green Gables
—L.M. Montgomery

MINI-LOBSTER ROLLS

½ pound lobster meat, fresh preferred

½ cup finely chopped celery

¼ cup finely chopped green pepper

¼ cup mayonnaise or enough to moisten

8 finger rolls

Combine all ingredients, except rolls. • Slice rolls on top instead of on the sides. • Spoon mixture into the rolls. Yield: 8 rolls

IRISH SCONES

2½ sticks plus 2 tablespoons butter, cut into small pieces

5½ cups all-purpose flour

¾ cup sugar

¼ cup baking powder

1½ cups sour milk (add 1 teaspoon or so of lemon or orange to regular milk)

½ cup plain yogurt

2½ tablespoons caraway seeds

1¼ cups currants

1 yolk of large egg, beaten

Preheat oven to 350°. • In a mixing bowl, combine butter, flour, sugar and baking powder until it resembles coarse meal. • In another bowl, mix together the sour milk and yogurt. • Add to the flour mixture, stirring quickly but gently with a fork. • Turn sticky dough onto a floured board. • Pour caraway seeds and currants on top. • Quickly knead them in, working the dough as little as possible. • Divide the dough into 4 equal parts. • Pat each part into a 1-inch-thick circle. • Cut each circle into 8 pie-shaped wedges. • Place on lightly floured baking sheets. • Brush tops with beaten egg yolk. • Bake for 15 minutes or until golden brown. Yield: 32 scones

CHERRY PECAN BREAD

8 ounces cream cheese, softened

2 sticks butter

1½ cups sugar

1½ teaspoons vanilla extract

4 eggs

2¼ cups all-purpose flour, sifted

1½ teaspoons baking powder

1 8-ounce jar maraschino cherries, chopped

½ cup chopped pecans

Preheat oven to 325°. • Blend cream cheese, butter, sugar and vanilla. • Add eggs one at a time, mixing well after each addition. • Set aside ¼ cup flour. • Mix baking powder with remaining 2 cups of flour. • Gradually add flour mixture to cream cheese mixture. • Coat chopped cherries with all the reserved flour. • Add to batter. • Grease a 10-inch bundt pan. Sprinkle chopped nuts around the pan. • Pour in batter. • Bake for 1 hour. • Cool for about 5 minutes. • Remove from pan. Yield: 1 loaf

SAND TARTS

1½ sticks butter, at room temperature
1¼ cups sugar, sifted
¼ teaspoon salt
1 egg
1 egg yolk (reserve white for egg wash)
1 teaspoon vanilla extract
½ teaspoon nutmeg
3 cups all-purpose flour
Sugar

Cream butter until soft. • Gradually add the sugar and blend until mixture is creamy. • Beat in salt, egg, egg yolk, vanilla and nutmeg. • Slowly sift the flour into the butter mixture until well blended. (The last of the flour may have to be kneaded in by hand.) • Chill the dough for several hours. • Preheat the oven to 375°. • Roll dough out to a ¼-inch thickness. • Cut into shapes with cookie cutters. • Brush the tops of the cookies with beaten egg white and sprinkle with sugar. • Bake on greased cookie sheets for 8 minutes or until golden brown. • Serve with cookie dips (see Tea-Time for Tots at Home on page 147). Yield: 4 dozen

OREO COOKIE CHEESECAKES

20 Oreo cookies
16 ounces cream cheese, at room temperature
¾ cup sugar
2 tablespoons all-purpose flour
3 eggs
¾ cup sour cream
3 tablespoons sugar

Preheat oven to 350°. • Line 16 muffin cups with paper liners. • Separate 16 cookies in two, leaving the Oreo's cream filling on each cookie half and placing any half into each cup liner. • Make crumbs out of the 4 whole cookies. • Set aside.

In bowl of electric mixer, combine cream cheese, sugar, flour and eggs. • Beat for 4 minutes. • Place 1 tablespoon of the mixture on top of each cookie half. • Sprinkle cookie crumbs on top. • Add the remaining cheese mixture on top of the crumbs. • Bake for 20 minutes. • Remove from oven.

Combine the sour cream and sugar. Spread each cake with the mixture. • Return to the oven for 4 minutes. • Remove from the oven and place remaining cookie halves on top of each cheesecake. • Store in the refrigerator. • Serve chilled. Yield: 16

Mini-Lobster Rolls (left), Oreo Cookie Cheesecakes (front of plate), and Whoopie Pies

WHOOPIE PIES

CAKES

1 stick butter, softened
1 cup sugar
2 cups all-purpose flour
1½ teaspoons baking soda
½ teaspoon salt
½ cup cocoa
1 egg
1 cup milk
1 teaspoon vanilla extract

Preheat oven to 350°. • Cream butter and sugar. • Sift together flour, baking soda, salt and cocoa. • Add to creamed mixture. • Add egg, milk and vanilla and mix until smooth. •

Drop by rounded teaspoons onto ungreased cookie sheet. • Bake for 7 to 9 minutes. • Cool on waxed paper.

FILLING

1 stick butter
1 cup confectioners' sugar
1 cup marshmallow creme
1 teaspoon vanilla extract

Beat all ingredients together. • Spread on half the cakes. • Top with remaining cakes. Yield: 12

You are going out to tea today,
So mind how you behave;
Let all accounts I have of you
Be pleasant ones, I crave.

Don't spill your tea, or gnaw your bread,
And don't tease one another;
And Tommy musn't talk too much,
Or quarrel with his brother.

Say, "If you please," and "thank you Nurse,"
Come home at eight o'clock;
And Fanny, pray, be careful that
You do not tear your frock.

Now, mind your manners, children five,
Attend to what I say;
And then, perhaps, I'll let you go
Again another day.

Under the Window
—Kate Greenway

A Book Lover's Tea

Mushroom Pâté

Cardamom Braid

Meringue Mushrooms

Maple Pecan Scones

Linzer Cookies

Chocolate-Cherry Tart

TEA-TIME IS AN IMPOR-tant occasion at The Inn at Cedar Crossing. A dozen or more times a year, owner/innkeeper Terry Wulf honors local authors and poets at a special tea. "We have so many published writers and other talented people in the arts here," says Terry, "that we thought we would do our part to feature them."

Literary gourmets, hungry for food-for-thought, are treated to volumes of edible palate pleasers cooked up in the inn's kitchen, which also serves daily breakfasts, lunches and dinners. The book-lover's tea-time usually features one author speaking about his or her book as well as writing and publishing in general.

The recipes offered here are complementary to two books that have been fêted at the inn: *The Loving Spice of Life* by family saga and romance writer Adeline Edmunds and *Out on a Limb* by naturalist writer Roy Lukes. The Mushroom Pâté, Mushroom Meringues and Maple Pecan Scones were chosen to complement the nature theme of Lukes' books and the sweet treats were in order with the light and romantic twist to Edmunds' work.

The tea is served buffet style and once guests have their plates and their teacups filled, they listen to the storytellers. Later, books are signed and questions answered.

The Inn at Cedar Crossing is an 1884 Victorian brick vernacular-style building that once housed a tailor, an apothecary shop, and a soda fountain. It has the ambiance of an historic hotel, thoughtfully decorated with a flair for country elegance. Plump, down-filled pillows, whirlpools, and heirloom collectibles are a few guest-room amenities. Bowing again to Terry's affinity for local talent, there are craft items from local artisans accenting rooms. Some of the works are for sale.

Beyond the inn is the Lake Michigan shoreline and environs of Door County, famous for its cherry production. These serene wooded areas must have inspired Roy Lukes to write about nature. Spectacular limestone bluffs along the water's edges most assuredly stimulated some of the conflict and resolution in Adeline Edmunds' amorous writings. The writers at any of the inn's teas and even the inn itself will coax your own penchant for penning your thoughts, observations, or imaginings in a diary, a novel, or that travel postcard you've been meaning to send!

The Inn at Cedar Crossing
336 Louisiana Street
Sturgeon Bay, WI 54235
Phone: **(414) 743-4200**
Rooms: **9**
Tea-Time: **On special occasions**

A BOOK LOVER'S TEA AT HOME

- Invite guests by writing party information on a blank bookmark.
- Make a centerpiece, using stacks of the author's books, flowers and props that give clues to the book's content.
- If you're inviting people who are strangers to one another, use name tags. Cut them out in the shape of an open book. Use straight pins to fasten onto clothing.

MUSHROOM PÂTÉ

1½ pounds domestic mushrooms, brushed clean, not washed
½ pound shiitake mushrooms, stems removed
¾ cup chopped shallots
2 tablespoons butter
2 tablespoons Dijon-style mustard
1 tablespoon minced garlic
1 tablespoon dried tarragon or 3 sprigs fresh
½ teaspoon salt
⅛ teaspoon pepper
8 ounces cream cheese, softened
1 cup grated Swiss cheese
6 egg whites

Preheat oven to 375°. • Coarsely chop mushrooms and shallots. • Sauté in butter until softened. • Add mustard, garlic, tarragon, salt and pepper. • Mix well. • Add the cream cheese and Swiss cheese. • Place ingredients in bowl of food processor. • Purée until very fine. • Slowly, while processor is running, add the egg whites 1 at a time. • Place into a well-oiled, 9x5-inch loaf pan or bundt pan. • Place into a larger pan for a water bath. • Water should come halfway up the sides of the smaller pan. • Cover over both pans with foil. • Bake for 1 hour or until tester inserted in center comes out clean. • Serve with crackers or toast points. Yield: 3 cups

CARDAMOM BRAID

2 cups warm milk
2 eggs
2 small packages active dry yeast
1 stick butter, softened
½ cup sugar

1 1/2 teaspoons salt

1 teaspoon cardamom

6 cups flour

Butter

Sugar

Preheat oven to 350°. • Combine milk, eggs, yeast, 1 stick butter, sugar, salt and cardamom. • Add enough flour to make a moderately stiff dough. • Knead. • Place in a greased bowl and let rise until doubled in size. • Punch down and divide into 3 equal parts. • Divide each part into thirds. • Roll into long ropes. • Braid, tucking ends under. • Place braids on greased cookie sheets. • Cover with dish towel and let rise in warm place until doubled in size. • Bake for 25 to 30 minutes or until golden brown. • Remove from oven. • Brush with melted butter and sprinkle with sugar. • Cool completely. • Yield: 3 loaves

In America, we call them tea carts or tea wagons. In England they refer to them as tea trolleys.

MERINGUE MUSHROOMS

4 egg whites

1 teaspoon vanilla extract

1/2 teaspoon cream of tartar

1 cup sugar

1/4 cup unsweetened cocoa powder

1 cup semi-sweet chocolate morsels

Preheat oven to 250°. • Line cookie sheets with parchment paper. • Beat egg whites, vanilla and cream of tartar until soft peaks

Chocolate Cherry Tart and Mushroom Pâté

nilla and cream of tartar until soft peaks form. • Gradually add sugar and continue beating. • (You still want soft peaks.) • Put egg white mixture into a pastry bag fitted with a 1/2-inch round tip, filling bag half full.

To form mushroom tops, hold tip about 1/2 inch from the paper and squeeze, letting the meringue spread out and mound like a mushroom cap onto the prepared pan. Dip finger in water, so that you can easily pull the tip away and flatten the point that forms. • Make caps until half the meringue is used. • Dust very lightly with cocoa sifted from a small strainer. • To form stems, squeeze meringue onto the prepared pan, pulling up as you squeeze. • Make them 1 1/2 to 2-inches long. • Bake meringues for 2 hours. • Don't let them brown. They should be completely dry. • Cool completely.

Melt chocolate morsels over low heat. • Meanwhile, with a sharp knife, trim the point off each stem, made when forming each meringue. Spread the melted chocolate on the underside of each mushroom cap and attach stems. When the chocolate hardens, it glues the mushrooms together. Yield: 24 to 36

Handmade arts at The Inn at Cedar Crossing include a quilt, Cardamom Braid, Linzer Cookies, and a taste of literature.

LINZER COOKIES

3 cups all-purpose flour
2½ teaspoons cinnamon
½ teaspoon cloves
1 teaspoon salt
2½ sticks butter
2 cups ground almonds
2 cups ground walnuts
Grated peel of 1 lemon
1⅔ cups sugar
1 egg
1 yolk of large egg
2 cups raspberry jam

Combine all ingredients, except eggs and jam, in a large mixing bowl. • Add egg and egg yolk. • Dough should hold together. • Chill for 1 hour. • Preheat oven to 350°. • On lightly floured surface, roll out half the dough to an ⅛-inch thickness. • With a 2½-inch heart or round cookie cutter, cut out cookies. • Place cookies on a greased baking sheet about 1 inch apart. • Spread each with ½ teaspoon jam to within ¼ inch from the edge. • Roll out remaining dough. • Cut out cookies. • Follow with a 1-inch cutter to cut out centers. • Reuse dough from centers in another recipe. Place rings on top of jam-covered bottoms. • Bake for 10 to 12 minutes or until golden brown. Yield: 45 to 50

You can freeze grated lemon and orange peel for future use. Wrap in plastic in teaspoon-size portions and freeze.

MAPLE PECAN SCONES

3 cups all-purpose flour
1½ tablespoons baking powder
¾ teaspoon salt
1½ sticks unsalted butter
1 cup chopped pecans
⅓ cup milk
⅔ cup pure maple syrup, plus more for brushing

Preheat oven to 350°. • Combine flour, baking powder and salt. • Cut in butter with pastry blender. • Add pecans. • In separate bowl, whisk together milk and syrup. • Slowly pour liquid into dry ingredients while mixing until combined. • Dough should be firm. • Roll out dough on floured surface 1½ inches thick. • Cut scones with 3-inch round biscuit cutter. • Brush tops with additional maple syrup. • Place on greased and floured cookie sheet. • Bake for 15 to 20 minutes or until golden. Yield: 12

CHOCOLATE-CHERRY TART

Cherries are indigenous to the inn's area. So they are usually on the menu in some form or another.

DOUGH

1½ cups all-purpose flour
2 tablespoons sugar
¾ teaspoon salt
1 stick plus 2 tablespoons butter
Yolks of 2 large eggs
3 tablespoons water

Preheat oven to 300°. • Combine flour, sugar, salt and butter. • In separate bowl, whisk together yolks and water. While whisking, slowly add to flour mixture. • Mix only until dough holds together. • Do not overmix. • Roll out onto a lighly floured surface to a ¼-inch thickness. • Place into an ungreased 10-inch tart pan. • Line with parchment paper and pie weights. • Bake for 15 to 20 minutes or until lightly golden brown. • Cool on rack. • Remove weights and parchment paper. • Make filling.

FILLING

½ stick butter
1½ ounces unsweetened chocolate
2 eggs
1½ tablespoons light corn syrup
¾ cup sugar
¼ teaspoon salt
⅛ cup heavy cream
½ teaspoon vanilla extract

Melt butter and chocolate separately. • Set aside. • Beat together eggs, corn syrup, sugar and salt. • Add chocolate and butter to egg mixture. • Stir in cream and vanilla. • Pour into prebaked shell. • Bake for 20 to 25 minutes or until just set. • Cool on rack. • Prepare topping.

TOPPING

2½ cups frozen sweetened cherries, well drained
¼ teaspoon almond extract
1 teaspoon vanilla extract
¾ teaspoon lemon juice
¼ cup sugar
2 tablespoons cornstarch

Bring cherries to a boil. • Add extracts and lemon juice. • Combine sugar and cornstarch. • Add to cherries. • Stir until it is thickened. • Cool slightly. • Pour onto tart. • Chill. • Garnish with chocolate curls.

CHOCOLATE CURLS

Melt 1 cup semi-sweet chocolate morsels. • Using a spatula, spread a thin layer onto cookie sheet. • Chill just until firm. • Using flat edge of knife, curl the chocolate off the sheet. Yield: 12 to 14 slices

The Business Tea

Shrimp Tea Sandwiches

———

Scones of Choice

———

Fruit Tarts with Crème Anglaise

———

Pumpkin Bread

———

Banana Nut Bread

THE CLOCK STRUCK 5 AND it was tea-time at The Bailiwick Inn. Executives of the Hamilton Insurance Company had just checked into their rooms—each an individual portrait of eighteenth-century Colonial America with replicas of plush featherbeds and goose-down pillows. Darjeeling and raspberry brews spouted from cozy-clad teapots into china cups, complementing the cheerful palaver in the parlor.

Innkeeper Anne Smith served the sandwiches and freshly baked scones and then let everyone help themselves. Hamilton Insurance was taking over the inn for a few days and the pampering had just begun.

The Bailiwick Inn is a splendid ex- ample of an urban Colonial inn in an historic area. Anne and her husband, Ray, spent a great deal of money and time to bring the old Joshua Gunnel house to life. Built during the late 1700s, the inn is a decorator's dream. There's just the right mixture of old and new in every room here and oil-on-canvas portraits of Anne and Ray in period garb hang in different parlors.

Every guest room flaunts replica brass-covered keyholes, and many have sinks with hand-painted designs in the porcelain bowls. Leather chairs, built-in bookcases, and crystal chandeliers tell only a part of the story. Outside, a brick-walled garden filled with flowers invites you to take tea in the warmer weather.

Small business meetings at inns are becoming more and more popular as executives find the atmosphere at inns more conducive to brainstorming. Part of that atmosphere is due to the pampering the corporate guest receives while away from home, and since tea is served at inns as a matter of course, it has become a part of many business meetings. Business people also find tea waiting for them on arrival after a day of traveling.

At The Bailiwick, I joined the briefcase crowd, drinking tea from a

Tea means business at The Bailiwick Inn.

Wedgwood china cup that was modeled after a pattern used in the Colonies in the New World, and soon heard the informal business group getting even more informal. The ubiquitous suits and ties were sinking into plush Edwardian, Georgian, and Colonial-inspired upholsteries. They were many moods away from the sterile office with its rolling, swivel, tight-weave chairs and bright lights.

I gazed out the window for a moment at the courthouse across the street where George Washington's will rests in peace. I knew, if he were still around today, he'd choose Anne and Ray's place to call an informal meeting of the Continental Congress with tea at the head of the table.

The Bailiwick Inn
4023 Chain Bridge Road
Fairfax, VA 22030
Phone: **(703) 691-2266**
Rooms: **14**
Tea-Time: **5:00–6:00** P.M. **for inn guests**

SHRIMP TEA SANDWICHES

8 ounces cream cheese, beaten
8 ounces small shrimp, finely diced
1 clove garlic, finely chopped
¼ cup finely chopped chives
¼ teaspoon salt
Freshly ground pepper
1 stick butter
Juice of half a large lemon
2 teaspoons chopped fresh parsley
20 slices brown bread

In medium bowl, mix together cream cheese, shrimp, garlic, chives, salt and pepper. • In separate bowl, cream butter, adding lemon juice and parsley. • Spread butter mixture on 10 slices bread, followed by a layer of the cream cheese mixture. • Top with remaining slices. • Remove crusts. • Cut each sandwich into 4 triangles. Yield: 40

FRUIT TARTS WITH CRÈME ANGLAISE

Top with fruits such as strawberries, grape halves, sliced bananas, mandarin oranges, blueberries or raspberries. Layer a coating of glaze over the fruit.

TART SHELLS

2 cups all-purpose flour
⅛ teaspoon salt
½ teaspoon sugar
1½ sticks unsalted butter, chilled and cut into bits
2 to 3 tablespoons ice water

In bowl of electric mixer, combine flour, salt, sugar and butter on low speed of electric mixer (paddle attachment preferable). • Beat for 8 minutes or until the mixture is the consistency of fine cornmeal. • Add up to 3 tablespoons of water. The pastry will roll from the sides of the bowl. • Remove the pastry to a lightly floured surface and shape into a ball. • Cover with waxed paper and chill for 30 to 45 minutes. • Preheat oven to 450°. • When dough is chilled, roll out to an ⅛-inch thickness. • Cut circles with a 2-inch cutter and line each muffin tin cup with a circle. • Bake for 8 minutes or until golden. Make filling.

SANDWICH SAVVY

Expect 30 finger or triangle sand-wiches, or 40 square sandwiches from 1 loaf (20 slices) of bread. Plan on 3 sand-wiches per person.

Hannah Marie Country Inn

***

Make them as dainty as possible: they should be two-mouthful affairs. Be adven-turous with the fillings; but remember colour as well as taste. Pinwheel sand-wiches look like miniature slices of a Swiss roll—make the fillings contrast with the colour of the bread. Cut slices lengthwise from loaf and cut off crusts. Spread each slice with the filling and roll lengthwise. Chill before cutting across into pinwheels. For white bread, try jam, pâté, creamed fish, bloater paste, Gentlemen's Relish. For brown, choose cream cheese, egg or cress.

Dining with Dickens

***

Thin ribbon tied around each finger sandwich provides a handle for lifting the sandwiches off the plate daintily.

***

Use a heart cookie cutter to make inter-estingly shaped sandwiches.

Mad River Inn

***

To thinly slice homemade bread for proper tea sandwiches, freeze the bread after baking and slice, while frozen, with an electric knife.

Dairy Hollow House

***

It's usually best to cut the crusts from tea breads after you assemble the sand-wiches and before you cut them. This way, the ingredients end up all the way into the corners.

Bee & Thistle

CRÈME ANGLAISE FILLING

3 egg yolks

¼ cup sugar

1 tablespoon cornstarch

1 cup milk

¼ teaspoon vanilla extract

In double boiler over hot water, heat egg yolks and sugar, stirring with a whisk until the mixture turns to ribbons. • Dissolve cornstarch in milk. Add to egg mixture. • Add vanilla and mix until thick. • Remove from heat. • Put bowl on ice. • Stir until cold. • Cover. • Fill each tart with the Crème Anglaise filling. • **Fruit Glaze:** If fruit is green or yellow in color, use 2 tablespoons apricot jam with 1 teaspoon water. Pour enough to cover fruit. • If fruit is red, purple, or blue, use 2 tablespoons red currant jelly and 1 teaspoon water. Yield: 72

PUMPKIN BREAD

3½ cups all-purpose flour

2 teaspoons baking soda

1½ teaspoons salt

1 teaspoon nutmeg

1½ teaspoons pumpkin pie spice

1 teaspoon cinnamon

½ teaspoon cloves

1 cup nuts, chopped

4 eggs, slightly beaten

⅔ cup water

1¾ cups pumpkin purée

3 cups sugar

1 cup vegetable oil

A fanciful featherbed

Preheat oven to 350°. • In large bowl, mix and sift dry ingredients. • Add nuts and mix. • Combine eggs with water, pumpkin, sugar and oil. • Pour mixture into dry ingredients and blend lightly. • Pour into 2 greased 9x5-inch loaf pans. • Bake for 1 hour or until tester inserted in center comes out clean. Yield: 2 loaves

THE BUSINESS TEA AT HOME

- Use desk blotters as the place mats.
- If the tea is being served during the meeting, serve with thermal pots so that the meeting can go on uninterrupted.
- Teas are great ideas for having the people you work with to your house. Suggest the possibility for your next departmental meeting.

Innkeeper Ray Smith prepares for tea while the delightful brew is kept warm in a homespun cozy.

Banana Nut Bread
This recipe is best cooked a day ahead.

2 cups all-purpose flour
½ teaspoon salt
1 teaspoon baking soda
1 stick butter
1 cup sugar
2 eggs, beaten
1 cup (3 medium) mashed bananas
½ cup sour milk

¾ cup walnuts, chopped coarsely
½ teaspoon grated lemon peel

Preheat oven to 350°. • In medium bowl, sift together first 3 ingredients. • In large bowl, cream butter and sugar; add eggs. • Mix in dry ingredients alternately with mashed bananas and sour milk. • Add nuts and lemon peel. • Pour into a greased and floured 9x5-inch loaf pan. • Bake for 70 minutes on rack below center of oven. • Bake until tester inserted in center comes out clean. Yield: 1 loaf

The Breakfast Tea

Chilled Mixed Fruit Soup

Rolled-Oat Breakfast Scones

Monterey Morning Cheese Rolls

English Cream-Coddled Eggs

*Pacific Coast Pimiento and Green Chili
Quiche*

Spicy Pear Muffins

Laura's Lemon Tea Bars

PERHAPS THE CLOSEST thing to having breakfast in a garden somewhere on the English coast is to have it at Old Monterey Inn. Here a veritable paradise of greenery and fronds, a sea of impatiens and wisteria vines, and redwood trees surround you. There's an acre of landscaped gardens to behold as you sip your morning tea—perhaps the full-bodied, eye-opening English Breakfast. The inn itself is an elegant English Tudor country house built in 1929.

Ann and Gene Swett have lived in this house with their five children for 25 years. When the kids started going off on their own, the Swetts redecorated the home and turned it into a bed & breakfast. In a short time, they captured the Mobil 4-star rating.

The inn's ten rooms are designer showcases, offering various themes. The turn-of-the-century Serengeti room is done in patterns by designer

Ralph Lauren. There's a "mosquito-netting" crown canopy and a copy of *The Making of the African Queen* by Katharine Hepburn sitting next to a lady's pith helmet. Three large antique hatboxes are stacked totem-pole style with a round glass top to form a side table. The scene makes you feel as though some bold but delicate adventurer is about to ride off in a Land Rover, but not before satisfying her appetite for a spot of tea and sweet rewards. You can fulfill your own safari fantasies here and take tea in the afternoon, catching the warm breezes that blow in off the bay. You might even hear barking sea lions as waves crack against the shore.

Breakfast is a full-fledged affair, whether you take it in the garden or in your room. The inn's breakfast tea includes an assortment of beverages and a combination of British and Pacific Coast dishes, cooked up by Gene. In England, they take a tea break called "elevenses." If they had an Old Monterey breakfast in them, they wouldn't have to stop at 11 A.M. for mid-morning snacks.

Old Monterey Inn
500 Martin Street
Monterey, CA 93940
Phone: **(408) 375-8284**
Rooms: **10**
Tea-Time: **Breakfast, and 2:30 P.M. for arriving inn guests**

A BREAKFAST TEA AT HOME

- Serve this tea-time as you would if it were an evening dinner party. In other words, relax in the family room with your guests first before serving tea and sitting them at the dining room or breakfast table. First, offer a beverage as each guest arrives, such as the Chilled Mixed Fruit Soup. Then, pass around an eye-opening appetizer such as the Monterey Morning Cheese Rolls.
- Add lighted candles to the breakfast table for elegance, even if it is already a bright morning.
- Make the centerpiece a large basket of breakfast breads and sprinkle oatmeal and finely chopped granola around the base.

CHILLED MIXED FRUIT SOUP

1 cup cranberry cocktail juice
½ cup orange juice
¼ teaspoon vanilla extract
1 cup apple juice
½ cup pineapple juice
½ cup strawberries
1 cup coarsely cut peaches
1 cup bananas
½ cup each: chopped bananas, seedless grapes, pineapple chunks, peaches and melon balls

In food processor, purée first 8 ingredients. • Keep chilled. • When ready to serve, add remaining fruit to the mixture. • Serve in soup bowls, garnished with fresh mint leaves. Yield: 4 cups

ROLLED-OAT BREAKFAST SCONES

1 cup all-purpose flour
1 cup old-fashioned rolled oats
½ teaspoon baking soda
½ teaspoon salt
1 teaspoon cream of tartar
1 tablespoon sugar
¼ cup shortening
½ cup milk

Preheat oven to 425°. • Mix together flour, oats, baking soda, salt, cream of tartar and sugar. • Add shortening and milk, and with fork mix to a soft dough. • Roll out on floured board to a ½-inch thickness. • Cut into triangles. • Place on greased cookie sheet. • Bake for 15 minutes or until lightly browned. • Serve warm with butter and preserves. Yield: 8 to 12

MONTEREY MORNING CHEESE ROLLS

1 cup milk
2 tablespoons butter
⅛ teaspoon salt
⅛ teaspoon pepper
1 cup all-purpose flour
4 eggs
¾ cup grated extra sharp cheddar cheese, divided

Preheat oven to 375°. • Combine milk, butter, salt and pepper in a 3-quart saucepan. • Bring to a boil. • Remove from heat. • Add flour and stir until mixture forms a ball. • Beat in eggs, 2 at a time until the dough is smooth. • Add ½ cup grated cheese. • Spoon equal portions into 4 well-greased, 6-ounce custard cups. • Cover tops with remaining cheese. • Bake for 45 minutes. (Do not open oven door while baking.) Yield: 4

The Serengeti Room

A tasty kaleidoscope: quiche, fruit soup, and cheese rolls

ENGLISH CREAM-CODDLED EGGS

In the British tradition, Old Monterey often serves these in elegant small porcelain egg cups. • For each cup:

1 large fresh egg
⅛ teaspoon half-and-half
½ teaspoon cream cheese
⅛ teaspoon salt
⅛ teaspoon white pepper
½ teaspoon freshly chopped or dried chives

Combine all ingredients, except chives, mixing well. • Chill overnight. • In the morning, whisk to lighten and add fresh chopped chives. • Place in individual lightly greased egg cups, filling ¾ full. • Place cups in pan of boiling water, with water covering just to the lid. • Cook exactly 7 minutes. • Remove cup and loosen lid slightly. • Serve immediately.

PACIFIC COAST PIMIENTO AND GREEN CHILI QUICHE

6 extra large eggs
1¼ cups sour cream
1 tablespoon cream sherry
½ cup pimientos, drained and chopped
¾ cup green chilies, drained and chopped
2 tablespoons dried onions
1¼ cups grated cheddar cheese
1 9-inch pie shell

Preheat oven to 425°. • Mix together eggs, sour cream and sherry. • Add pimientos, chilies and onions. • Mix well. • Add cheddar cheese. • Pour into pie shell. • Bake for 40 to 45 minutes or until golden brown. • Serve warm or cold. Yield: 8 servings

Spicy Pear Muffins

4 large pears
1 cup sugar
½ cup vegetable oil
2 large eggs
2 teaspoons vanilla extract
2 cups all-purpose flour
2 teaspoons baking soda
2 teaspoons cinnamon
1 teaspoon nutmeg
1 teaspoon salt
1 cup raisins
1 cup walnuts
Confectioners' sugar

Preheat oven to 325°. • Peel and dice pears. Set aside. • Cream together sugar, oil, eggs and vanilla. • In another bowl, mix together flour, baking soda, cinnamon, nutmeg and salt. • Add to egg mixture and blend. • Do not overmix. • Fold in raisins, walnuts and pears. • Turn into a muffin tin and bake for 30 minutes or until golden brown. • Dust with confectioners' sugar. Yield: 12

Laura's Lemon Tea Bars

Crust

1½ sticks margarine
1½ cups all-purpose flour
⅓ cup sugar
¼ teaspoon salt

Mix all ingredients until smooth and spreadable. • Spread into bottom of a greased 8x4-inch baking pan.

Filling

3 eggs
1½ cups sugar
⅛ teaspoon salt
1 tablespoon grated lemon peel
¼ cup fresh lemon juice
Confectioners' sugar

Preheat oven to 350°. • Mix together all ingredients, except confectioners' sugar, until smooth. • Pour over crust. • Bake for 20 to 30 minutes or until set. • Cool on rack. • Dust with confectioners' sugar. • Cut into 1x2-inch rectangles. Yield: 16

Save old tea leaves to throw over fireplace ashes to keep down the dust when you clean the hearth.

Five

HOLIDAY AND SEASONAL TEAS

YOU CAN FIND ALMOST ANY EXCUSE TO SIT DOWN AND have a cup of tea. But when you're expecting company to join you—a lot of company—you may need more than a teapot and a few cups. Holidays and the seasons of the year present ideal settings for holding a tea. The Tea Council of the United States even suggests serving a barbecue tea in summertime!

When there is a lot of excitement and a special occasion, such as with teas served during a holiday or special season, it's easy for the basic ingredient—the tea—to get lost under all the exciting foods and merriment. But, if you make tea the center of attraction by putting it on its own special table or in a decorated punch bowl, you will draw attention to it. The tea does the rest. Once your guests start enjoying the tea, there's no doubt about what's the catalyst for the celebration and why.

Think of not-so-celebrated holidays and seasonal events to hold a tea. Have a Kentucky Derby Tea or celebrate the annual tennis tournament at Wimbledon, England, by holding a tea at the tennis courts, something they do occasionally at the Corner House on Nantucket. Have a Presidential Tea or a Columbus Day Tea. When school starts, have a Back-to-School Tea.

As you will see in this chapter, inns know how to make the most of tea-time by connecting it to the time of year. Remember that tea for no reason except for the season is a perfectly wonderful excuse to share a "cuppa."

Colorful threads and regional foods weave a tapestry of celebration at Geneva on the Lake.

A High-Energy Spring Tea

Red Clover Tea

Fresh Strawberry Blossom Tea

Homestyle Sesame Crackers

Hearty Nut-Mix Melt

Oatmeal Almond Muffins

Strawberry Walnut Tea Bread

TUCKED HANDSOMELY into the shadows of the majestic White Mountains is one of the smallest towns in America. As spring unfolds here in Lower Waterford, daffodils trumpet to life, leading a chorus of young buds pushing through the slumberous earth. *New Life*. The music of the season—played by nature as well as the sweet breath of a talented innkeeper—is filled with promises of great personal harmony. *Rebirth*. Swaying to a gentle rhythm, the waves of Vermont clover softly blanket the meadows. *Nurturing*. Jubilant treasures of a yielding land festoon the mornings once again. *Renewal*.

It's springtime in Vermont and the countryside around Rabbit Hill Inn awakens your body and soul. The time is right for outdoor activity and exercise, and for storybook afternoons when you take spring and a cup of tea by the hand. At Rabbit Hill Inn, the season's promises are fulfilled—the new life, rebirth, nurturing, renewal, tea-time and music—always the music.

They call you by name as you enter the 1785 inn, even though they haven't met you yet. Oh, so refreshing is this springtime attitude. At the center of such hospitality are innkeepers John and Maureen Magee. Canadian Olympic athletes are often guests at the inn, but it is the Magees who capture the gold here.

Hours before tea-time, John, Maureen and the zestful spring season encourage you to meander footloose on Rabbit Hill's fifteen acres and beyond. Indulge in a frolicsome trek past a busy beaver colony. Hasten your stride, but stop to caress a periwinkle or a morning glory. Bicycle past Lower Waterford's eight houses, its honor-system library, an eighteenth-century post office, and a white-steepled church. Stop for a picnic lunch at an old graveyard and then pedal on to open road. Ride to a park where mountain climbing is popular. Then go for the tea to restore your energy.

A spring tea at the inn is fortified with restorative gifts: new friends and power-packing foods to keep you up and running. Tea in the parlor is lovely, graced with the ever-present candlelight and fresh-cut spring flowers. Tea in the inn's *gemütlich* After-Sports Lounge can be accompanied with checkers or a puzzle. You can then amble down to the Connecticut River (200 yards away) for trout and bass fishing or a breezy canoe ride. Filled with tea-time energy, put plenty of oomph behind those oars, but stop awhile to absorb the surrounding landscape.

Oh, how quickly the days pass at Rabbit Hill—no matter what you're doing. As twilight falls, you hear the music of the night. You wait with anticipation for the dining room doors to open because Maureen and John keep the room off limits all day to create surprise for their special dining experience.

Once you're seated, classical notes wing their way into the dining room where a gourmet chef's repertoire is being served. Maureen serenades from the parlor with her melodious silver flute. In an inn that's bursting with spring fever, she offers her lyrical friendship until dinnertime ebbs and the tulips sleep.

Back in your room, the candles are lit, the bed turned down, and a soft-sculpture heart is on the pillow. The music is still playing, but from a classical tape this time. You blush with childish delight. From working out and playing hard to taking tea and dining, Rabbit Hill has offered a seasonal renaissance. You're only aching now to exercise your applause for the Magees and their most precious of country inns.

Rabbit Hill Inn
Lower Waterford, VT 05848
Phone: **(802) 748-5168**
Rooms: **18**
Tea-Time: **2:30 P.M. daily**

A HIGH-ENERGY SPRING TEA AT HOME

- Have guests dress in their warm-ups and sneakers, and preface your tea with an activity: a volleyball match, a hike, a softball game.
- Use pretty colored athletic sweat bands for napkin rings.
- An energy tea, says Maureen, should include some fresh or dried fruits, whole grains, nuts and food that is, "delectable yet high in complex carbohydrates and low in fat." Shy away from serving items filled with sugar and lacking in nutrition.

FRESH STRAWBERRY BLOSSOM TEA

| 40 fresh strawberries (tops only), rinsed |
| 2 cups cold water |

Preheat oven to 150°. • Remove the green leaves from the tops of the strawberries. (Reserve berries for use in Strawberry Walnut Tea Bread on page 171.) • Spread the leaves out evenly on a baking pan. • Place in oven for 10 to 15 minutes or until leaves are dry and crumbly. • Bring 2 cups of cold tap water to a boil. • Remove from heat and immediately add dried leaves. • Cover and set aside in a warm place for 7 to 10 minutes. • Strain and serve. Yield: 2 cups

HOMESTYLE SESAME CRACKERS

| 1 cup whole-wheat flour |
| 1 cup unbleached all-purpose flour |
| 1½ teaspoons baking powder |
| 1 teaspoon salt |
| ¼ cup plain yogurt |
| 1 tablespoon butter |
| 2 tablespoons sesame seeds |
| ⅔ cup ice water (scant) |

Preheat oven to 350°. • Sift together twice, flours, baking powder and salt. • Cut in yogurt. • Melt butter in sauté pan. • Add sesame seeds and stir until toasted. • Add seeds and butter to flour mixture. • Stir in ice water to form dough. • Knead lightly, about 20 strokes. • Roll out on floured surface to an ⅛-inch thickness. • Cut with 2-inch cookie cutters. • Prick each cracker all over with a fork. • Bake on greased cookie sheets for 10 minutes or until golden

RED CLOVER TEA

Red clover is the state flower of Vermont. So the folks at Rabbit Hill enjoy treating guests to a native beverage. You can grow red clover in your own garden.

| 1 gallon cold water |
| 3 cups red clover blossoms, rinsed |
| ¼ cup fresh mint leaves, shredded |
| ¼ teaspoon grated lemon peel |

In a large kettle, bring the water and red clover blossoms to a quiet boil. • Reduce heat and simmer 20 minutes. • Remove from heat and strain. • Add mint and lemon peel. The tea will be light green. • You may add a touch of Earl Grey tea to enrich the color and body. Yield: 16 cups brown. • Cool on rack. • Serve with a low-fat cheese such as Neufchâtel, Camembert and part-skim mozzarella. Yield: 60

HEARTY NUT-MIX MELT

½ cup pine nuts

¾ cup whole, blanched almonds

1 cup pecan halves

½ cup whole walnuts, cut in fourths

3 tablespoons butter

2 cloves garlic, crushed

1 teaspoon Worcestershire sauce

2 teaspoons curry powder

⅛ teaspoon cayenne pepper

Preheat oven to 350°. • Place all nuts in a bowl. • Melt butter in saucepan and stir in garlic, Worcestershire, curry powder and cayenne pepper. • Drizzle butter evenly over nuts and toss to coat evenly. • Spread nuts in a baking dish. • Bake for 15 to 20 minutes or until golden brown. (Stir every 5 minutes to toast evenly.) • Cool completely. Yield: 3 cups

OATMEAL ALMOND MUFFINS

A generous portion of oatmeal in this recipe yields a protein-packed sweet bread.

1 cup old-fashioned oatmeal

1 cup sour cream

1 stick (scant) butter, melted

¾ cup honey

2 eggs

1 cup unbleached all-purpose flour

1 teaspoon baking powder

½ teaspoon baking soda

½ teaspoon salt

½ cup sliced almonds

Preheat oven to 375°. • Mix together oatmeal and sour cream. • Add melted butter, honey and eggs. • Mix well. • Sift flour, baking powder, baking soda and salt into the mixture. • Add almonds. • Mix until just combined. • Pour into greased muffin tins, distributing the batter evenly. • Bake for 20 minutes or until golden. Yield: 12

STRAWBERRY WALNUT TEA BREAD

1 pint fresh strawberries, rinsed

1 cup unbleached all-purpose flour

¾ cup whole-wheat flour (preferably stone-ground)

¼ teaspoon baking powder

1 teaspoon baking soda

1 teaspoon salt

2 tablespoons wheat germ

1 stick butter

¾ cup sugar

2 eggs

⅓ cup water

½ cup chopped walnuts

Preheat oven to 350°. • In small non-stick sauté pan, mash half the strawberries. • Cook on medium heat for 3 to 4 minutes or until juices dry up. • Set aside to cool. • Mash remaining berries; add to sautéed berries. • Sift together flours, baking powder, baking soda and salt. • Mix in wheat germ. • In separate bowl, cream butter and sugar. • Add eggs and water, then mix. • Add wet ingredients to dry ingredients. • Fold in strawberries and nuts. • Turn into a greased 8x4-inch loaf pan. • Bake for 1 hour or until tester inserted in center comes out clean. Yield: 1 loaf

Victorian Summer Daze Tea

Tomato and Aged Cheddar Sandwiches

———

Crab and Olive Tea Sandwiches

———

English Tea Cinnamon Scones

———

Nectarine-Almond Pudding

———

Swiss Roll with Lemon Curd

———

Raspberry-Blueberry Cream Tart

STRAINS FROM THE SINGING voice of a grass canary flow exuberantly through guest rooms. How perfectly period of the Victorian Villa. Grass canaries were a favorite of Queen Victoria. Sam's soprano spreads like the morning sun, which shadows and highlights the grandiose sculpting on regally carved beds and then reaches far enough into a hallway to naturally light the frosted and crystal globes that are Victorian Villa's trademarks.

Innkeeper Ron Gibson is an unofficial curator of the Victorian era, "with something new to learn about that time every day," he says, reaching for the breakfast room regulator clock, which he winds faithfully. That's why he enjoys putting on Victorian holidays as much as his guests enjoy being at the inn to participate. Whether it's Christmas with Dickens, a New Year's celebration, a Valentine's weekend, two days of sleuthing about with Sherlock Holmes, or simply ambling about the inn, one feels like a Victorian occupant of the 1876 mansion. The Victorian Villa in winter is cloaked in quietly lit solitude. And in summer, the shutters fly open to welcome in days of dapper gents and sophisticated ladies.

Iced herb and fruit teas are served during Victorian Summer Daze, an annual time when guests crank out homemade ice cream, listen to the oompah of John Philip Sousa melodies under a romantic gazebo, eat scrumptious dinners and bountiful breakfasts, and play old-fashioned lawn games such as candlelight croquet. (Ron's research into the period yielded a line drawing depicting Victorians playing croquet at night. So he, too, had candleholders welded to the inn's wickets.)

Barbershop harmony fills the air and yarns are told from liar's benches during the weekend. The inn's aura evokes childhood memories of helping to squeeze fresh lemons for lemonade or going out to pick dew-frosted berries. Tea is also packed into the picnic hampers that couples tie to the backs of bicycles built for two. Others can just sit idly with a cup of golden tea in their hands and pretend to be happy vagabonds, traveling through history, far from the pressures of home.

I left the Victorian Villa comforted in knowing that I am only a plane ride away from the nineteenth century. I can return any time, and the people there will understand why I've come.

The Victorian Villa
601 North Broadway Street
Union City, MI 49094
Phone: **(517) 741-7383**
Rooms: **10**
Tea-Time: **4:00 P.M. daily for inn guests and on special occasions**

SUMMER DAZE TEA AT HOME

- Hold the event at a park and bring in some tandem bicycles.
- Ask everyone to wear vintage clothing. Pass out straw hats and barbershop arm bands you can make with wide satin ribbon.
- Rent an ice cream maker and give everyone the experience of making their own.
- Hire a barbershop quartet.

TOMATO AND AGED CHEDDAR SANDWICHES

Use fresh garden-ripened summer tomatoes.

1 cup grated, extra sharp cheddar cheese
½ cup diced fresh tomato
Mayonnaise
8 thin slices bread, crusts removed

Combine cheese, tomato and enough mayonnaise to moisten thoroughly. • Spread mixture on 4 slices of bread. • Top with remaining bread; cut each sandwich into 4 triangles or serve on croissants. Yield: 16

CRAB AND OLIVE TEA SANDWICHES

French bread gives this tea sandwich a different twist.

8 ounces cream cheese, softened
¼ pound fresh or frozen crab meat, thoroughly drained
½ cup pitted black olives, drained and chopped
40 slices cocktail rye bread or French baguette
1 medium cucumber, peeled and cut into 20 thin slices
1 bunch fresh watercress sprigs (about 4 ounces)
1 tablespoon coarsely shredded lemon peel

In a large bowl, beat cream cheese until smooth. • Stir in crab meat and olives until well combined. • Spread 1 teaspoon of crab mixture onto each bread slice. • Top 20 of the bread slices with 1 cucumber slice and 1 watercress sprig. • Sprinkle lemon peel atop watercress. • Top with remaining bread slices to form sandwiches. Yield: 20

ENGLISH TEA CINNAMON SCONES

4 cups all-purpose flour
¼ cup sugar
4 teaspoons baking powder
1 teaspoon salt
½ teaspoon cream of tartar
⅔ cup butter
1⅓ cups light cream
1 large egg
Milk
½ teaspoon cinnamon mixed with ½ teaspoon sugar

Front to back: Nectarine Almond Pudding; Raspberry-Blueberry Cream Tarts; English Tea Cinnamon Scones; and Tomato and Aged Cheddar Sandwiches on a croissant

Preheat oven to 425°. • Combine flour, sugar, baking powder, salt and cream of tartar. • Cut in butter. • In separate bowl, beat together cream and egg and add to butter mixture. • Mix lightly with a fork. • Turn out onto floured surface and knead 5 to 6 times. • Divide in half and pat out to a ¾-inch thickness. • Cut into 2-inch rounds. • Brush tops with milk; dust with cinnamon/sugar mixture. • Bake for 12 to 15 minutes or until golden. Yield: 24 to 30

The average American drinks 180 cups and glasses of tea per year.
Tea Council of the U.S.A.

NECTARINE-ALMOND PUDDING

| 5 tablespoons butter |
| 1/2 cup sugar |
| 3 eggs |
| 1 teaspoon vanilla extract |
| 1/2 teaspoon almond extract |
| 2 1/2 cups all-purpose flour |
| 3 tablespoons baking powder |
| 1/2 cup milk |
| 1 1/2 cups puréed nectarines (about 8) |
| Whole almonds |
| Fresh fruit |

Combine butter, sugar, eggs and extracts. • Beat well. • Add flour and baking powder; blend in milk and nectarines. • Place whole almonds in pattern in bottom of a well-greased 4-to 6-cup mold. Pour in batter. • Place mold in large saucepan over medium heat; add water halfway up the sides of the mold. • Cover. • Steam for 1 1/2 hours. • Add a baker's glaze if desired. Garnish with fresh fruit. • Serve cold. Yield: 20 small servings

SWISS ROLL WITH LEMON CURD

Prepare and chill lemon curd before preparing cake. Use recipe below or your favorite packaged lemon curd.

LEMON CURD

| 1/2 stick unsalted butter |
| 1/2 cup sugar |
| 1/2 cup fresh lemon juice |
| 4 egg yolks |
| 1 tablespoon grated lemon peel |

In heavy saucepan, combine butter, sugar, lemon juice and egg yolks. • Cook over very low heat, stirring constantly until mixture thickens enough to heavily coat the back of a spoon. Do not let mixture boil. • Pour into small bowl and stir in lemon peel. • Chill until ready to use. Yield: 1 cup

CAKE

| 2 tablespoons butter, divided |
| 2 tablespoons all-purpose flour |
| 6 tablespoons sugar |
| 4 eggs |
| 1/2 cup self-rising flour |
| 2 tablespoons superfine sugar |
| Lemon curd |

Prepare and chill lemon curd before baking cake. • Preheat oven to 400°. • Grease bottom of 11x17-inch jellyroll pan with 1 tablespoon butter. Line the pan with waxed paper. • Let paper hang over sides. • Brush remaining butter on paper and sprinkle with 2 tablespoons flour.

Beat sugar and eggs together until light and fluffy. • Sift flour over the eggs, a little at a time, folding gently but thoroughly with a rubber spatula. • Do not overmix. • Pour into prepared pan, spreading evenly. • Bake for 10 minutes or until golden brown. • Remove cake. • Dust evenly with superfine sugar. • Turn over onto clean waxed paper. • Peel off baking paper. • Spread evenly with lemon curd and roll up. • Cool to room temperature. • Cut into 1/2-inch slices. Yield: 10

Ripe berries and ice-cold tea whisper summer daze.

RASPBERRY-BLUEBERRY CREAM TART

Using berries for tea-time desserts was very popular in Victorian summertimes. If you have a pick-your-own field near your home, gather the berries fresh for this traditional tart. Victorian Villa also makes this recipe as individual tarts.

PASTRY

1¼ cups all-purpose flour

¼ cup sugar

1 egg yolk

1 stick chilled butter, cut in small pieces

Preheat oven to 425°. • Sift flour into bowl. • Make a well and pour in the sugar. • Add egg yolk to well. • Cut in chilled butter with pastry blender until mixture resembles coarse crumbs. • Gather dough together and knead a few times until dough is smooth. • Cover with plastic and wrap; chill for 30 minutes. • Roll pastry out to fit a 10-inch flan pan. • Place in pan and line pastry with foil and pie weights. • Bake for 8 minutes. • Remove foil and weights and bake 5 minutes longer. • Cool.

VANILLA CREAM FILLING

¾ cup sugar

5 tablespoons all-purpose flour

¼ teaspoon salt

2 cups milk

6 egg yolks, beaten

2 teaspoons vanilla extract

1 pint blueberries

1 pint raspberries

2 tablespoons blueberry jelly

2 tablespoons raspberry jelly

2 teaspoons water

In a medium saucepan, stir together sugar, flour and salt. • Add milk. • Cook over low heat, stirring constantly, until thickened and boiling. • Remove from heat. • Add ½ cup hot milk mixture to beaten egg yolks. • Return all to saucepan. • Cook over low heat, stirring until thickened. • Do not allow to come to a boil. • Remove from heat and stir in vanilla. • Cover surface with plastic wrap and allow to cool. • Pour cream into pastry crust. • Arrange the raspberries and blueberries on top of cream. • Mix blueberry jelly and raspberry jelly with 2 teaspoons of water. Brush mixture over fruit to glaze. Yield: 12 slices

Tea by the Sea

Feta Cheese Cups

Cheese Straw Daisies

Date-Nut Lemon Sandwiches

Chocolate Chip Meringue Cookies

Chocolate Streusel Bars

I F YOU EVER WONDERED what it might be like to live out a nineteenth-century illustration depicting a Victorian seaside holiday, dream no more. You can make it happen at Cape May and at one of the premiere small Victorian inns in America, The Mainstay. Visiting here is like opening your grandmother's personal cache of seaside vacation letters and watching the words on the handwritten pages leap into life. Oh, modern automobiles do pass by and pedestrians stroll side-by-side in the latest fashions, but it's the pace, the surrounding architecture, and the furnishings of the inn that make you part of Cape May's living archives.

Mainstay innkeepers Sue and Tom Carroll are pioneers in the field of

bed & breakfast innkeeping in America. In 1970, they opened their home to guests who longed for the old-fashioned beach atmosphere. Back then, there was no guideline for new innkeepers to follow, and so they helped pave the way for this new kind of hospitality that was only in the budding stage in America.

Massive pieces of antique furniture complement the inn's fourteen-foot ceilings. The Carrolls are ever-present among their treasures and their guests, at the breakfast table and during tea. "We began serving tea fifteen years ago to get our house guests to mingle," recalls Sue.

Most of the year, tea is served in the dining room, often following a guided tour of the inn for overnight guests and non-inn guests alike. In summer, tea is served from ornate urns on the inn's munificent front porch. Chairs and tables abound with sweets served from salvers and tea carts. The Atlantic Ocean is only a block away and you can watch bathers returning from their day of surf and sand.

You might steal away as I did and sip tea in the inn's belvedere. This spacious, all-glass perch has two built-in seat cushions, enough for a few other "tea-totaling" inn guests to have joined me. But no one noticed me slip away, because I did so with great dispatch up the long fold-down stairs to the top of The Mainstay where I had a view of Cape May and a wonderful brew all to myself.

The Mainstay Inn
635 Columbia Avenue
Cape May, NJ 08204
Phone: **(609) 884-8690**
Rooms: **12**
Tea-Time: **4:00 P.M. Tuesday, Thursday, Saturday and Sunday for inn guests and drop-ins**

TEA BY THE SEA AT HOME

- Serve cookies from antique children's beach pails. Line the pails with foil.
- Use children's new beach pails as ice buckets.
- Add a replica of a Victorian fan to each place setting for cooling summer breezes while sipping the tea.

FETA CHEESE CUPS

Thin white bread
Melted butter
1 large egg, beaten
4 ounces cream cheese, softened
¼ pound crumbled feta cheese
½ teaspoon basil

Preheat oven to 350°. • With favorite biscuit cutter, cut rounds of white bread to fit miniature muffin tins. • Brush both sides of bread with melted butter. • Fit a piece of bread into each cup. • Mix remaining ingredients and fill each cup with a heaping teaspoon. • Bake for 20 minutes or until slightly browned. Yield: 24

It has been said that tea is suggestive of a thousand wants, from which spring the decencies and luxuries of civilization.

"To Think of Tea"
Agnes Repplier

CHEESE STRAW DAISIES

8 ounces sharp cheddar cheese, grated and at room temperature
1 cup shortening
1/4 teaspoon cayenne pepper
2 teaspoons salt
1 tablespoon water
1/3 cup Romano cheese, grated
2 cups sifted all-purpose flour
1 teaspoon baking powder

Preheat oven to 375°. • In bowl of electric mixer, mix cheddar cheese until creamy. • Add shortening and blend well. • Add pepper, salt, water and Romano cheese. • Blend together. • Sift flour and baking powder twice and slowly add to cheese mixture. • Add mixture in portions to pastry bag fitted with large star tip and squeeze small daisies onto ungreased cookie sheet. • Bake for 15 minutes or until set and golden. Yield: 70 to 80

DATE-NUT LEMON SANDWICHES

3 egg yolks
1/2 cup sugar
Juice and grated peel of 3 lemons
8 ounces cream cheese, softened
1 cup crushed pecans
Date-nut or whole-wheat bread, thinly sliced

Cook yolks, sugar and lemon juice over medium heat, stirring constantly until thickened. • Add grated peel. • Cool. • Mix in cream cheese and nuts. • Spread on bread. • Remove crusts. Yield: 1½ cups spread

Innkeeper Sue Carroll's star-shaped tea breads

CHOCOLATE CHIP MERINGUE COOKIES

2 egg whites
1 teaspoon vanilla extract
1/4 teaspoon cream of tartar
1/4 teaspoon salt
3/4 cup sugar
6 ounces semi-sweet chocolate morsels

Preheat oven to 300°. • Beat egg whites, vanilla, cream of tartar and salt until stiff peaks form. • Gradually beat in sugar until mixture is very stiff and glossy. • Fold in chocolate morsels. • Drop from a teaspoon onto a baking sheet lined with brown paper. • Bake for 25 minutes or until golden. Yield: 24

CHOCOLATE STREUSEL BARS

1³/₄ cups unsifted all-purpose flour

1¹/₂ cups confectioners' sugar

¹/₂ cup unsweetened cocoa powder

2 sticks cold butter

1 8-ounce package cream cheese, softened

1 14-ounce can sweetened condensed milk

1 egg

2 teaspoons vanilla extract

¹/₂ cup chopped walnuts

Preheat oven to 350°. • In large bowl, combine flour, sugar and cocoa. • Cut in butter with pastry blender until crumbly (mixture will be dry). • Reserve 2 cups crumb mixture. • Press remainder of crumb mixture onto bottom of 13x9-inch baking pan. • Bake for 15 minutes. • In large bowl, beat cream cheese until fluffy. • Gradually beat in condensed milk until smooth. • Add egg and vanilla. • Mix well. • Pour over prepared crust. • Combine nuts with reserved crumb mixture. • Sprinkle evenly over cheese mixture. • Bake for 20 minutes or until bubbly. • Cool and chill. • Cut into bars. • Store covered in refrigerator. Yield: 24

Tea and a penny farthing for your thoughts on the porch of The Mainstay

Frost-on-the-Pumpkin Tea

Gougère with Green Pepper Jelly

Onion Sandwiches with Homemade Mustard Mayonnaise

Pumpkin Nut Cookies

The Governor's Apple Bread with Cranberries

White Gingerbread Tea Cake

THE GOVERNOR'S INN CAPtured the fancy of tea aficionados in 1987. The National Tea Association decided to offer an award that year to a hotel, inn, or other service establishment for the presentation of afternoon tea. The Governor's took top honors. Teatime has always been a part of the hospitality showered on guests here by innkeeper-chefs Deedy and Charlie Marble. Their daughter, Jennifer, is the tea-time host. She often serves a blend of raspberry and black tea in striking china teacups and with Old World tea equipage, including a sugar bowl that once belonged to Queen Elizabeth II's grandfather.

Fall is a busy time as the inn buzzes with nonstop packing of gourmet picnic hampers for guests who have come to see Vermont's fall foliage. "Fall," says Deedy, "conjures up so many images—new Bonnie Doon knee socks for back-to-school, hot cider, crunching leaves underfoot, the autumn sun brilliantly reflecting the shimmering colors of the leaves and the chilly nights with warm comforters and log fires . . ." Kitchen kettles at the Governor's Inn work overtime, boiling up the fruits of the fall's harvest to enjoy throughout the winter. In fact, the fall brings green peppers in abundance and the little emerald puffs take over the inn's kitchen.

The Governor's onion sandwich brings back memories for me of the autumns my father took us all out to the country to pick bushels of onions from the dark, rich soil. If only back then we had had tea and The Governor's sandwiches to pack along!

The Governor's Inn
86 Main Street
Ludlow, VT 05149
Phone: **(802) 228-8830**
Rooms: **8**
Tea-Time: **3:00 P.M. daily for inn guests**

Cranberries spice an apple bread while pumpkin cookies peek through an antique tea tin.

GOUGÈRE WITH GREEN PEPPER JELLY

Gougère is a puff pastry with cheese. It resembles a savory, round bun. In Burgundy, France, Gougère accompanies many cellar wine tastings. Serve with green pepper jelly (see next recipe).

2 cups whole milk
2 sticks unsalted butter
1 teaspoon salt
2 cups all-purpose flour
8 eggs, at room temperature
2 cups grated sharp cheddar cheese
1/3 cup freshly snipped chives

Preheat oven to 375°. • In medium saucepan, bring the milk and butter to a slow boil. • Add the salt and heat until the butter is melted. • Remove the pan from heat. • With a wooden spoon, beat in the flour until well mixed and batter rolls away from sides of pan. • Transfer to bowl of electric mixer and beat at medium speed. • Add the eggs, 1 at a time, beating well after each addition. • Blend in cheese and chives. • Drop mixture by the teaspoonful onto a parchment-lined cookie sheet. • Bake for 35 minutes or until nicely brown and puffed. • (If you remove from the oven too soon, the Gougère will collapse.) • Serve with green pepper jelly. Yield: 64

GREEN PEPPER JELLY

1 cup ground green peppers
1 cup ground red peppers
1/4 cup ground hot pepper
6 1/2 cups sugar
1 1/2 cups cider vinegar
1 bottle Certo

Remove seeds from peppers. • Grind down and save the juice. (Measure ground peppers with juice.) • In saucepan, bring sugar, vinegar and peppers to a rolling boil. • Boil for 30 minutes. • Remove from heat and add Certo. • Cool and refrigerate in covered container. • The jelly should be the consistency of chocolate pudding. Yield: 3 to 4 cups

---

FROST-ON-THE-PUMPKIN TEA AT HOME

- Serve jams and preserves for scones in small, hollowed fresh pumpkins.
- Pick leaves, press them and use them under cheeses or tea cakes.
- Use small apple baskets to hold tea bags.
- Have a back-to-school tea for youngsters and give them each a new notebook to carry on the first day.

ONION SANDWICHES WITH HOMEMADE MUSTARD MAYONNAISE

MUSTARD MAYONNAISE

2 large egg yolks, at room temperature
4 teaspoons freshly squeezed lemon juice
2 tablespoons Dijon-style mustard
½ teaspoon salt
1½ cups extra virgin olive oil, divided (The Governor's uses Badia a Coltibuono)

In a bowl, with wire whisk, beat together the egg yolks, lemon juice, mustard, salt and ½ cup olive oil. • (Note: Add the remaining oil drop by drop, beating constantly.) • Beat the mayonnaise until it is emulsified. • Season with additional lemon juice, mustard or salt to taste. • It will keep 4 days in the refrigerator. Yield: 1⅔ cups

FOR THE SANDWICHES

24 thin slices white bread
1 cup mustard mayonnaise
1 large white onion, cut crosswise into 12 very thin slices
Salt to taste
1 cup minced fresh parsley leaves

With a 3-inch round cutter, cut out a round from each slice of bread. • Spread some of the mayonnaise generously on one side of each round. • Arrange a slice of onion on half of the rounds. • Sprinkle the onion with salt to taste. • Cover with the remaining rounds of bread. • Spread a thin layer of the remaining mayonnaise around the edges of the sandwiches and roll the edges in the chopped parsley. • Keep covered with a dampish tea towel in a plastic container. • Chill for about 6 hours. Yield: 12

PUMPKIN NUT COOKIES

Deedy thinks this recipe came from an heirloom box of old "receipts" she found in her grandmother's house.

½ stick unsalted butter, at room temperature
½ cup sugar
1 egg, beaten
½ cup pumpkin purée
1 cup all-purpose flour
1 tablespoon baking powder
½ teaspoon salt
1¼ teaspoons cinnamon
¼ teaspoon nutmeg
⅛ teaspoon ginger
½ cup raisins
½ cup chopped walnuts

Preheat oven to 350°. • Cream butter. • Add sugar gradually, mixing until light and fluffy. • Add egg and pumpkin. • Sift together flour, baking powder, salt and spices. • Stir into creamed mixture. • Add raisins and nuts. • Drop by teaspoon onto greased cookie sheet. • Bake for 14 minutes or until lightly browned. Yield: 24

"Oh, Marilla, I'm so glad we live in a world where there are Octobers . . . Look at these maple branches. Don't they give you a thrill—several thrills?"

—L.M. Montgomery, *Anne of Green Gables*

THE GOVERNOR'S APPLE BREAD WITH CRANBERRIES

½ stick sweet butter, softened
1 cup sugar
2 eggs
1 cup sour cream
2 teaspoons freshly grated lemon peel
3 cups all-purpose flour
4 teaspoons baking powder
1 teaspoon baking soda
½ teaspoon salt
2 cups peeled and chopped apples, cores removed
1½ cups chopped cranberries (drain slightly)
½ cup chopped walnuts

Preheat oven to 350°. • Cream together butter and sugar until light and fluffy. • Beat in eggs, sour cream and lemon peel. • Sift together flour, baking powder, baking soda and salt. • Add to egg and butter mixture. • Fold in apples, cranberries and walnuts. • Pour into prepared 10½x5½-inch pan. • Bake for 1 hour or until tester inserted in center comes out clean. • Cool in pan for 15 minutes. • Wrap in waxed paper and chill overnight. Slices best when chilled. • Serve at room temperature. Yield: 1 loaf

WHITE GINGERBREAD TEA CAKE

Spice cakes are great for fall. This is a light, moist cake that looks pretty. Since it's made in a tube pan, The Governor's uses the center as a flower vase. Pick fall flowers, wrap them in a wet towel and place in the center of the cake.

2 cups all-purpose flour
1 cup sugar
1 stick sweet butter, at room temperature
1 teaspoon cinnamon
½ teaspoon ginger
½ teaspoon mace
¼ teaspoon salt
½ teaspoon baking soda
½ teaspoon baking powder
1 egg
½ cup buttermilk

Preheat oven to 350°. • Mix together flour, sugar and butter until mixture resembles coarse meal. • Add ½ teaspoon of the cinnamon. • Blend. • Set aside 1 cup. • To the rest of the mixture, add the ginger, mace, salt, baking soda, baking powder and remaining cinnamon. • Mix together, then add egg and buttermilk, beating till smooth. • Pour batter into greased 10-inch tube pan. • Sprinkle reserved crumb mixture evenly over top. • Bake for 40 minutes or until tester inserted in center comes out clean. • Cool and serve. Yield: 16 to 20 slices

After-the-Ski Tea

Snow Peas Stuffed with Herb Cheese

Artichoke Cheesecake Spread

Cranberry Eggnog Tea Bread

White Chocolate Almond and Apricot Scones

Alpine Maple Cream Tarts

Linzer Torte

Pumpkin Roll

Bourbon Balls

THE VIEW FROM THE BACK of The Mad River Inn is breathtaking, majestic, beckoning. A mountainscape fills the frame as far as the eye can see. "Come," this section of the Green Mountains seems to be whispering, with a wide grin tilted at the picture-postcard valley below. "If you ski, try our downhill and cross-country trails. If you canoe, navigate our river. If you bike, pedal past our wildflower blooms. And if you hike, touch our ferns that layer the forest floor like lace cloths. Tread on our soil in autumn and see nature's most astonishing color wheel."

I listened to the mountain and found the Mad River area (so-called because the river flows north instead of south) to have everything one could want from the outdoors. In addition, the town of Waitsfield is chockablock with specialty food, clothing, crafts, and gift shops. But the reward at the end of the day was the real sweetener to this area they appropriately call Sugarbush: The Mad River Inn. And I was there just in time for tea. In fact, Annie Reed was filling tassies with a lemon mixture, while a Linzer Torte was just settling down after 45 minutes of puffing and swelling into its regal shape.

Innkeepers Rita and Luc Maranda and Rita's sister, Annie, work the magic that happens at Mad River. Although Mad River holds a variety of afternoon teas from traditional to wedding and holiday, snow so prolifically surrounds the 1900s house that an après-ski tea is so appropriate for this inn.

One knows it's time for tea when the lights go dim and the Victorian facade of The Mad River Inn starts to look like a Currier & Ives painting. Inside, wet ski wear dries, while all through the house is the scent of fragrant potpourri, harmonizing with the strains of classical music coming through speakers in the background.

Tea-time treats are cooked up by Annie, a creative chef, who is also hailed for her artful dinners, served on special occasions. Tea is served in the dining room, which is transformed into a country tea room at 4 P.M. The room is decorated with floral swag poufs and tablecloths bursting with lilac and rose patterns. An antique buffet proudly displays tea caddies and assorted tea bags and cocoa in woven baskets. A teacart carries antique teapots, creamers, sugar bowls and dessert plates.

Taking tea at The Mad River inspires you to make the pastime a regular habit, long after your visit. The Mad River innkeepers know that feeling well. They actually opened the inn because of Rita, Luc and Annie's passion for taking tea. "We wanted to recapture our first tea-time experience," recalls Rita. And they do— every day.

The Mad River Inn
P.O. Box 75
Pine Road off Route 100
Waitsfield, VT 05673
Phone: **(802) 496-7900**
Rooms: **8**
Tea-Time: **4:00–6:00 P.M. daily for inn guests**

SNOW PEAS STUFFED WITH HERB CHEESE

25 medium-large, blemish-free snow peas
6 ounces soft cream cheese, at room temperature
1 teaspoon onion powder or 3 scallion heads, chopped
1 clove garlic, finely chopped
½ cup mixture of chopped fresh basil, dill, parsley

Blanch peas in boiling water (45 seconds). • Drain and rinse. • Place in bowl of ice water for 1 minute. • Drain. • Dry on a towel. • Combine remaining ingredients in a bowl. • Mix well. • Using a sharp knife, split the snow peas on curved side. • Using a pastry bag, fill each pea with the cream cheese mixture. Yield: 25

ARTICHOKE CHEESECAKE SPREAD

PAN PREPARATION

2 tablespoons butter, softened
¼ cup fine dry bread crumbs
¼ cup Parmesan cheese
2 tablespoons fresh or dry herbs, finely chopped

Grease a 9-inch springform pan with the butter. • Mix together remaining ingredients. • Coat bottom of pan, setting aside remaining mixture.

CHEESECAKE

16 ounces cream cheese, at room temperature
1 cup crumbled feta cheese
3 large eggs
1 cup sour cream

14 ounces artichoke hearts, drained and chopped, (reserve 3 hearts)

1 small red pepper, chopped (reserve 4 small strips)

1 small green pepper, chopped

6 scallion heads, plus ½-inch green tops from each, chopped

1 large clove garlic, crushed

1 teaspoon crushed dried tarragon

1 tablespoon fresh or dried basil

6 basil leaves for garnish

¼ cup chopped parsley for garnish

Preheat oven to 375°. • In food processor, beat cream cheese until fluffy. • Add feta cheese, eggs and sour cream. • Beat until smooth. • Add chopped artichokes. • Beat in red and green peppers, scallions, garlic, tarragon and basil. • Spoon mixture into prepared pan. • Bake for 40 minutes or until golden brown. • Cool to room temperature. • Chill for at least 2 hours. • Remove from pan. • Pat reserved crumb coating mixture on outside of cheesecake. • Garnish with artichokes, red pepper strips, basil leaves and parsley. • Serve with toast points or crackers. Yield: 1 cheesecake

CRANBERRY EGGNOG TEA BREAD

2 eggs

1 cup sugar

1 cup eggnog (without rum or rum flavor added)

1 stick butter, melted

1½ teaspoons rum extract

1 teaspoon vanilla extract

1 cup whole-wheat flour

1¼ cups unbleached all-purpose flour

2 teaspoons baking powder

½ teaspoon salt

¾ teaspoon nutmeg (freshly ground is best)

¾ cup fresh cranberries, rinsed

1 teaspoon all-purpose flour

Preheat oven to 350°. • Grease bottom of 9x5-inch loaf pan. • In food processor, beat eggs; add sugar, eggnog, butter, rum and vanilla extracts. • Blend well. • In a large bowl, add flours, baking powder, salt and nutmeg. • Mix well. • Add wet ingredients until dry mixture is moistened. • Combine the cranberries with 1 teaspoon flour and fold into the mixture. • Bake for 45 minutes or until tester inserted in center comes out clean. • Cool completely. Yield: 1 loaf

Pumpkin Roll and Linzer Torte warmed by a Mad River hearth

A snowfall for tea-time

WHITE CHOCOLATE ALMOND AND APRICOT SCONES

2 cups all-purpose flour
1 cup whole-wheat flour
½ cup sugar
½ teaspoon salt
¾ teaspoon baking powder
¾ stick cold unsalted butter
2 medium eggs
¾ cup half-and-half
2½ teaspoons almond extract
9 ounces quality white chocolate, cut into bite-sized pieces
1½ cups chopped toasted, slivered almonds
1½ cups chopped dried apricots

Preheat oven to 350°. • In a large bowl, stir together flours, sugar, salt and baking powder. • Cut the butter into small pieces. • Using two knives, cut the butter into flour mixture until it resembles coarse crumbs. • In a separate bowl, stir together eggs, cream and almond extract. • Add the cream mixture to the flour mixture and knead until well mixed. • Knead in chocolate, almonds and apricots. • On a lightly floured surface, roll out dough to a ½-inch thickness. • Cut the dough into hearts, with 3-inch, heart-shaped cookie cutter. • Place hearts on an ungreased cookie sheet. • Bake for 15 to 20 minutes or until lightly browned. Yield: 12

ALPINE MAPLE CREAM TARTS

Mad River often garnishes the tarts with edible pansies. This is a basic crust that requires no rolling.

TART SHELLS

1 cup all-purpose flour
1 cup whole-wheat flour
⅔ cup confectioners' sugar
1 stick butter
1 egg yolk
2 tablespoons water
2 teaspoons almond extract

In large bowl, mix flours, confectioners' sugar and butter until crumbly. • In another bowl, lightly mix egg yolk with water and almond extract. • Slowly add to flour mixture, forming a smooth ball with your hands. • If mixture is too dry, add a little water. • Press 1 tablespoon of dough into bottom and halfway up the sides of ungreased muffin cups.

FILLING

12 ounces cream cheese, softened
½ cup maple syrup (dark grade is best)
1 egg
½ teaspoon cinnamon
2 tablespoons confectioners' sugar

Preheat oven to 350°. • Combine all ingredients in food processor and blend well. • Pour about 2 tablespoons of filling into each pastry-lined muffin cup. • Bake for 20 minutes or until firm. Yield: 15

FRUIT GLAZE

In saucepan, combine 4 tablespoons apricot jam with 4 tablespoons water and 1 teaspoon almond extract. • Bring to a boil, while stirring constantly. • Strain out lumps; brush glaze onto fruit with pastry brush.

LINZER TORTE

This is especially good to make in the winter when fresh fruit is scarce.

¾ cup unbleached all-purpose flour, divided
¾ cup almonds
¾ cup whole-wheat flour
1 stick butter
½ cup confectioners' sugar
1 egg
1 teaspoon cinnamon
1 teaspoon grated lemon peel
1 teaspoon almond extract
1½ cups raspberry preserves (or apricot, blackberry or blueberry)
Confectioners' sugar

Preheat oven to 350°. • Grease a 9-inch springform pan. • In food processor, mix ¼ cup of the unbleached flour with the almonds until finely chopped. • Set aside. • In food processor, mix together remaining unbleached flour, whole-wheat flour, butter and sugar until creamy. • Add nut mixture, egg, cinnamon, lemon peel and almond extract. • Blend. • Remove dough from processor and place into a bowl. • Wrap ⅓ of the dough and put in freezer. • Take remaining ⅔ dough and cover bottom of springform pan and 1 to 1½ inches up sides. • Spread preserves over bottom.

Remove dough from freezer, roll out on floured surface to a ¼-inch thickness. • Cut long strips about ½-inch wide and ¼-inch thick. Form a lattice pattern on top of torte. A spatula helps to scoop up strips of dough. Don't worry if they break—just patch them together. They look great once they are baked.

Bake for 45 minutes or until light golden brown. • Cool for 10 minutes. • Remove sides from springform pan. • Dust torte lightly with confectioners' sugar. Yield: 10 servings

AFTER-THE-SKI TEA AT HOME

- In addition to all the wonderful recipes from Mad River, you may also want to include a traditional after-ski, melted-cheese fondue dish for this tea. Skiing and fondue go together well.
- Provide tea-time guests with hot-water foot warmers to toast their toes.
- Serve tea in mugs so that skiers can wrap cold hands around a large surface.

PUMPKIN ROLL

3 eggs

1 cup sugar

⅔ cup pumpkin purée

1 teaspoon lemon juice

¾ cup all-purpose flour

2 teaspoons cinnamon

1 teaspoon baking powder

½ teaspoon ginger

½ teaspoon salt

½ teaspoon nutmeg

1 cup finely chopped pecans

1 cup sifted confectioners' sugar, plus additional for dusting

8 ounces cream cheese, softened

½ stick butter, softened

½ teaspoon maple extract

½ cup heavy cream, whipped

Preheat oven to 375°. • In large bowl of electric mixer, beat the eggs on high for 5 minutes or until thick. • Gradually beat in sugar. • Stir in pumpkin and lemon juice. • In separate bowl, sift together flour, cinnamon, baking powder, ginger, salt and nutmeg. • Fold into pumpkin mixture. • Spread in greased and floured 15x10x1-inch jellyroll pan. • Sprinkle with nuts. • Bake for 15 minutes. • Immediately invert cake onto towel sprinkled with enough confectioners' sugar to lightly cover towel. • Roll up cake and towel, jellyroll style, starting from short side. • Cool completely. • Unroll cake. • In small bowl of electric mixer, beat 1 cup confectioners' sugar, cream cheese, butter and maple extract on medium speed until smooth. • Fold in whipped cream. • Spread over cake. • Reroll cake. • Cover and chill. • To serve, cut cake into 1-inch slices. Yield: 10 to 12 servings.

BOURBON BALLS

1 cup butter, softened

½ cup confectioners' sugar

½ teaspoon salt

1 teaspoon almond extract

1 tablespoon bourbon

2 cups all-purpose flour, sifted

1½ cups nuts, finely chopped (almonds, pecans, walnuts)

Confectioners' sugar

Preheat oven to 350°. • Mix together butter and sugar until light and fluffy. • Add salt, almond extract, bourbon, flour and nuts. (If too sticky, add flour. If too dry, add bourbon.) • Shape dough into 1-inch balls. • Place on ungreased cookie sheet. • Bake for 12 to 15 minutes. • Do not overcook. Balls are done when firm to the touch and very light brown. • Cool for 5 minutes. • While still warm, roll in confectioners' sugar. Yield: 48

A Caroler's Tea

Pimm's Cup Punch

Victorian Chocolate Lace Cookies

Gouda Cheese en Croûte

Cranberry Tarts

ALONE GULL WINGS ITS
way over the cupolas of Cape
May's Painted Ladies. The tide
ebbs, and the vacated wooden board-
walk creaks underfoot as the winter
wind whips. But it's a bright, sunny
day, and in the middle of December
the water is reflecting as many colors
as a Monet painting. The seashore is
not the first place one thinks of
spending the Christmas holidays or
the cold months. However, once you
step onto the shores of this seaside
resort in the off-season, you'll discover that there are still plenty of
ways to build yourself a sandcastle.

I found tea-time at the Manor
House to satisfy my sandbox yearn-
ings. The Victorian parlor was
bustling with holiday guests, who
were exchanging funny stories and
singing Christmas carols. Innkeeper

Tom Snyder—not the player piano
tinkling songs from yesteryear—was
at the center of attention. Tom has
an incredible sense of humor and a
knack for keeping his guests laughing
and singing.

Tom and his wife, Mary, were in
the process of writing a cookbook
called *Tom's Puns and Mary's Buns.*
That alone will tell you how wonderfully funny this pair can be. At
breakfast, Tom serves up Mary's buns.
She's in the kitchen cooking away

The addition of lemon (in tea) was a Russian habit introduced by Queen Victoria's eldest daughter, who was the Consort of the Emperor of Prussia.

Morrison House, Alexandria, Virginia

while Tom, clad whimsically in colorful suspenders that have become his trademark, does a veritable stand-up comic routine between courses.

So, why should tea-time be any less spirited, especially during the holidays? The Manor House is decked in elegant and unusual fresh holiday dressings, brought in and arranged by a Pennsylvania stylist. Fragrant boughs trim doorways and highlight the magnificent oak staircase in the foyer. There is so much cheer going on, that tea-time is often a stand-up affair. Everyone, teacup in hand, is busy meeting everyone else. Tom and Mary make it that way. Tom has a talent that automatically brings together perfect strangers of all ages.

Tom and Mary know how to do things in style and yet without pretense. There are comforting guest touches everywhere. A hinged picture frame offers two choices for the next day's breakfast such as Eggs Mornay or Blueberry Pancakes. You write in your selection before you retire. Each

evening, you go to the credenza, anxious to know what's on tomorrow's menu. The people at the Manor House give you more than one reason to get up in the morning.

An antique barber's chair is in the inn's sitting room, but it's not for haircuts. It's more symbolic of another one of Tom's pastimes, singing in a local barbershop quartet.

No, they just won't let you leave Manor House without a song in your heart, a few puns in your pocket and plenty of buns under your belt.

Manor House Inn Cape May
612 Hughes Street
Cape May, NJ 08204
Phone: **(609) 884-4710**
Rooms: **12**
Tea-Time: **4:30 P.M. daily for inn guests**

A CAROLER'S TEA AT HOME

- Place a decorated holiday wreath at the center of the table. The Pimm's Cup Punch can sit in the middle of the wreath.
- Use small wreaths to encircle teapots.
- Make copies of the lyrics to Christmas carols you want to sing and pass them out to guests for a sing-along.
- As everyone leaves, give them a song for their heart by sending them home with a musical bell ornament for their Christmas tree.

Gouda Cheese en Croûte, Victorian Chocolate Lace Cookies, and Cranberry Tarts

PIMM'S CUP PUNCH

In addition to tea, this somewhat "peppy," not-too-sweet libation helps guests get into a British holiday mood.

⅓ bottle Pimm's No. 1 Cup
⅔ bottle ginger beer
Cucumber strips
Lemon wedges

In a large punch bowl or pitcher, mix together Pimm's Cup and ginger beer. • Garnish each serving with 1 cucumber strip and 1 lemon wedge. Yield: 20 punch cups

VICTORIAN CHOCOLATE LACE COOKIES

⅔ cup butter
2 cups quick oats
1 cup sugar
⅔ cup all-purpose flour
¼ cup corn syrup
¼ cup milk
1 teaspoon vanilla extract
¼ teaspoon salt

Preheat oven to 350°. • Melt butter in a medium saucepan over medium heat. • Remove from heat. • Stir in oats, sugar, flour, corn syrup, milk, vanilla and salt. • Drop by the teaspoonful 3 inches apart on foil-lined cookie sheet. • Bake for 5 to 7 minutes or until lightly browned. • Let cool.

FILLING

2 cups chocolate morsels

In a double boiler, melt chocolate morsels over hot (not boiling) water. • Stir until smooth. • Spread on one cookie and top with another. Yield: 18

When preparing finger sandwiches in advance, keep them from drying out by placing them in a shallow container lined with a damp towel and waxed paper. Refrigerate.

GOUDA CHEESE EN CROÛTE

This afternoon treat can also be served as an appetizer or hors d'oeuvre. You can substitute with brie cheese and chopped apricot preserves. Serve on a cheese board and decorate with fruit or other edible garnishings.

| 1 package prepared crescent rolls |
| 1 round gouda cheese |
| Stone ground mustard |

Preheat oven to 350°. • Roll together 2 pieces of the dough to make one flat piece. • Place cheese on top in center and spread cheese with mustard. • Roll out two more pieces of dough and place on top of cheese. • Fold and pinch sides together. • Bake for 15 minutes or until lightly browned. Yield: 10 servings

CRANBERRY TARTS

| 1 9-inch prepared pastry shell |
| 2 cups fresh or frozen cranberries |
| ¾ cup sugar |
| 3 tablespoons all-purpose flour |

Preheat oven to 350°. • Grease mini-muffin tins. • Roll out pastry to a ¼-inch thickness and cut out disks with a 2-inch round cookie cutter to fit tins. • Place in tins. • In medium saucepan over low heat, mix together cranberries, sugar and flour until slightly thickened. • Place about 1 teaspoon of cranberry mixture into each cup.

TOPPING

| ⅓ cup all-purpose flour |
| ⅓ cup sugar |
| 2 tablespoons butter |
| Whipped cream |

In medium bowl, combine flour, sugar and butter with hands. • Sprinkle crumbs over the tarts. • Bake for 20 minutes or until lightly browned. • Just before serving, top with a dollop of freshly whipped cream. Yield: 36

A Victorian Christmas Tea

Chicken and Ham Holiday Pâté

Rum Raisin Cheddar Spread

Walnut-and-Cheese Stuffed Cucumbers

Almond Brittle Bars

"I T WAS THE BEST OF times . . ." Yes, indeed, I had a Dickens of a holiday during my trip to historic Cape May. The seaside town has several inns that host afternoon tea and I was there to sample tea-time during the annual Dickens Christmas Extravaganza. For three days, there were discussions and plays and much banter about Dickens novels, headed by noted Dickens expert Dr. Elliot Engel.

Cape May at Christmas is literally a tale of two cities—nineteenth-century Cape May eclipses the twentieth-century town. Touted as the area with the largest collection of Victorian frame buildings in the United States, Cape May is ideal for experiencing holidays of the past. White lights outline the sugary architecture of inns,

shops, restaurants and private homes as if it were a Dickens village come to life.

At The Queen Victoria, innkeepers Joan and Dane Wells are Christmas history buffs who recreate Victorian Christmas trees. Ornaments are handmade by guests, reflecting trinkets of the early, middle and late Victorian periods. Early Victorian trees were ornamented with fruits, nuts, winter buds, pretzels and decorated eggs, symbolizing pagan fertility. The mid-

dle Victorian era saw trees with hand-made and glass-blown trinkets; crocheted snowflakes; scrap fabric and ribbons; doilies; candles in tin holders; and colorful, candy filled cornucopias. The late Victorian years hosted trees with mass-produced trinkets, heralding the Industrial Revolution.

I pondered each of the trees while mingling with other tea-time guests, who I noted, were also having the "best of times" at The Queen Victoria.

The Queen Victoria
102 Ocean Street
Cape May, NJ 08204
Phone: **(609) 884-8702**
Rooms: **27, including suites and cottage**
Tea-Time: **4–6 P.M. daily for inn guests**

I got a letter from my old Great Aunt. It read: 'Of
course, I'll understand if you can't, but if you find
some time, how wonderful if we could have a little
chat and share a cup of Christmas tea . . ."
I . . . stopped beside the wooden house that held the
Christmas cup. "Come in! Come in!" she laughed
the words. She took me by the hand. . . .
She was passionately interested in everything I did.
She spoke with candor and good grace. Then,
defying the reality of crutches and straightened
knee, on wings of hospitality, she flew
to brew the tea.

A Cup of Christmas Tea
—Tom Hegg

A VICTORIAN CHRISTMAS TEA AT HOME

- Most of us aren't historians, but we can interpret some Victorian tree ornaments. Cones (or cornucopias) of sweets were hung on Victorian trees. Include an ornament-making session with the tea by letting guests make and decorate their own cone ornaments. Shape thin cardboard into a cone. Cover the cone with an assortment of colored papers or Victorian decals. Add lace around the edge and top with a satin ribbon for hanging. Fill with tiny tea sweets and let your guests take their ornaments home.
- Include a storytelling during tea-time. Ask guests to bring a favorite short Christmas story and have each read it aloud.

CHICKEN AND HAM HOLIDAY PÂTÉ

Colorful layers in this pâté make it a festive choice for the holidays. Just make sure you have a brick handy!

2 whole uncooked chicken breasts, skinned, boned, and each cut into 3 horizontal slices
½ to ¾ pound thin bacon
½ pound cooked ham, thinly sliced
2 tablespoons minced shallots (or white part of scallions)
2 tablespoons chopped fresh parsley per layer
⅛ teaspoon thyme per layer

⅛ teaspoon savory per layer

¼ large bay leaf crumbled per layer

¼ teaspoon unflavored gelatin per layer

2 tablespoons cognac

¼ cup dry white wine

Parsley, chopped

Preheat oven to 350°. • Pound chicken breasts flat and thin. • Line an 8x4-inch loaf pan with enough bacon to cover. • Follow with a layer of chicken and one of ham. • Sprinkle shallots, parsley and seasonings over the ham, followed by gelatin, ending with bacon on top. • Repeat layers. • Pour cognac and then wine over all. • Seal the pan with foil. • Place in a large shallow pan with hot water halfway up the pan. • Bake for 1 hour and 15 minutes.

Remove from oven. • Loosen foil. • Place a brick on top to compress the layers. • Refrigerate overnight. • Remove brick and any fat solids from loaf. • To unmold, run a knife round the edge of the loaf. Place a platter over the pan and then reverse, giving a slight jerk to dislodge. • Spoon the jellied juices from the ends over the loaf. • Sprinkle with parsley. Yield: 14 slices

Rum Raisin Cheddar Spread

Spread on sweet breads or serve with crackers, raw vegetables and fruit wedges.

1 cup raisins

⅓ cup rum

8 ounces sharp cheddar cheese, shredded

6 ounces cream cheese

Soak raisins in rum for 1 hour. • Process cheddar and cream cheese until smooth. • Add raisins and rum; blend well. Yield: 1½ cups

Walnut-and-Cheese Stuffed Cucumbers

8 ounces cream cheese

3 ounces bleu cheese

1 tablespoon dry sherry

2 tablespoons minced parsley

⅛ teaspoon garlic powder

½ cup chopped walnuts

3 large cucumbers (each 8 inches long)

In a food processor, cream cheeses together. • Add next 3 ingredients. • Process until well blended. • Stir in walnuts. • Store in covered container in the refrigerator overnight. • Next day, wash and cut cucumbers into 1-inch thick slices. • Hollow centers. • Spoon mixture into each cucumber slice. Yield: 24

Tea-time gifts under an old-fashioned tree

ALMOND BRITTLE BARS

COOKIE CRUST

2 sticks butter

2 cups sugar

3 teaspoons grated orange peel

3 eggs

¼ cup milk

4 teaspoons vanilla extract

7 cups all-purpose flour

⅛ teaspoon salt

Preheat oven to 400°. • Cream butter. • Add sugar and orange peel. • Beat well. • Add eggs, milk and vanilla. • Beat in flour and salt. • Pat dough into two greased jellyroll pans. • Prick dough at 1-inch intervals with a fork. • Bake for 13 to 15 minutes or until golden brown. • Cool while preparing filling and almond topping.

Mulled Holiday Tea Punch

Combine in saucepan 1 quart brewed Darjeeling tea with 4 cups apple juice, 2 cups dry red wine, ½ cup sugar, ½ teaspoon nutmeg and ½ teaspoon ground allspice. Bring to a boil. Serve warm with clove-studded oranges. Yield: 2½ quarts

Thorwood, Hastings, Minnesota

FILLING

1 cup apricot jam

3 teaspoons brandy

Stir together jam and brandy in a cup and brush mixture over cooled cookie crust.

TOPPING

2 sticks plus 2 tablespoons butter

1 cup plus 2 tablespoons sugar

¼ cup honey

½ teaspoon salt

½ cup heavy cream

2 teaspoons vanilla extract

¼ teaspoon lemon juice

4 cups sliced blanched almonds

Preheat oven to 400°. • In a heavy large saucepan, melt butter. • Add sugar, honey and salt. • Cook over low heat, stirring constantly until sugar dissolves. • Increase heat to medium. • Add the cream and bring the mixture to a boil, stirring constantly with a wooden spoon until mixture is smooth. • Remove from heat and stir in vanilla, lemon juice and almonds. • Pour over the cookie crust, spreading in an even layer. • Bake for 15 to 20 minutes or until bubbly and golden brown. • Cool completely and cut into rectangles. Yield: 90 cookies

New Year's Eve Tea

Wild Mushroom Tartlets

———

Beggar's Purses with Lobster Filling

———

Prosciutto and Pear Cornets with Ginger Cream

———

Hazelnut Sables

———

Chocolate Chestnut Torte

———

Fruit Tartlets with Pastry Cream

I'VE SPENT SEVERAL NEW Year's Eves at country inns with my husband. After the busy holidays and year-end business commitments, inns have provided us with soothing getaways. We've come to accept the happy fact that we're going to be at an inn on New Year's Eve, possibly for many future new years. We find the inns both restful and invigorating. We feel renewed when we leave. The inn setting provides us with inspiration to delineate new goals. We bring pad and pen along and after great discussion, write down our next year's ambitions. When we get home, we type them up and put them into one of those clear-covered, term-paper folders, keeping them in view all year.

I must say, however, that we had never discussed our goals over tea at an inn on New Year's Eve. I mean isn't this the season of bubbly?

Well, innkeepers Chris and Ted Sprague announced they were going to serve a tea before their traditional New Year's Eve dinner at the Newcastle Inn. It made sense as dinner was a long way off. As guests arrived for the holiday fête, out came the pots of premium English Earl Grey and yes, even some bubbly circulated as a taste of what was to come.

The Spragues' assortment of holiday tea-time treats were a harbinger that good things were on the way for their guests in the year ahead. Tables were decorated with hats and noise-makers in keeping with the inn's casual elegance. One table hosted a white rabbit—a gift from one of the inn's guests. Good luck, indeed.

The Newcastle Inn
River Road
Newcastle, ME 04553
Phone: **(207) 563-5685**
Rooms: **15**
Tea-Time: **On special occasions**

A NEW YEAR'S EVE TEA AT HOME

- New Year's Eve is a perfect time to have a tea, especially if you're planning a long evening. Starting with tea allows your guests to enjoy the evening meal more than if they have been drinking alcoholic beverages long before dinner.
- At each place setting use a wrist watch as a napkin ring, with the clock's hands at midnight. This means you will have to gather watches from everyone in the house. Borrow some if you need more or buy broken ones at garage sales.

WILD MUSHROOM TARTLETS

Use individual tin tartlet shells. The recipe is doubled compared to the filling. Use the extra shells for the Fruit Tartlet recipe on page 204 or freeze remaining shells for future use.

TART SHELLS

2 cups all-purpose flour
1/8 teaspoon salt
1/2 teaspoon sugar
1 1/2 sticks unsalted chilled butter, cut into small squares
3 tablespoons ice water

In small bowl of electric mixer, combine flour, salt, sugar and butter on low speed until mixture resembles cornmeal. • Add ice water slowly. • The pastry will roll away from the sides of the bowl. • Remove pastry from bowl; place on a floured surface and shape into a ball. • Cover with plastic wrap and chill for 30 minutes. • Preheat oven to 425°. • Roll out pastry to an 1/8-inch thickness. • Cut into 3-inch rounds, and line tartlet forms. • Prick dough lightly with a fork. • Place forms on baking sheet. Line with foil and fill each form with rice. • Bake for 5 to 10 minutes or until golden brown. • Cool on rack. Yield: 40 shells

FILLING

3 tablespoons unsalted butter
1 leek, thinly sliced
1 ounce dried porcini mushrooms, soaked in hot water for 30 minutes, drained and finely chopped
1 pound mushrooms, finely chopped
2 tablespoons all-purpose flour
3 tablespoons Madeira
1/2 cup crème fraîche
Salt and pepper
1/4 cup minced parsley leaves

Preheat oven to 375°. • In a large skillet, melt butter and cook leeks, covered, for 10 minutes. • Add the porcini and chopped mushrooms. • Cook, stirring until all liquid is evaporated. • Stir in flour and cook for 2 minutes. • Stir in Madeira, crème fraîche, salt and pepper to taste. • Cook, stirring, for 5 minutes. • Remove from heat. • Stir in parsley. • Divide the filling among the shells. • Bake for 10 minutes. • Loosen the tartlets from the tins and serve warm. Yield: 20

BEGGAR'S PURSES WITH LOBSTER FILLING

5 shallots

½ stick sweet butter

1 cup cooked lobster meat, chopped

½ teaspoon salt

¼ teaspoon pepper

Juice of 1 lemon

1 pound phyllo pastry sheets

2 sticks unsalted butter, melted

Preheat oven to 350°. • Peel and finely chop shallots. • Cook in ½ stick butter until soft. • Combine lobster meat, shallots, salt, pepper and lemon juice. • Place 1 phyllo sheet on work surface. • Brush lightly with melted butter. • Top with 2 more sheets, buttering each layer. • Cut stacked sheets into 4-inch squares. • Place 1 teaspoon lobster filling in center of each square. • Gather corners together over center and crimp firmly to form purses. • Transfer to baking sheets, spacing 1 inch apart. • Brush tops lightly with melted butter. • Repeat process until all ingredients are used. • Bake for 25 minutes or until crisp. Yield: 50

Ringing in the new year with a different kind of brew

Left: Hazelnut Sables and Fruit Tartlets. Middle: Chocolate Chestnut Torte. Right: Shortbread, caviar on toast, Wild Mushroom Tartlets, Beggar's Purses, and Prosciutto and Pear Cornets.

Prosciutto and Pear Cornets with Ginger Cream

3 ounces cream cheese, softened
2 tablespoons heavy cream
1 teaspoon grated fresh ginger
1 teaspoon grain mustard
4 firm pears
Juice of 2 lemons
¼ pound prosciutto, sliced paper-thin, cut in half

In bowl of electric mixer, beat together cream cheese, cream, ginger and mustard until smooth. • Halve, core and cut each pear lengthwise into 8 pieces. • Toss gently with lemon juice to coat. • Spread each pear slice with ½ teaspoon of cream cheese mixture. Wrap pear in 1 slice of prosciutto. Yield: 32

Hazelnut Sables

To remove skins from hazelnuts, place in a 350° oven for 12 to 15 minutes or until skins split. When cool, rub between hands or with a towel to remove skins.

½ cup whole hazelnuts, toasted, skinned and cooled
⅔ cup confectioners' sugar
1½ sticks unsalted butter
2 tablespoons confectioners' sugar
½ teaspoon vanilla extract
2 egg yolks
⅛ teaspoon salt
2 cups all-purpose flour
1 egg, beaten with 1 teaspoon water
Chopped, toasted and skinned hazelnuts

In food processor, finely grind hazelnuts with ⅔ cup sugar. • In separate bowl of electric mixer, cream butter with 2 tablespoons confectioners' sugar until light and fluffy. • Add vanilla, egg yolks and salt, beating until the mixture is combined. • Beat in hazelnut mixture. • Beat in flour. • Continue beating until well combined and dough is formed. • Cover with plastic wrap and chill for 6 hours or overnight. • Preheat oven to 350°.

Work with ¼ of the dough at a time, keeping remaining dough in refrigerator. • Roll dough out ¼-inch thick. • Cut into desired shapes with cookie cutters and transfer immediately to a greased baking sheet. • Chill cookies on baking sheets for 30 minutes. • Remove from refrigerator and brush cookies lightly with the beaten egg. • Sprinkle cookies with chopped hazelnuts. • Bake for 15 to 20 minutes or until pale golden yellow. • Remove to rack to cool. Yield: 48 cookies

For a more formal afternoon tea (circa 1780) to which friends and visitors were invited, the tea table was placed in the formal parlor next to the fireplace for warmth in the winter or closer to a window for light in the warmer months. Silver and porcelain tea equipage created a fashionable setting, presented on a table sometimes covered by a fine linen tablecloth. A servant passed the cups of tea and refreshments to the guests on a waiter or tray. Along with conversation, afternoon tea was accompanied by music and games such as cards and backgammon—activities which might last until supper. Afternoon tea provided a social occasion when John Carlyle and his family and friends gathered to hear the news and gossip of the day.

From Carlyle House Historic Park, Alexandria, Virginia

CHOCOLATE CHESTNUT TORTE

1 pound vacuum-packed whole chestnuts
⅓ cup heavy cream
¾ cup sugar
1 stick unsalted butter, softened
10 ounces semi-sweet chocolate, melted
6 large eggs, separated
⅛ teaspoon salt

Preheat oven to 350°. • Line bottom of greased 9-inch springform pan with waxed paper. • Grease paper and dust with flour. • In food processor, purée chestnuts until smooth. • In large bowl, whisk together chestnut purée and cream until smooth. • Whisk in sugar and butter. • Stir in chocolate. • Whisk in egg yolks, one at a time, beating well after each addition. • Beat egg whites with ⅛ teaspoon salt until meringue forms stiff peaks. • Whisk about ⅓ of the meringue into the chocolate mixture to lighten it; gently fold in remaining meringue. • Pour batter into prepared pan; smooth top. • Bake for 45 to 55 minutes or until top of torte is cracked. • Cool on rack for 15 minutes. • Remove sides of pan. • Invert onto serving platter. • Cool completely.

GLAZE

6 ounces semi-sweet chocolate, finely chopped
½ cup heavy cream

Add chocolate to a small bowl. • In a saucepan, bring cream to a boil. • Pour over chocolate. • Stir mixture until chocolate is melted and smooth. • Spread glaze evenly over top and sides of torte. Yield: 10 to 12 servings

FRUIT TARTLETS WITH PASTRY CREAM

Make the tart shells using recipe for Wild Mushroom Tartlets on page 200.

PASTRY CREAM

1 cup milk
1/3 cup sugar
3 egg yolks
2 tablespoons all-purpose flour
1 1/2 teaspoons vanilla extract
Strawberries, kiwis and clementines (or mandarin oranges)

Place milk in a saucepan and bring to a slow boil. • Meanwhile, with wire whisk, beat the sugar and egg yolks together until mixture whitens. • Gently stir in flour with whisk. • Add vanilla. • Pour hot milk into the egg and sugar mixture, beating all the while with whisk. • Pour mixture back into the saucepan and bring to a boil, stirring constantly with whisk. • Boil for 1 minute longer, stirring constantly. • Pour mixture into a bowl and rub surface of cream with butter to keep a skin from forming as it cools.

Place one tablespoon of filling into each tartlet shell. • Place fruit decoratively on top. • Use 1 strawberry per shell. • Slice kiwi and place 3 or 4 slices on top in a circular fashion. • Peel clementines and use 3 to 5 sections according to how they fit into each shell. Yield: 20

GLAZE

For strawberry tartlets, melt 4 tablespoons of red currant jelly with 1 tablespoon water. • Brush tops of strawberries with glaze. • For clementine tartlets, melt 4 tablespoons orange marmalade with 1 teaspoon water. • Strain; brush tops with glaze. • For kiwi tartlets, melt 4 tablespoons apricot preserves with 1 teaspoon water. • Strain; brush tops of kiwi fruit with glaze.

We blew up balloons, sprinkled gold confetti and strewed gold streamers. Then we sat in front of the fire and poured the tea and ate epicurean delights we had never before tasted.

—Chris Sprague, The Newcastle Inn, Newcastle, Maine

Tea for a Mardi Gras

French Quarter Beignets

New Orleans Poppy Seed Corn Muffins

Mardi Gras Pralines

Bayou Cinnamon Twists

I T WAS THE DEAD OF WINter when we arrived at Geneva on the Lake. But as we entered the Italianate inn and former monastery, the season came to life. The Schickel family, which owns this inn with all the amenities and earmarks of a small Mediterranean resort, has something special planned for guests most weekends of the off-season. On the schedule the weekend I visited was a Mardi Gras celebration, complete with a tea and a costume contest.

The Mardi Gras weekend began Friday evening with a New York State wine tasting in the Loft room with its fabulous views of the second-largest of the state's Finger Lakes: Seneca Lake. The wine-tasting was followed by dinner in the Lancelotti dining room, already enlivened by the voice of a melodious young soprano, singing Broadway tunes.

Next day at 4 P.M., guests participated in a mask-making workshop served up at tea-time in the Leonardo da Vinci room. A fire in the carved marble fireplace warmed the room, where a business conference of Corning Glass executives had been held the previous afternoon. Geneva on the Lake effectively caters to major corporations that book several days for a conference in a setting that proves productive and restful.

We worked on our masks with supplies provided by the inn: glitter, glue, feathers, paints and shiny plastic charms. My husband, Tom, and I had never made a Mardi Gras or any other mask before. Tom and innkeeper Bill Schickel proved more artistic than I. The tea, however, kept me going. Meanwhile, the beignets (pronounced ben-yays) and other Louisiana treats put everyone into the Mardi Gras spirit. While we knew our disguises would fool others later that evening, there was no masking our enjoyment of the moment.

A tea table was set buffet style with a silver tea set reflecting the colorful flames of the fire. Tea was served with traditional Louisiana goodies as was the dinner that night. Cajun specialties and gumbo soups were offered by waitresses dressed as street mimes

Lake view from the patio of Geneva on the Lake

in black and white from head to toe. A jazz band sounded the evening's entertainment.

The presence of the Schickel family—Norbert, Marion, their son Bill and his wife, Trina—added to the cordial spirit and good feeling we received at this inn. Norbert and Marion are always around, mingling with the guests just enough so you know they are there. Having had 13 children of their own, they know just how to make everyone happy.

All the guest accommodations at Geneva on the Lake are suites, complete with a sitting room, and many have small kitchens. The Schickels invested a great deal since taking over the vacated monastery in the early 1980s. They moved walls and repaired arches and columns. They revived the sculptured gardens and restored six terra-cotta urns—originally imported from Italy—to their positions atop pedestals, overlooking Seneca Lake to the east and the inn's

pool to the west. There's a huge, columned patio adjacent to the gardens—just right for sipping a cold drink when the warm breezes blow. Really, it's so festive here that it's Mardi Gras any day of the year.

Geneva on the Lake
1001 Lochland Road
Geneva, NY 14456
Phone: **(315) 789-7190**
Rooms: **29 suites**
Tea-Time: **On special occasions**

A MARDI GRAS TEA AT HOME

- Buy solid, fabric-covered, Zorro-style masks in a variety of colors. Lay out sparkles, glitter, feathers and any other frills, and let your guests make their own masks.
- Decorate the tea table festively with beads, streamers and confetti.
- Play Dixieland and jazz music.

FRENCH QUARTER BEIGNETS

Beignets are traditionally served with café au lait, a popular Southern beverage. But they also go wonderfully with tea.

½ cup milk
1 package active dry yeast
½ cup warm water
¼ cup sugar
1 egg
½ teaspoon nutmeg
⅛ teaspoon salt
5 cups all-purpose flour, divided
1 tablespoon butter, melted
Vegetable oil
Confectioners' sugar

Sugar-covered beignets, New Orleans Poppy Seed Corn Muffins, and Bayou Cinnamon Twists

In a small saucepan, heat milk until bubbles form. • Remove from heat. • Cool to room temperature. • In a large mixing bowl, dissolve yeast in water. • Add milk, sugar, egg, nutmeg and salt. • Gradually beat in 3 cups of flour and the melted butter until the batter is smooth. • Add enough of the remaining flour to make the dough manageable. • Knead until smooth. • Cover dough in bowl with lid and set in a warm place to rise until doubled in size, about 1 hour.

On a lightly floured board, roll out dough to make a ¼-inch thick 15x10-inch rectangle. • Cut dough into 3½x3-inch rectangles. • Set dough aside in a warm place to rise until doubled in size, about 45 minutes. • In a large skillet, heat 2 inches of vegetable oil to 350°. • Fry dough squares, turning until puffy and golden brown. • Drain. • Sprinkle with confectioners' sugar. • Serve warm. Yield: 15

NEW ORLEANS POPPY SEED CORN MUFFINS

¾ cup all-purpose flour
2½ teaspoons baking powder
½ teaspoon salt
2 tablespoons sugar
1¼ cups cornmeal
1 egg
2 to 3 tablespoons butter, melted
1 cup milk
½ cup Parmesan cheese, divided
¼ cup poppy seeds

Preheat oven to 400°. • Combine flour, baking powder, salt, sugar and cornmeal. • Mix egg with melted butter and milk. • Combine with dry ingredients and ¼ cup Parmesan cheese. • Pour into greased mini-muffin pan. • Sprinkle with remaining Parmesan cheese and poppy seed. • Bake for 25 to 30 minutes or until golden. Yield: 24

MARDI GRAS PRALINES

1 cup firmly packed light brown sugar
2 cups sugar
3/4 cup light cream
1 teaspoon grated orange peel
2 1/4 cups pecans
2 tablespoons butter
1/8 teaspoon salt
1 teaspoon vanilla extract

In a medium saucepan, combine sugars with cream and orange peel. • Bring to a boil over medium heat, stirring occasionally. • Continue boiling until mixture reaches 228° on a candy thermometer. • Stir in pecans, butter and salt. • Cook, stirring continuously until candy dropped into cold water forms a soft ball, 236° on the candy thermometer. • Remove pan from heat. • Cool for 10 minutes. • Stir in vanilla. • Beat until almost thick, then drop by the tablespoonful onto a greased cookie sheet. • Cool completely. Yield: 32

BAYOU CINNAMON TWISTS

4 cups all-purpose flour
1/4 cup sugar
1 teaspoon salt
1/2 teaspoon cardamom, crushed
1/2 teaspoon nutmeg
1 package cake or dry yeast
2 eggs, beaten well
3/4 cup warm water (85°)
3 sticks butter, beaten
Cinnamon
Confectioners' sugar

Combine flour, sugar, salt, cardamom and nutmeg. • Make a ring. Add melted butter. • Dissolve yeast in eggs and water. • Work yeast/egg mixture into the dry ingredients. • Knead for several minutes until smooth. • Set aside for 30 minutes. • Roll out on floured board. • Dot with beaten butter. • Roll and fold several times. • Chill for 30 minutes. • Preheat oven to 350°. • Roll out and cut into 6-inch-long strips; twist and shape them into S-curls. • Dust with cinnamon and confectioners' sugar. • Bake for 30 minutes on a greased cookie sheet or until brown. Yield: 24

A Valentine's Day Tea

Ginger Peach Ring

Sam Hill (Sour Cream) Cake

Swedish Granola Tea Ring

Coconut Butter Pastry Rolls

BACK WHEN STAGECOACHES rolled into the town of Marshall, Michigan, they stopped at The National House Inn. I arrived in my own four-wheeler, and as soon as I walked into the lobby, I noticed the fir floors and exposed beams, which set a rustic and romantic mood. Guest rooms are furnished in Victorian and Colonial decor and, no doubt, when the inn first attracted visitors in 1835, tea was as popular a beverage as it is today.

Innkeeper Barbara Bradley, who became the inn's fourteenth keeper in 1984, serves tea every day. She has more than a dozen special "lecture teas" a year, including talks on antique dolls and linens, Russian tea-pots, Christmas toys and decorations. "I feel tea should be more than just conversation," opines Barbara.

The Valentine's tea included a lecture by a local collector on antique Valentines. The Victorians created their flirtatious love notes at home until commercial manufacturers ushered in the age of paper Valentines. The first American manufacturer was Esther Howland, who in 1848 set up production in Worcester, Massachusetts. By 1860, the American stationery firm of Berlin and Jones offered a lace-paper Valentine for the suitor who wanted to propose marriage by way of messenger. The ornately cut card contained a silhouette of a gentleman proposing. His intended was to attach to the card a gold paper ring with the printed word, *Accept.*

Antique Valentines studied during this season do enhance the holiday atmosphere and as Barbara says, make for more than mere mundane conversation as the tea is poured.

National House Inn
102 South Parkview
Marshall, MI 49068
Phone: **(616) 781-7374**
Rooms: **16**
Tea-Time: **4:00 P.M. and on special occasions**

Ginger Peach Ring

2 fresh peaches, peeled and cut into small pieces
½ cup all-purpose flour
1 cup firmly packed dark brown sugar
½ cup shortening
2 eggs
½ teaspoon baking soda
¼ cup unsulfured molasses
2½ cups all-purpose flour, sifted
1 teaspoon baking powder
½ teaspoon allspice
½ teaspoon cinnamon
1 teaspoon ginger
½ teaspoon salt
¾ cup milk
Confectioners' sugar
Whipped cream or sour cream

Preheat oven to 375°. • Place cut peaches into a bowl and dredge with ½ cup flour. • Cream together brown sugar and shortening until light and fluffy. • Beat in eggs, 1 at a time. • Add baking soda to molasses and stir into sugar mixture. • Sift together flour, baking powder, allspice, cinnamon, ginger and salt. • Add to mixture alternately with milk, until well combined. • Add peaches. • Pour into greased and floured bundt pan. • Bake for 40 minutes or until tester inserted in center comes out clean. • Sprinkle with confectioners' sugar. • Serve with whipped cream or sweetened sour cream. Yield: 12 slices

A VALENTINE'S DAY TEA AT HOME

- Make this a couples-only tea on a Sunday afternoon right around Valentine's Day. Serve heart-shaped cookies and candies in addition to these recipes.
- Fill a basket with 3-inch paper hearts, each with a question on the heart regarding a romantic piece of trivia such as, "Who wrote *Romeo and Juliet*? (Answer: Shakespeare)" or, "Why is the wedding band worn on the fourth finger of the left hand?" (Answer: A vein from that finger leads directly to the heart.) It's fun developing the questions. Put the basket out and invite anyone to reach in and try and guess the answers.

Sam Hill (Sour Cream) Cake

Graham cracker crumbs
½ stick butter
⅓ cup sugar
2 eggs
½ cup milk
¾ cup all-purpose flour
1 teaspoon grated lemon peel
⅓ cup sugar
2 cups sour cream
Fresh sliced strawberries

The heart remembers with antique valentines at National House Inn.

Preheat oven to 350°. • Sprinkle a greased 8-inch cake pan with graham cracker crumbs. • Cream together butter and sugar. • Beat in eggs, 1 at a time. • Add milk, flour and lemon peel; blend well. • Pour into pan and bake for 10 minutes or until tester inserted in center comes out clean. • Turn cake onto serving plate and cool. • Mix sugar with sour cream and spoon into center of cake. • Arrange strawberries around top in a pleasing pattern. • Serve chilled. Yield: 8 to 10 slices

SWEDISH GRANOLA TEA RING

This is a delicious cake with a cherry filling and honey topping.

2 packages active dry yeast
½ cup warm water (105°–115°)
1 egg
¾ cup lukewarm milk (scalded then cooled)
¼ cup honey
¼ cup butter, softened
2 cups granola, slightly crushed
3½ cups all-purpose flour, divided (plus ½ cup if needed)
1 teaspoon salt

Dissolve yeast in warm water in a large bowl. • Stir in egg, milk, honey, butter, granola, 2 cups flour and salt. • Stir vigorously until blended. • Stir in enough remaining flour to make dough easy to handle. • Turn dough out onto lightly floured surface. • Knead until smooth and elastic, about 5 minutes. • Place in greased bowl. • Cover and let rise in a warm place until doubled in size, about 90 minutes. • Meanwhile, prepare cherry filling and honey frosting.

CHERRY FILLING

1 cup crushed granola
1 cup finely chopped maraschino cherries

Combine ingredients and set aside.

HONEY FROSTING

¾ cup confectioners' sugar
2 tablespoons honey
2 tablespoons butter, softened
1 tablespoon milk
½ cup chopped nuts

Mix all ingredients, except nuts, until smooth and of spreadable consistency. • Set aside. • Punch down dough. • Divide into halves. • On lightly floured surface, roll each half into a 15x9-inch rectangle. • Spread each with cherry filling. • Roll up tightly beginning with widest part. • Pinch edge of dough into roll to seal. • With sealed edge down, shape each roll into a ring, pinching ends together. • Place on greased baking sheet. • With kitchen scissors, make cuts ⅔ of the way through the ring at 1-inch intervals. • Let rise until doubled in size, about 1 hour. • Preheat oven to 350°. • Bake for about 20 minutes or until golden brown. • Cool, then spread with honey frosting and sprinkle with nuts. Yield: 2 rings

Coconut Butter Pastry Rolls

4½ cups all-purpose flour, (plus ½ cup if needed)

⅓ cup sugar

1½ teaspoons salt

¼ teaspoon nutmeg

1 teaspoon grated orange peel

1 package active dry yeast

1¼ cups milk

½ stick butter

2 eggs (reserve 1 yolk)

½ teaspoon vanilla extract

½ stick butter, softened

Ginger Peach Ring

In large bowl of electric mixer, combine 2 cups of the flour, sugar, salt, nutmeg, orange peel and dry yeast. • In saucepan, heat milk and ½ stick butter until milk is warm (it is not necessary to melt butter). • Add milk/butter mixture, eggs and vanilla to dry ingredients. • Mix at low speed until moistened. • Beat 3 minutes at medium speed. • By hand, stir in remaining flour, using extra if needed to make dough easier to handle. • Cover. • Let rise in warm place until light and doubled in size, about 90 minutes.

Punch down dough. • Roll out on floured surface to form a 14-inch square. • Spread half the dough with butter to within 2 inches of edges. • Fold dough in half and then in quarters. • Seal edges. • Repeat process, using remaining butter. • Cover and set aside for 15 minutes. • Prepare filling.

Filling

½ cup sugar

3 tablespoons butter

1 cup flaked coconut

Reserved egg yolk

Blend sugar with butter. • Add coconut and egg yolk. • Mix well. • Divide dough into thirds. • Roll out each third on floured surface to form a 9-inch circle. • Cut each circle into 12 wedges. • Place a scant teaspoon of the filling in the center of each wedge and roll up, starting from the widest end. • Place, point-side down, on ungreased baking sheets. • Cover and let rise until doubled in size. • Preheat oven to 400°. • Bake for 10 to 12 minutes or until golden. Yield: 36

MORE TEA-TIME AT THE INN

Many inns hold a regularly scheduled afternoon tea or a welcome tea for arriving overnight guests. Here is a sampling. If you would like another inn to be listed in future printings, please write to me at 5501 Granby Road, Rockville, MD 20855.

MID-ATLANTIC

AARON BURR HOUSE
80 West Bridge Street
New Hope, Pennsylvania 18938
(215) 862-2343

ANGEL OF THE SEA
5-7 Trenton Ave.
Cape May, New Jersey 08204
(800) 848-3369

BEAVER CREEK HOUSE
Beaver Creek Road
Route 9, Box 330
Hagerstown, Maryland 21740
(301) 797-4764

GENESEE COUNTRY INN
948 George Street
Mumford, New York 14511
(716) 538-2500

HABERSHAM COUNTRY INN
6124 Routes 5 and 20
Canandaigua, New York 14424
(716) 394-1510

J.P. MORGAN HOUSE
2920 Smith Road
Canandaigua, New York 14424
(800) 233-3252

THE KING'S COTTAGE
1049 East King Street
Lancaster, Pennsylvania 17602
(717) 397-1017

SEA CREST BY THE SEA
19 Tuttle Ave.
Spring Lake, New Jersey 07762
(201) 449-9031

THE TYLER SPITE HOUSE
112 West Church Street
Frederick, Maryland 21701
(301) 831-4455

THE WEDGWOOD INN
111 West Bridge Street
New Hope, Pennsylvania 18938
(215) 862-2570

THE WHITEHALL INN
1370 Pineville Road
New Hope, Pennsylvania 18938
(215) 598-7945
Strawberry teas and musical teas

THE WHITE SWAN TAVERN
231 High Street
Chestertown, Maryland 21620
(301) 778-2300

MIDWEST

THE CHICAGO PIKE INN
215 East Chicago Street
Coldwater, Michigan 49036
(517) 279-8744

GARTH WOODSIDE MANSION
R.R. 1
Hannibal, Missouri 63401
(314) 221-2789

OLD CHURCH HOUSE INN
Mossville, Illinois
(309) 579-2300

OLD LAMPLIGHTER
276 Capital Ave. NE
Battle Creek, Michigan 49017
(616) 963-2603
Tea by reservation once a month

THE REDSTONE INN
504 Bluff Street
Dubuque, Iowa 52001
(319) 582-1894
Also served to the public

SWEET BASIL HILL FARM
15937 W. Washington St.
Gurnee, Illinois 60031
(708) 244-3333

NEW ENGLAND

THE COL. BLACKINTON INN
203 North Main Street
Attleboro, Massachusetts 02703
(508) 222-6022

HAWTHORN INN
9 High Street
Camden, Maine 04843
(207) 236-8842

THE MAINE STAY
34 Maine Street
Kennebunkport, Maine 04046
(207) 967-2117

THE TERRACE TOWNEHOUSE
60 Chandler Street
Boston, Massachusetts 02116
(617) 350-6520

THE WHITE HART INN
The Village Green
Salisbury, Connecticut 06068
(203) 435-0030

SOUTH

HILLTOP HOUSE
Route 7, Box 180
Greenville, Tennessee 37743
(615) 639-8202

MISSOURI INN
Florence, South Carolina
(803) 383-9553

THORNROSE HOUSE
531 Thornrose Avenue
Staunton, Virginia 24401
(703) 885-7026

SOUTHWEST

ANNIE'S B&B
4224 W. Red Bird Lane
Big Sandy, Texas 75237
(214) 298-5433
Special theme teas

PEPPERTREES B&B
724 E. University Blvd.
Tucson, Arizona 85719
(602) 622-7167

PUEBLO BONITO B&B
138 W. Manhattan
Santa Fe, New Mexico 87501
(505) 984-8001

WEST COAST and HAWAII

BENBOW INN
445 Lake Benbow Drive
Garberville, California 95440
(707) 923-2124
English tea-time

BRITT HOUSE
406 Maple Street
San Diego, California 92103
(619) 234-2926
Formal afternoon teas

BLUE LANTERN INN
34343 Street of the Blue Lantern
Dana Point, California 92629
(714) 661-1304

COBBLESTONE INN
(Junipero between 7th and 8th)
P.O. Box 3185
Carmel, California 93921
(408) 625-5222

THE GABLES
4257 Petaluma Hill Road
Santa Rosa, California 95404
(707) 585-7777

THE GINGERBREAD MANSION
400 Berding Street
Ferndale, California 95536
(707) 786-4000

THE GOSBY HOUSE
643 Lighthouse Ave.
Pacific Grove, California 93950
(408) 375-2095

CANADA

THE MANOA VALLEY INN
2001 Vancouver Ave.
Manoa, Hawaii 96822
(800) 634-5115

PETITE AUBERGE
863 Bush Street
San Francisco, California 94108
(415) 928-6000

OAK BAY BEACH HOTEL
1175 Beach Drive
Victoria, British Columbia V8S 2N2 Canada
(604) 598-4556

INDEX

Gail Greco is a prolific food journalist and the author of fifteen cookbooks, including *Tea-Time Journeys*. She has traveled the world for recipes and entertaining ideas and has become well-known through her award-winning PBS-TV series, *Country Inn Cooking with Gail Greco*. Home is the historic waterfront village of Annapolis, Maryland, and when she is there, the author especially enjoys taking tea by the quiet waters of the Chesapeake Bay at London Town House and Gardens, a former inn in an eighteenth-century trading port. *Tea-Time at the Inn*, one of Gail's first books, continues to be her most popular cookbook.